A Practical Guide to

A Practical Guide to

Finbarr O'Connell and Ethna Kennon

Chartered
Accountants
Ireland

Published in 2017 by
Chartered Accountants Ireland
Chartered Accountants House
47–49 Pearse Street
Dublin 2
www.charteredaccountants.ie

ISBN 978-1-910374-38-2

Typeset by Datapage
Printed by Turner's Printing Company, Longford, Ireland

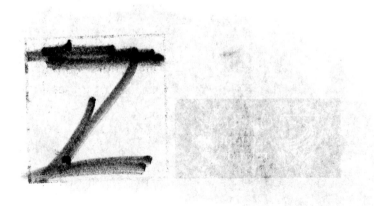

Contents

Introduction   xi

Acknowledgements   xv

1. Registration and Administration

. . . . . able   24

VAT Groups   25

VAT Deregistration   29

Conclusion   29

Appendix 1.1 – Form TR2   31

2. Supplies of Goods   **35**

Introduction   37

Supplies of Goods   37

VAT Registration Threshold   41

Deemed Non-supplies of Goods   42

Place where Goods are Supplied   43

Intra-Community Supplies   44

Exports of Goods to non-EU Countries   45

Distance Sales   46

Supply and Installation of Goods   47

Intra-Community Acquisitions (ICAs)   48

Triangulation   50

Statistical Obligations in Relation to EU Transactions   52

Imports of Goods from Outside the European Union   52

VAT56 Authorisation   53

Summary of VAT Issues Impacting on Irish Businesses
operating in an International Context   54

Conclusion   55

3. **Supplies of Services**   57

    Introduction   59

    How to Determine if 'Services' are being Supplied   59

    Intangible Assets and Transfer of Business Relief   60

    Self-supplies of Services and Services Supplied through Agents   60

    Place where Services are Supplied   61

    Exceptions to the General Place of Supply Rules   68

    Use and Enjoyment Rules   71

    Mini One Stop Shop ('MOSS')   71

    VAT Recovery   72

    Conclusion   73

4. **VAT on Property**   75

    Introduction   77

    THE OLD VAT ON PROPERTY RULES (PRE-1 JULY 2008)   77

    Supplies of Immovable Goods (Land and Buildings)   78

    Requirements for VAT to Arise   78

    Transactions involving 'Long Leases'   79

    Accounting for VAT on Long Leases   81

    Long Leases: VAT Treatment of Landlords' Expenses   82

    Transactions involving 'Short Leases' and the 'Waiver
    of Exemption'   83

    THE NEW VAT AND PROPERTY RULES (POST-1 JULY 2008)   85

    Sales of Property – What is Regarded as a Sale?   85

    When is a Sale of Property Subject to VAT?   86

    Letting of Property   93

    THE 'TRANSITIONAL' VAT ON PROPERTY RULES   95

    Supplies of Freeholds – Transitional Measures   96

    Sales of Reversionary Interests (No Second Supply Rule) –
    Transitional Measures   96

    Assignments or Surrenders of Long Leases – Transitional Measures 97

    Waivers of Exemption – Transitional Measures   98

    THE CAPITAL GOODS SCHEME   99

    'Intervals'   99

    Operation of the Capital Goods Scheme   100

    Capital Goods Scheme Adjustments   102

COMMON VAT ISSUES TO WATCH FOR IN PROPERTY
TRANSACTIONS 103
1. Determining an Accurate History of the Property 103
2. Catering for Changes in Timing 104
3. Disregarded Transfers of Property 105
4. Transfer of Business

111
11. Leases versus Licences 112
12. Holiday Homes 112
13. Tenant Dilapidations 112
14. Private (Non-business) Use of Property 113
15. Premiums Paid by Landlords or Tenants 113
Conclusion 114
Appendix 4.1: Connected Parties 114

5. VAT Recovery **117**
Introduction 119
VAT Recovery – General 119
How VAT is Reclaimed 122
Non-deductible VAT 124
Partial VAT Recovery 125
Timing of the VAT-recovery Rate Calculation 129
VAT Exemption 129
VAT-exempt Traders 131
Conclusion 132

6. Other Common VAT Issues **135**
Introduction 137
Ensuring the Correct VAT Rate is Used 137
Value of Transactions for VAT Purposes 141
Cash Receipts Basis 148

Common Invoicing Issues 148
Expressing Doubt on the VAT Treatment of a Transaction 149
Asset Finance and Financial Services 150
Requirement to Retain Records 150
VAT Cash-flow Issues 151
Conclusion 152

7. **Revenue Audits and Other Interventions** **153**
Introduction 155
Types of Revenue Intervention 155
What to Do on Receiving Notification of a Revenue Audit 157
The Revenue Audit Process 157
E-audits 159
Qualifying Disclosures 161
Preparing for the Revenue Audit 163
The Opening Meeting of the Audit 164
The Audit Settlement 164
'No Loss of Revenue' 167
Self-correction 168
Innocent Error 169
Technical Adjustments 169
Statutory Penalties 170
Inability to Pay 170
Revenue Powers 170
Tax Tips Relating to the Revenue Audit Process 172
Conclusion 174
Appendix 7.1 – Sample Notification of a Revenue Audit 175

8. **Receivers, Liquidators and Mortgagees in Possession** **177**
Introduction 179
VAT Review on Appointment of an Insolvency
Practitioner or Mortgagee in Possession 179
VAT Obligations of Liquidators 181
VAT Obligations of Receivers 182
VAT Obligations of Mortgagees in Possession (MIPs) 183

VAT Obligations or Issues particular to Insolvency and
Property Transactions   183

Entitlement of Insolvency Practitioners and Mortgagees
in Possession to Input Credit   184

Other VAT Issues arising in Insolvency Situations   185

in relation to VAT   198

General Principles of European Union Law   199

Ireland's General Anti-avoidance Rules   205

Mandatory Disclosures   206

Base Erosion and Profit Shifting (BEPS)
Project – (VAT Implications)   208

Conclusion   209

10. Relevant Contracts Tax (RCT)   **211**

Introduction   213

What is Relevant Contracts Tax?   213

Why it is Important from a VAT Perspective to
get RCT Right   213

When Does Relevant Contracts Tax Apply?   214

What Happens when Relevant Contracts Tax Applies?   227

The Impact of RCT on the VAT Treatment of Certain
Construction Operations   228

The 'Two-thirds Rule' and Relevant Contracts Tax   229

Relevant Contracts Tax in the Context of Insolvency   230

Conclusion   230

Appendix 10.1: Extract from Revenue Guidance Note for
School Boards of Management on dealing with RCT/VAT   231

Appendix A. VAT Rates Applied in Member States of
   the European Union   237

Appendix B. Revenue VAT Information Leaflet: Transfer
   of Business   241

Appendix C. Revenue VAT Information Leaflet: Bad Debts
   (excluding hire-purchase)   253

Index   261

Introduction

Value-added tax (VAT) has an impact on everyone. Businesses must generally account for it on their supplies and consumers pay it on most things they purchase.

...... income tax or stamp duty, for example) and for that reason many of the concepts and the application of the rules are still being teased out. In addition, as a tax on transactions, VAT law has struggled to deal with changes in society and technology, how goods and services are bought and sold, and how people consume those goods and services. When VAT was introduced in Ireland in 1972, the internet as we know it did not exist.

In Ireland today, the key sources of VAT legislation are the Value-Added Tax Consolidation Act 2010 (VATCA 2010), which consolidated and replaced VAT legislation that was introduced in Ireland from 1 November 1972, as well as various VAT Regulations.

Compared to legislation for other tax heads, the VATCA 2010 (which is amended from time to time by the Finance Acts) is relatively short, with only 125 sections and eight schedules. The schedules to VATCA 2010 are where the main lists of activities that attract each of the different VAT rates (or VAT exemption) are found. It is worth noting that as the 'default' rate of VAT in Ireland is currently 23%, the listings in the schedules of activities attracting other VAT rates or VAT exemption are normally interpreted narrowly.

Tax Tip Revenue's extensive non-statutory index of the VAT rates applicable in Ireland to different products and services can be found on www.revenue.ie.[1]

---

[1] See http://www.revenue.ie/en/tax/vat/rates/index.jsp

> **Tax Tip** If you are reading VAT provisions in a pre-2010 agreement that refers to old legislative references from the 1972 VAT Act, you can map these to their counterparts in VATCA 2010 by referring to the destination table on the Revenue website.[2]

Generally, secondary legislation in the form of Regulations (most notably the Value-Added Tax (VAT) Regulations 2010 (S.I. No. 639 of 2016)) give more detail to the provisions in VATCA 2010. For example, VATCA 2010 requires a supplier to issue valid VAT invoices in certain circumstances (see sections 66 and 67 VATCA 2010) and the VAT Regulations 2010 specify the time limits for issuing the invoice and the particulars that need to be shown (see regulations 20–23). VAT invoicing procedures are discussed in more detail in **Chapters 1** and **6**.

VAT law is full of grey areas where good arguments can be made for completely different VAT treatments when analysing the same transactions. It can still be quite difficult to determine the following with respect to a transaction:

- Where is it regarded as taking place for VAT purposes?
- When is the transaction regarded as taking place?
- Is it a supply of goods or services, or both?
- Does the transaction give rise to VAT recovery on related costs?
- Which party is responsible for remitting VAT on the transaction?

The answers to such questions can have a fundamental impact on the VAT treatment applied to a transaction and yet it is easy to find examples where these issues are not clear cut. Even after many years of case law at the level of the European Court of Justice, there are many questions still to be answered.

Consequently, VAT is a tax with which business managers and many practitioners are not comfortable and it is often not given the attention it deserves. However, like it or not, VAT is a tax that businesses certainly cannot afford to ignore.

VAT can be seen as a high-risk tax. Take, for example, a very large trading company in Ireland with turnover of €100 million and profits of €8 million. The corporation tax liability for that company would likely be approximately €1 million (12.5% of €8 million). Assuming the company sells goods or services that are subject to VAT at the standard rate, the amount of sales

---

[2] See http://www.revenue.ie/en/practitioner/law/notes-for-guidance/vat/index.html. Accessed February 2016.

VAT that the company should be accounting for could be up to €23 million (€100 million @ 23%). It is probably fair to say that an error in calculating the VAT liability for the company is likely to have a more significant consequence for the company than an error in calculating the corporation tax liability. This is only logical, as the rate of VAT (23%) is higher than the rate of corporation tax (12.5%) and VAT is generally based on turnover, which is typically much larger than the profit figure. In addition, a company could be

[text obscured]

...they earn to taxing them ...spend. Accordingly, Revenue devote significant resources to ensuring that the right amount of VAT is paid by businesses with VAT audits and other periodic checks being far more common than those in relation to other taxes.

It is worth noting the current global focus on large corporations and where they pay their taxes. Concepts such as base erosion and profit shifting (BEPS) and country-by-country reporting have become everyday talking points for businesses. The obligations of businesses to pay the correct amount of VAT in the right locations need to be considered in this context.

Throughout this book, we have tried to identify potential risks and opportunities for Irish businesses in dealing with VAT based on our experience of dealing with large and small businesses, sole traders as well as PLCs. We hope that these tips will assist you and your clients.

Acknowledgements

We would like to sincerely thank Michael Diviney, Director of Publishing with Chartered Accountants Ireland, for his guidance and encouragement throughout this collaboration. We would also like to thank M~~~~ ~~~~~

her ~~~~~~ ~~~ ~~~ ~~~~~

- Introduction
- Who Needs to Register for VAT in Ireland?
- The VAT Registration Process
- VAT Invoices
- Filing VAT Returns
- Annual Return of Trading Details
- VAT Due and Payable
- VAT Groups
- VAT Deregistration
- Conclusion
- Appendix 1.1 – Form TR2

Introduction

Value-added tax (VAT) is sometimes regarded as a complex, even mysterious, tax. VAT differs in many key ways from other taxes such as corporation tax, income tax, etc. Prior to the introduction of VAT, Ireland operated wholesale and turnover taxes. It is a condition of EU member ship that each Mem...

..., a trader can be required to be VAT-registered and remit VAT to the Revenue Commissioners ('Revenue') on the value of transactions carried out, even where the trader is in a significant loss-making position with respect to those transactions.

VAT is levied at each stage of production and distribution and for VAT purposes, business transactions are categorised as either:
- 'supplies of goods' (e.g. sales of equipment, tangible assets, land, etc.); or
- 'supplies of services' (e.g. catering, construction services, consultancy services, etc.).

Broadly, in a business transaction that is carried out in Ireland, the seller A is registered for VAT, charges VAT on the value of the transaction to its customer B and remits this VAT to Revenue. The rate of VAT charged depends on the type of transaction that A is carrying out. If B is an end user, or 'consumer', that is not incurring the expenditure for business purposes, the VAT paid by B is typically an absolute cost to it and is retained by the Exchequer. However, if B is VAT-registered and is incurring the expenditure as a cost component of its own business sales, then, in the normal course, B can reclaim from Revenue the VAT that B has paid to A on the purchase. B then charges VAT on the value of its own sales to its customers and, again, the VAT rate applied depends on the type of sales transaction that B is carrying out.

In practical terms, the starting point for ensuring that a trader is meeting its VAT obligations in Ireland is to consider whether the trader is required to be VAT registered here. Therefore, in this chapter we look at the broad categories of traders that are obliged to VAT register in Ireland, the VAT registration procedure itself and also the procedure for registering multiple traders as a 'VAT group'. We then outline key aspects of Irish VAT administrative rules, including the criteria for valid VAT invoices and the procedure for filing VAT returns to Revenue.

In order to determine if a VAT registration is required, the following questions should be considered:

1. Will the Relevant Transactions be within the Scope of VAT?

As already noted, VAT is a tax on business transactions and 'business' is interpreted very broadly, i.e. generally a loss-making business is taxed in the same manner as a profitable one, etc. However, there are many transactions that are not subject to VAT. For example, where a person sells their home (principal private residence) in a straightforward transaction to another party, the vendor would typically not be acting in a business capacity. Such a transaction is outside the scope of VAT altogether. For that reason, VAT does not apply. Therefore, if someone is not acting in a business capacity, or is not deemed to be acting in a business capacity under the legislation, then VAT should not arise.

2. Will the Transactions be Exempt from VAT?

The main source of Irish VAT legislation is the Value-added Tax Consolidation Act 2010 (VATCA 2010), Schedule 1 of which sets out many VAT-exempt activities. Doctors, dentists, schools, hospitals, funeral undertakers, insurance companies, banks, etc., are all examples of persons involved in VAT-exempt activity. VAT-exempt activities are business activities that are technically within the scope of VAT (because they are carried out in a business capacity) but are expressly exempted in law from a VAT charge. Thus, solely on the basis that VAT-exempt supplies are involved, there is no obligation to register for or account for VAT in respect of those supplies.

However, VAT exemption is limited by law solely to the VAT-exempt activity itself. Therefore, a business carrying out a range of activities may be regarded as carrying out VAT-exempt sales on which no VAT is charged and also non-exempt sales that trigger a VAT registration obligation and on which VAT must be remitted to Revenue.

Also, as we will see later in this chapter, a business carrying out VAT-exempt sales may trigger a VAT registration obligation if certain purchases are made (particularly from outside Ireland).

Once VAT-registered, the business continues to apply VAT exemption to its VAT-exempt activities but files VAT returns to record the non-exempt transactions it carries out.

3. Will the Transactions be Subject to VAT in Ireland?

There is no obligation

... . on purchases via a regular VAT return).

4. Who will be the Person Accountable for VAT?

The general rule is that the supplier is the party that is required to account for any VAT arising on sales made in Ireland. In order to do this, the supplier registers for VAT in Ireland and files returns here.

There are cases, however, where the recipient of a supply is liable to account for VAT rather than the supplier. For example, supplies of scrap metal by businesses to scrap metal dealers are dealt with by 'reverse charge' in Ireland, i.e. instead of the supplier charging VAT, the customer 'self-accounts' for the VAT arising by recording this in its own VAT return. It is therefore possible that a person who is only involved in the supply of scrap metal would not be required to register for VAT in Ireland.

> **Tax Tip** It is important to know when there is an obligation to register for VAT in Ireland. Even if there is no obligation to register, it is worth considering if a VAT registration may be attractive where there are grounds to register. For example, would a VAT registration make it possible to obtain refunds of VAT on costs incurred, etc.?

Who Needs to Register for VAT in Ireland?

VAT legislation uses the terms 'taxable person' and 'accountable person'. A taxable person is any 'entity' (e.g. sole trader, company, etc.) carrying on any business activities. Taxable persons who make supplies of VATable goods or services within the State are known as 'account-able persons' and must register for VAT. However, persons whose sup-plies are below the annual thresholds (€75,000 for goods, €37,500 for services) are not accountable persons unless they elect to be so.

Note: The €75,000 threshold only applies where at least 90% of the per-son's annual turnover is derived from supplies of goods. The legislation states that a person should register when turnover from VATable sup-plies exceeds or is likely to exceed the relevant threshold in a continu-ous period of 12 months.

Although not provided for in legislation, Revenue concessionally accept that, for the purposes of deciding if a person is obliged to register for VAT, the actual turnover of the business may be reduced by an amount equivalent to the VAT borne on purchases of stock for re-sale, as illus-trated in **Example 1.1** below:

EXAMPLE 1.1: CALCULATION OF REVISED BUSINESS TURNOVER

Annual purchases of stock for re-sale   €49,200 (VAT inclusive)
[€40,000 plus €9,200 of VAT at the
standard rate]

Actual turnover	€80,000 (VAT inclusive)
Less VAT on stock for re-sale	(€9,200)
'Revised business turnover'	€70,800

As the 'revised business turnover' is below the registration limit of €75,000 after the deduction of €9,200 VAT charged to it on pur-chases of stock, the business is not obliged to register.

Tax Tip In practice, although the VAT legislation states that an entity is an accountable person when its turnover is "likely" to exceed the relevant threshold, Revenue will generally accept that a person will not be required to register for VAT until they reach the relevant threshold in question.

The VAT registration thresholds in Ireland are lower than in a number of other countries; it is important to remember that the thresholds apply to annual turnover and not to profits and that therefore it does not take a lot of trading activity to reach them.

In addition to traders exceeding the turnover thresholds, entities also need to register for VAT in Ireland in the following circumstances, as they become 'accountable' persons.

- **Goods acquired into Ireland from other EU countries**

  If not already registered for VAT, any taxable persons who make intra-EU acquisitions of goods in excess of €41,000 in a

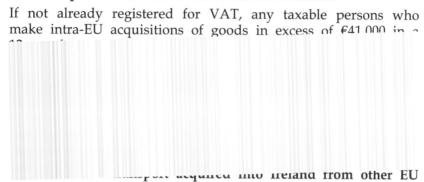

  ...port acquired into Ireland from other EU countries

The intra-Community acquisition of 'new means of transport' into Ireland makes the acquirer an accountable person and always subject to VAT on the acquisition, regardless of the value of the transactions or the taxable status of the person. 'New means of transport' are defined in section 2 VATCA 2010 as being intended for the transport of persons or goods and comprise either motorised land vehicles with an engine cylinder capacity exceeding 48 cubic centimetres or a power exceeding 7.2 kilowatts, vessels exceeding 7.5 metres in length and aircraft with a take-off weight exceeding 1,550 kilograms. To be considered 'new', the means of transport must also have been supplied within six months of first entry into service for land vehicles (three months in the case of vessels and aircraft) or if this condition has not been met, it cannot have travelled more than 6,000 kilometres in the case of land vehicles, been sailed for more than 100 hours in the case of vessels or flown for more than 40 hours in the case of aircraft. (Although outside the scope of this book, it should be noted that vehicle registration tax may also become payable on the registration of vehicles in Ireland, whether the vehicles are considered 'new means of transport' or not.)

- **Services received in Ireland from abroad**

  Taxable persons and government or public bodies who receive services from persons established outside the State are generally required to VAT register. (We look at examples of these services in **Chapter 3**.)

- **Supply and install contracts**

  Taxable persons, a Department of State or local authority, or a body established by statute that acquires goods that are supplied and installed in Ireland by a supplier not established in the State are required to be VAT-registered.

- **Construction services subject to relevant contracts tax (RCT)**

  'Principals', as outlined in RCT law, who receive certain construction operation services in Ireland from sub-contractors, are also accountable persons.

  Note: this applies to all such sub-contractors, including those established within the State. For construction contracts subject to RCT, VAT is generally dealt with by way of 'reverse charge', i.e. the person receiving the service self-accounts for the VAT and the sub-contractor does not charge or collect the VAT. The reverse-charge rule does not apply to haulage for hire (of materials, etc.). We look at the interaction between VAT and RCT rules in further detail in **Chapter 10**.

- **Construction services received from connected parties**

  Taxable persons receiving certain construction services from connected parties are obliged to account for the VAT arising on such supplies by way of reverse charge (even in cases where RCT may not apply). In practice, however, supplies of construction services between connected parties are commonly subject to RCT and therefore are already subject to a 'reverse charge' regardless of this provision.

- **Scrap metal sales**

  As outlined above, certain dealers in scrap metal are obliged to account for reverse-charge VAT on the purchase of certain goods from suppliers.

- **Premises providers**

  Landowners and certain premises providers in Ireland who allow either mobile traders onto their property or non-Irish established promoters to supply admissions to certain events for short periods of time, have obligations to report certain information to Revenue. If they fail to do so within specified timeframes then they may become accountable persons, and could be held liable for the VAT due by the mobile trader or promoter.

- **Public bodies**

  Public bodies and the State may be held to be accountable persons in respect of the activities in which they engage. From 1 July 2010, many supplies of goods and services by local authorities became subject to VAT, including the provision of off-street car parking, waste collec-

- **Greenhouse gas emission allowances**

  The EU has introduced a market-based system for greenhouse gas emission allowance trading (the EU emissions trading system or 'EU ETS') in order to promote cost-effective reductions of greenhouse gas emissions and help combat climate change. Broadly, if a company (e.g. power station operator) required to reduce its emissions has exceeded its targets, it can sell the surplus 'allowances' (or else buy allowances if it has not met its obligations). Supplies of greenhouse gas emission allowances are dealt with by way of 'reverse charge', even where the supplier and recipient are both established in the State. This is an important provision, as the values in these types of transactions are typically very large, and it has a large impact on cash flow in this industry while also providing a measure of protection for Revenue (as there is a lot of potential for VAT fraud in such transactions).

- **Mail order sales of goods**

  'Distance sellers' are traders that are not established in the State and that supply and deliver goods such as mail-order goods directly to the public in the State from another EU Member State. These traders are accountable persons when the level of these supplies into Ireland exceeds, or is likely to exceed, the calendar-year threshold of €35,000.

- **Telecommunications, radio and television broadcasting, and electronic services**

  Suppliers of broadcasting, telecommunications and electronic services (e.g. online suppliers of downloadable software) that are established outside of Ireland are liable to account for Irish VAT on supplies made to consumers in Ireland. Before 1 January 2015, this only applied to suppliers outside the EU. An optional system known as 'MOSS' allows suppliers of such services to account for VAT in each of the EU Member States (without the need to file VAT returns in each country) by submitting VAT returns in one EU Member State. The EU country in question then allocates the VAT to the remaining EU Member States accordingly. More detail on MOSS is outlined in **Chapter 3** and there is also extensive information available on Revenue's website (www.revenue.ie).

Non-Irish Established Traders

It is important to note that the annual VAT registration thresholds that apply to Irish-established businesses do not apply to those businesses established outside the State. Therefore, any level of activity in the State by such a business will trigger an obligation to register for VAT (unless either Irish VAT law applies VAT exemption to the activity or a reverse charge applies to the supplies in question). Set out in section 23 VATCA 2010, a relief is available that removes the obligation for a non-established trader having to register for Irish VAT in relation to intra-Community acquisitions of goods into Ireland if they make an onward taxable supply of the goods to a VAT-registered customer in Ireland. This is generally known as 'consignment stock relief', or 'call off stock relief', and it effectively removes the obligation for the supplier to VAT register with respect to the acquisition of the goods into Ireland and their sale here, instead obliging the VAT-registered customer in Ireland to account for VAT on the transaction.

Agents

Agents (and intermediaries) are often used to sell goods and services. The VAT treatment applied to the supplies made by agents depends on the status of the agent. Agents are generally either 'disclosed' or 'undisclosed'.

Disclosed Agents In disclosed agent scenarios, the purchaser is aware that the agent is acting for the vendor. When the sale takes place, the vendor will typically issue an invoice directly to the purchaser for the goods or services. The agent will issue an invoice to the vendor for their services. An example of a disclosed agency arrangement is where a customer is introduced to an insurance (or other financial services) provider by an intermediary and the customer knows that it is buying the insurance product from the provider. For VAT purposes, the provider will be deemed to provide the insurance or financial services in question to the customer.

Undisclosed Agents In undisclosed agent scenarios, the purchaser believes they are dealing directly with the agent (i.e. they are unaware

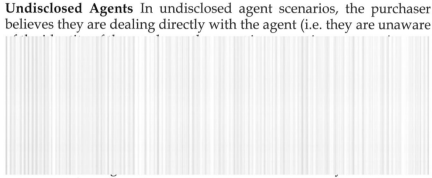

customer takes place, the vendor will issue a VAT invoice to the agent for the consultancy services. The agent will, in turn, issue an invoice to the purchaser for the same consultancy services. This invoice to the customer will include the agent's commission (i.e. the agent will take a mark-up). The invoices raised will typically attract the same rate of VAT such that the agent's commission is effectively taxed for VAT purposes at the same rate as the consultancy services.

> **Tax Tip** It is vital to determine if an agent is acting in a disclosed or undisclosed capacity as the VAT treatment can change significantly.

Farmers

Farmers are only obliged to register for VAT when they engage in certain activities. They may also elect to register for VAT, in which case they use their VAT registration to remit VAT on sales and reclaim VAT on farming expenditure in the normal manner. The rules relating to the intra-Community acquisition of goods and the receipt of services from abroad also generally apply to farmers. (We consider these general rules for cross-border supplies of goods and services in more detail in **Chapters 2** and **3** respectively.)

Where a farmer remains unregistered for VAT, he or she may be entitled to receive what is known as a 'flat-rate addition', which is an amount that the farmer receives from VAT-registered purchasers on top of the price agreed for the sale of agricultural goods or services. This effectively compensates the farmer for not being registered for VAT (as VAT on most costs/expenses cannot be recovered).

The flat-rate addition is currently 5.2% and the purchaser can reclaim this amount from Revenue, provided the purchaser is itself incurring the expenditure for activities that are subject to VAT (e.g. a supermarket retailer). Flat-rate farmers can also reclaim from Revenue VAT that they have paid on the construction, alteration, extension, etc., of farm buildings.

Farmers who are registered for VAT (either because they elect to be or are obliged to) can reclaim VAT under standard VAT recovery rules (which we consider in more detail in **Chapter 5**) through their VAT returns. However, they are then not entitled to the flat-rate addition. For that reason, it is important for farmers to consider their net position under both options (i.e. proceeding with a VAT registration or proceeding as a flat-rate farmer) in order to determine the preferred option. Where farmers are making intra-Community acquisitions or purchasing reverse-charge services from abroad, it is possible to ring-fence the VAT registration to deal with these transactions without impacting on the farmer's flat-rate addition.

If a farmer wishes to retain his or her status as a flat-rate farmer but also wants to engage in other, non-farming activities, then it may be possible to carry out these non-farming activities through a different entity. For example, a farmer could potentially incorporate a company and the company could carry on the relevant trade. Alternatively, it may be possible for the farmer to carry on the non-farming activities through a partnership (with his or her spouse or child) and generally this should not impact on the farmer's own status as a 'flat-rate' farmer.

Partnerships, Co-ownerships and Joint Ventures

Where an individual trades in their own name or a company is formed to carry on an activity, it is normally very clear who should be registered for VAT, i.e. who the accountable person is. However, it can be less straightforward where a number of persons or entities are collectively involved in making supplies.

Partnerships are treated as a single taxable person in Ireland for VAT purposes. For example, a law firm or accounting firm will usually have a single VAT registration for the activity it carries out. Each of the partners in a partnership could also be involved in other activities outside of the partnership and could therefore be registered separately in respect of these activities. In addition, a person could be involved in a number of different partnerships, each with its own VAT registration.

Tax Tip If you are a member of a partnership, it is important to understand what VAT liabilities you could be responsible for (in addition to the many other commercial and tax implications). For example, if the partnership was unable to meet its VAT liabilities, could Revenue seek the full payment from an individual partner?

The same VAT number typically remains in place for partnerships and co-ownerships, although members/partners may join and leave for as long as there is at least one common co-owner or partner before and after any change.

A joint venture (JV) is sometimes also considered as a taxable person. A JV typically arises where a purchaser wants to acquire a range of goods or services from a 'single' entity (although in reality the supplies would typically be made by a number of different parties). For example, a government department may want to award a contract to a person to design, construct and operate infrastructure (such as a toll road) for a period of time. Several parties that are experts in their own industries (e.g. finance, construction, maintenance) may come together to form a JV vehicle in order to make the supply to the government department. In many cases, the JV will take the form of a company, although this may not always be the case, e.g. an unincorporated JV. Depending on the arrangements, each party may make supplies to the JV entity (and issue VAT invoices to it) and the JV in turn will typically VAT register, make supplies and issue VAT invoices to the final customer (in this case the government department).

It is very important when dealing with such situations to clarify what is being supplied. The JV treatment outlined above is typically seen in public private partnership (PPP) scenarios and the VAT treatment arising can become quite complicated. The supplies to the final customer (e.g. government body) may involve a range of activities being provided for a single consideration, which may be paid over a long period of time. Issues such as VAT rates (including whether 'composite' or 'multiple' supplies are being made – see **Chapter 6**), the time when VAT becomes due and the application of RCT all arise in these scenarios and can be difficult to resolve.

> **Tax Tip** The VAT treatment arising in relation to any JV activities should be considered and agreed before the various parties commit to providing goods and services, as significant difficulties can arise in these scenarios.

Charities

Most approved charities are exempt from paying direct taxes, such as corporation tax and income tax, on the assumption that the funds are used for the purpose of the charity. There is no specific exemption from VAT for charities. However, their activities may fall within a VAT exemption (e.g. providing rented residential accommodation) or may be outside the scope of VAT if they are not considered to be acting in a business capacity.

We have seen in this chapter that even if a business is not obliged to be VAT-registered with respect to its sales, it may be required to VAT register where it receives goods or services from abroad.

If a charity that is not registered for VAT exceeds the threshold for intra-Community acquisitions (€41,000 in any continuous period of 12 months) in the course or furtherance of business, then it is generally obliged to apply the reverse-charge mechanism and self-account for VAT on acquiring the goods.

If a charity is not registered for VAT and is not acting in business, then there should be no obligation for it to self-account for VAT on receipt of services from outside Ireland (although it may be charged foreign VAT). If it is registered for VAT or is acting in business, then it will generally be obliged to self-account on receipt of the services, e.g. where it is VAT-registered with respect to its operation of charity shops and receives advertising or consultancy services from abroad.

> **Tax Tip** If you are dealing with a not-for-profit entity, you should consider whether there is any obligation to account for VAT on income generated. In our experience, Revenue will agree in many cases that an obligation for the charity to register for and account for VAT does not arise.

Holding Companies

There has been much debate about holding companies and what their VAT status is. A holding company is a company that owns shares in another company. It is generally accepted that the mere holding of shares is not a business activity for VAT purposes and, therefore, a

and therefore where such services are provided, the holding company would be obliged to register for and account for VAT, subject to the usual registration thresholds discussed earlier in this chapter. Such companies are sometimes referred to as 'active' holding companies. An active holding company should be entitled to recover VAT on costs it incurs which relate to its VATable activities. It is also typically obliged to self-account for VAT on receipt of services from outside Ireland.

There is a substantial amount of case law surrounding the question of VAT deduction on fees that relate to the issue, acquisition and disposal of shares by holding companies. Revenue's view has traditionally been that VAT on costs relating to all such transactions is irrecoverable as they are share related. Practitioners have consistently argued that such costs should be considered overheads of the business and if the business is a 'VATable one' (such as the provision of management services), then the VAT incurred on the relevant costs should in principle be recoverable. Following decisions in several Court of Justice of the European Union (CJEU) cases (e.g. Case C-465/03 *Kretztechnik*; Case C-16/00 *Cibo*), Revenue now typically accept that VAT recovery is possible in the following circumstances:
1. on costs relating to the issue of shares to raise finance for the VATable activities of a company;
2. on costs relating to the acquisition of shares in a subsidiary where it can be demonstrated that substantive and remunerated VATable services will be actively provided to that subsidiary. (**Note:** Revenue may still seek to restrict recovery of the VAT incurred on the basis that the company is involved in two activities, i.e. the holding of shares as well as the provision of VATable services.)

The evolving case law from the CJEU suggests that holding companies involved in the provision of VATable services should have greater VAT recovery than Revenue's current position.

> **Tax Tip** Consider whether including the holding company in a VAT group with its subsidiaries will improve or impact on the VAT recovery position for the group as a whole. (VAT grouping is discussed later in this chapter.)

Intending Traders

Traders who intend to make supplies that would normally be liable to VAT are commonly referred to as 'intending traders' for VAT purposes and should be entitled to register for VAT before they actually make supplies. This entitles them in principle to a deduction for VAT incurred on associated pre-trading expenditure, e.g. rent, professional fees, etc. However Revenue will often resist applications for backdating a VAT registration, so it is important that such applications are made in a timely manner and also Revenue can be expected to look for details of the intended trade.

EXAMPLE 1.2: INTENDING TRADERS

Where a new company has been established to distil and distribute premium whiskey it would likely be many years before any sales are made or VAT is charged. However, it should still be possible to register for VAT immediately and to begin reclaiming VAT in respect of the pre-trading costs. The EU VAT judgment in Case 268/83 *Rompelman* established the entitlement for an intending trader to recover VAT on costs incurred prior to making any supplies. The Rompelmans acquired an interest in commercial property and incurred VAT on the expenditure. They made a claim to recover the VAT on the basis that their intention was to make a taxable letting of the premises. The Dutch VAT authorities refused to refund the VAT. The CJEU confirmed that a person becomes a taxable person when they first intend to make taxable supplies. Therefore, where a person acquires an asset to use as part of a VATable economic activity (or future VATable economic activity) they should be entitled to register for VAT and recover VAT on expenses immediately. It is important to note that the intention of the parties is critical in such situations.

Revenue will typically look for firm evidence of a person's intention to make future taxable supplies when granting VAT registrations and/or issuing VAT refunds in advance of actual supplies having been made. Revenue are also permitted to require the payment of security (e.g. provision of a bond) in order to process a VAT refund or permit a trader to make VATable supplies in Ireland. As mentioned above, in

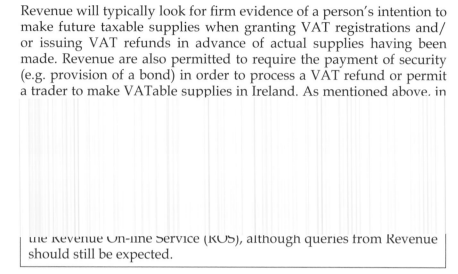

the Revenue On-line Service (ROS), although queries from Revenue should still be expected.

Practitioners should always be aware that information provided when registering for taxes may have a significant impact on how future transactions are regarded, as illustrated in **Example 1.3** below:

EXAMPLE 1.3: DOCUMENTATION OF INTENTION

Patricia acquired a commercial property in Dublin. At the time she acquired it, she was not quite sure whether she would redevelop it and then rent it, or redevelop it and then sell it. She wanted to get her VAT back on costs and when she submitted her application to register for VAT, she informed Revenue that she intended to develop the property and then to sell it, and that the sale would be VATable as the property would be newly completed.

When the development of the property was complete, Paula actually rented the property and accounted for VAT on the rents. A year later, she decided to sell the property as it had increased significantly in value. She had a discussion with her accountant about whether the profit would be subject to income tax or capital gains tax (CGT). Paula's accountant thought that, in addition to considering the impact of any accounting treatment applied, it could be difficult to argue that CGT should apply given that Paula had previously confirmed in her tax registration that her intention was to develop and sell the property.

Tax Tip Give consideration to the information included in tax registration applications to ensure that confirmations given are not misleading, as the information provided can have practical consequences. While submission of such applications is often done by the most junior members of staff, care is needed to ensure that all documentation correctly reflects the specific fact pattern.

The VAT Registration Process

Most VAT registrations are now carried out online via the Revenue On-line Service (ROS). While individuals and partnerships use Form TR1 and companies use Form TR2, both forms require broadly similar information about the taxpayer and the basis for the VAT registration. (See **Appendix 1.1** to this chapter for a copy of Form TR2.)

The VAT registration forms also ask whether the registration is being made because the person is electing to register or is obliged to register for VAT. In theory, because the obligation does not arise until the person exceeds or is likely to exceed the relevant VAT registration threshold, many people indicate that they are electing to register for VAT.

It is important to note that when a person cancels a VAT registration (e.g. they have ceased trading or their turnover has fallen below the threshold), they are obliged to review the three-year period prior to the cancellation, or, if shorter, the period of VAT registration. If the person has reclaimed more VAT from Revenue than paid to Revenue in the review period, the person is obliged to pay the difference to Revenue. However, this generally only arises where the person has 'elected' to register for VAT and not where the person was obliged to register.

Tax Tip When completing the VAT registration application, consider carefully whether it is an election or if it is compulsory; in the event that the VAT registration is cancelled, it would appear to be more advantageous where the person was obliged to register.

VAT Invoices

An Irish VAT invoice should contain the following details (per regulation 20 of the Value-Added Tax Regulations 2010[1] (the '2010 VAT Regulations'):

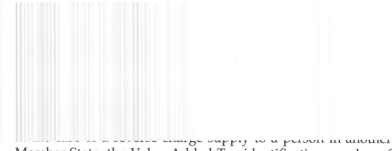

Member State, the Value-Added Tax identification number of the person to whom the supply was made and an indication that a reverse charge applies,

6. in the case of a supply of goods, other than a reverse charge supply, to a person registered for VAT in another Member State, the person's Value-Added Tax identification number in that Member State and an indication that the invoice relates to an intra-Community supply of goods,

7. the quantity and nature of the goods supplied or the extent and nature of the services rendered,

8. the date on which the goods or services were supplied or, in the case of early payment prior to the completion of the supply, the date on which the payment on account was made, in so far as that date differs from the date of issue of the invoice,

9. in respect of the goods or services supplied:
   • the unit price exclusive of VAT,
   • any discounts or price reductions not included in the unit price, and
   • the consideration exclusive of VAT.

10. in respect of the goods or services supplied, other than reverse charge supplies:
   • the consideration exclusive of tax for each rate (including zero-rate) of VAT, and
   • the rate of VAT chargeable.

11. the VAT payable in respect of the supply of the goods or services, except in the case of:
   • a reverse charge supply, or

---

[1] S.I. No. 639 of 2010.

- goods supplied:
  - under the margin scheme for second-hand goods, or
  - under the special scheme for auctioneers,
  - where the invoice should be clearly endorsed 'Margin Scheme – this invoice does not give the right to an input credit of VAT'.
12. in the case where a tax representative is liable to pay the VAT in another Member State, the full name and address and the Value-Added Tax identification number of that representative."[2]

Tax Tip You will note that where a supply is subject to Irish VAT, it is not a requirement to include the Irish VAT number of a customer on an invoice. However, when issuing a credit note, the Regulations state that this must be included.

Tax Tip It is important to be aware of the details required to be included on an invoice. First, a supplier will want to ensure that they are compliant with the law, as penalties can be imposed for issuing incorrect invoices. Secondly, a person can only take a VAT deduction or 'input credit' for expenditure when they are in receipt of a valid VAT invoice, so a purchaser will want to ensure that invoices received contain the information necessary to be considered as valid VAT invoices.

Filing VAT Returns

VAT is usually returned on a bi-monthly basis. Each calendar year is broken up into six taxable periods. VAT returns are due for each period on, or before, the 19th day of the month following the period. Where an accountable person submits his or her VAT return and pays any liability electronically (using ROS), then the deadline is extended by four days to the 23rd. It should be noted that when VAT returns are filed late, any interest due accrues from the 19th rather than the 23rd. Also, if an accountable person is obliged to file VAT returns but there are no transactions in a particular period, a VAT return should nevertheless be filed for the period, e.g. as a nil return. Penalties may be applied for incorrect or outstanding returns.

---

[2] Revenue, *Guide to VAT*, Invoices/Credit Notes. Available at www.revenue.ie/en/tax/vat/guide/credit-notes.html#section3 (accessed August 2016).

Typically, the returns are submitted as follows:

Period	VAT Return due by
Jan–Feb	19 Mar (23 if filing and paying on ROS)
Mar–Apr	19 May (23 if filing and paying on ROS)
May–Jun	19 Jul (23 if filing and paying on ROS)
Jul–Aug	19 Sep (23 if filing and paying on ROS)

€11,100, may be permitted by Revenue to submit returns every four months (tri-annual returns).

- Traders in a constant VAT repayment position may be allowed to submit returns on a monthly basis. This enables the trader to reclaim the VAT in a shorter time period.
- Traders may be permitted to submit an annual return (for a period specified by Revenue, not exceeding 12 months) on the condition that they set up a direct debit and pay a reasonable monthly amount towards their final liability. Where this option is chosen, it is important that the taxpayer monitors the expected final liability during the course of the year and compares this to the amounts paid by direct debit. If the shortfall at the end of the year is greater than 20% of the final liability, then interest becomes chargeable. It may, therefore, be necessary to increase the direct debit amounts prior to year end.

VAT 3 Returns

Regardless of when the VAT return is due, the same return form is used. VAT returns are relatively short when compared with other tax returns as there are only eight boxes to complete. The figures required are as follows:

Box T1 – VAT on supplies of goods and services (including reverse-charge VAT arising on certain purchases)
Box T2 – VAT on purchases
Box T3 – VAT payable (excess of output VAT over VAT deductions, if any)
Box T4 – VAT repayable (excess of VAT deductions over output VAT, if any)

Box E1 – Value of goods dispatched to other EU Member States (Intrastat)

Box E2 – Value of goods acquired from other EU Member States (Intrastat)

Box ES1 – Value of 'reverse-charge' services supplied to other EU businesses

Box ES2 – Value of 'reverse-charge' services acquired from other EU businesses

Box T1 – VAT on Supplies of Goods and Services (including reverse-charge VAT arising on certain purchases). It is important to consider that this box may contain more than just VAT amounts that have been charged to customers. It should also contain any VAT due on supplies that the accountable person was deemed to make in the relevant period. Such deemed supplies could include any of the following (the list is not exhaustive):

- VAT on goods acquired from outside the State;
- VAT on certain services received from outside the State;
- VAT on receipt of certain construction operations where the accountable person is a principal for RCT purposes;
- VAT on the acquisition of certain property interests, such as the assignment of a taxable 'legacy lease' or the purchase of the freehold in a property which is not 'new' for VAT purposes (but a joint option to tax has been agreed). VAT amounts may also be payable to Revenue in respect of property transactions under the 'Capital Goods Scheme'. (VAT and property rules, as well as the Capital Goods Scheme for property, are discussed in **Chapter 4**);
- VAT on goods previously used in the business, but which have been diverted to a private use (these are commonly referred to as 'self-supplies' and are considered in **Chapter 3**).

Box T2 – VAT on Purchases This box should contain any VAT that is deductible by the accountable person in the period in question. This could include the VAT paid on goods or services acquired from suppliers, and also any VAT that has been included in Box T1 of the return (see above) under the reverse-charge system. The recovery of any such VAT will be determined by the VAT status of the accountable person, e.g. they may be entitled to 100% VAT recovery or less, depending on what kind of business they are involved in and what the costs in question relate to (see list below). In order to support VAT recovery on expenditure, it is important that the person is also in possession of valid VAT invoices.

Non-deductible VAT

An accountable person may not deduct certain VAT, even when the goods and services in question are acquired or used for the purposes of a taxable business. Some of the items affected by this restriction include the following (as per section 60 VATCA 2010):

or accommodation or other entertainment services, where such expenditure forms all or part of the cost of providing an advertising service in respect of which tax is due and payable by the accountable person;
- entertainment expenses incurred by the accountable person, his or her agents or his or her employees (including corporate gifts);
- the purchase, hiring, intra-Community acquisition or importation of passenger motor vehicles generally, other than motor vehicles held as stock-in-trade, or for the purposes of the sale of those motor vehicles by a financial institution under a hire-purchase agreement, or for the purpose of hiring out the motor vehicles, or for use in a driving school business (see also entitlement to reclaim 20% of VAT on 'qualifying vehicles', addressed further in **Chapter 5**);
- the purchase, intra-Community acquisition or importation of petrol otherwise than as stock-in-trade;
- contract work involving the handing over of goods when such goods are themselves not deductible.

VAT recovery is dealt with in more detail in **Chapter 5**.

Boxes T3 and T4 are straightforward, in that Box T3 is used to record a net VAT liability due to Revenue (i.e. if Box T1 exceeds Box T2) and Box T4 is used to record a net VAT repayable position (i.e. if Box T2 exceeds Box T1).

The figures to be included in Boxes E1, E2, ES1 and ES2 are the VAT-exclusive figures (i.e. net of VAT amount in euros). Where the value of goods exceeds specified annual thresholds, the trader will also be obliged to complete statistical monthly Intrastat returns (see **Chapter 2**) to record cross-border EU trade. The annual values are €500,000 for arrivals and €635,000 for dispatches.

Annual Return of Trading Details

VAT-registered persons are also required to complete an annual form known as the 'Return of Trading Details'. This form is a statistical form that records the net value of goods and services acquired and supplied by the person, and is broken down by the different VAT rates that apply in Ireland. (VAT rates are addressed further in **Chapter 6**.) Failure to file this return can lead to delays in receiving VAT and refunds under other tax heads.

Tax Tip When preparing the bi-monthly (or other periodic) VAT returns, it is best practice to set out the information in each period to make it easier to prepare and file the annual return of trading details.

VAT Due and Payable

The time when VAT becomes due (the taxing point) is the earliest of the following events:
- The time when an invoice is raised (assuming the supplier is obliged to raise an invoice).
- The time when an invoice should have been raised. An accountable person is obliged to issue a VAT invoice to another accountable person, a business customer who carries on a VAT-exempt activity, public body and certain foreign customers (e.g. customers in other EU Member States who are liable to pay VAT on a 'reverse-charge' basis on the invoice in the other EU country) on or before the 15th day of the month following the supply (see below) or following the receipt of the payment (or part payment).
- The receipt of payment (if operating on the cash-receipts basis).

It is important to be able to determine when a supply has been made for VAT purposes. In most cases it is easy to determine when goods have been supplied. Section 19 VATCA 2010 contains a general rule that a 'supply' means the transfer of ownership of goods by agreement. Immovable goods (i.e. land and buildings) are generally deemed to be supplied when the conveyance is completed and payment is made, not when the contract is signed.

It can be more difficult to pinpoint exactly when a *service* has been supplied. For example, there could be a continuous supply of a service, such as ongoing consultancy advice provided over a prolonged period. Therefore, care needs to be taken to ensure the taxing point is not missed in relation to such services.

also what VAT rate applies (e.g. where there is a change of VAT rates), so it is important to be able to identify the relevant date.

VAT Groups

We have looked at the procedure for registering an entity for VAT. Two or more entities can apply to Revenue to be included in a VAT group registration (see section 15 VATCA 2010) whereby the members are effectively treated as a single entity for VAT purposes. The impact of this for the members of the VAT group is outlined further below, but we will first look at the conditions that must be met in order for VAT grouping to be permitted by Revenue.

It is important to note that granting a VAT group application (and de-grouping) is at the discretion of Revenue. Revenue will seek to ensure that the following conditions are satisfied before permitting VAT group registration:
- all of the proposed members of the VAT group must be established in the State;
- they should be closely bound by financial, economic and organisational links; and
- the grouping should be necessary and appropriate for the purposes of efficient and effective administration, including the collection of VAT.

The following should be noted in relation to VAT groups:
- a VAT group can contain individuals and partnerships, as well as corporate entities;

25

- a VAT group may include a person involved in VAT-exempt activities (e.g. lending, insurance, medical services, etc.) as well as 'pure' holding companies that do not engage in any economic activities;
- companies do not necessarily need to be in a legal group or corporation tax group to qualify;
- an Irish branch of a company incorporated (head office) in another country can be part of an Irish VAT group;
- not all EU Member States permit or recognise VAT groups; and
- Revenue can impose a VAT group (even where an application has not been made) in certain circumstances.

VAT groups generally become effective at the time Revenue process the application (i.e. from the current period), although technically it may be possible to backdate a VAT group registration. Backdating a VAT group application can be difficult in practice.

> **Tax Tip** There is evolving CJEU case law surrounding the application of VAT group rules to head offices and branches. As such, it may be necessary to consider the VAT impact in other countries as well as Ireland where it is proposed to include an entity (which is established abroad as well as in Ireland) in a VAT group.

Impact of VAT Group Registration

The following points should be borne in mind when considering group VAT registration:
1. The VAT group will nominate a single group 'remitter' that will be responsible for VAT compliance for the entire group. The remitter will be the only entity in the group to file a VAT return. The other members of the group are known as 'non-remitters'.
2. The group remitter must therefore lodge all VAT returns and make all payments for the entire group. *Note*: where VAT Information Exchange System (VIES) statements are required to be filed under sections 82 or 83 VATCA 2010, the VIES statements must be filed individually by the relevant entities. (VIES statements are addressed again in **Chapters 2** and **3**.)
3. VAT invoices are not necessary in respect of most transactions between the individual group members. This facilitates cash flow within the group as it allows one company to pay another company in the same VAT group without VAT arising. It should be noted that there is an exception in respect of the issuing of VAT invoices in the case of certain property disposals, e.g. freehold sales and very long

leases that are equivalent to freehold sales. (Property sales between VAT group members are considered further below and general VAT on property rules are addressed in **Chapter 4**.)

Each person in the group is jointly and severally liable in the event that timely payment of appropriate VAT is not made. *Note*: this joint and several liability is a significant disadvantage to joining a VAT group

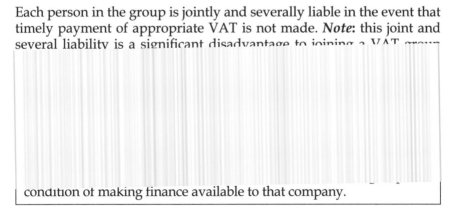

condition of making finance available to that company.

All VAT invoices issued by group members to third parties will show the VAT number of the individual entity making the supply. This is important and often overlooked. In other countries, members of a VAT group share a common VAT number. However, in Ireland, each person retains their VAT number; thus, from a systems perspective, it is necessary to ensure that these invoices can be raised.

Including a member that does not have full VAT recovery in a VAT group may affect the VAT recovery position of the overall VAT group, so this should be reviewed before proceeding with a VAT group application (as well as being monitored while the VAT group is in place).

If the VAT group collectively qualifies for a Section 56 certificate (previously known as '13B Certificate' and discussed in more detail in **Chapter 2**) then each member of the group will be entitled to a certificate.

Some of the potential benefits of creating a VAT group can be seen from the following example.

EXAMPLE 1.4: BENEFIT OF CREATING A VAT GROUP

Gamma Ltd and Delta Ltd are two Irish companies that are both wholly owned by the same individual. Gamma Ltd is involved in VAT-exempt training, while Delta Ltd is involved in providing consultancy services (which are subject to VAT). Both companies employ several staff. Some of the marketing and administration work for Gamma Ltd is carried out by the employees of Delta Ltd and at the end of each month an invoice for €10,000 is raised to Gamma Ltd for the provision of these services. If Gamma Ltd and Delta Ltd are not in a VAT group, 23% VAT will arise on top of the monthly invoice. Gamma Ltd will not be able to recover this VAT as it is solely engaged in VAT-exempt activities. However, if both companies are in a VAT group, there should be no obligation for a VAT invoice to be raised. This should result in a substantial saving for Gamma Ltd of €2,300 per month, or €27,600 per annum (subject to any other changes arising in relation to the overall recovery rate for the VAT group).

Sale of Property within a VAT Group

The sale of property from one entity to another within a VAT group is excluded from the usual VAT group relief provisions. VAT must be charged on the intra-group sale of a property (assuming VAT arises on the sale).

The company making the sale will issue a VAT invoice and the company purchasing the property will claim an input credit, assuming it is entitled to 100% VAT recovery. As the output VAT and input VAT will be recorded on the same VAT return, no payment to Revenue should actually be required where the VAT is fully deductible. If the acquirer of the property was only entitled to an 80% input credit, then only 80% of the VAT charged by the other VAT group member could be recovered by it and a payment to Revenue would be required.

> **Tax Tip** Consider carefully if a VAT group will assist in reducing administration and have a positive effect on cash flow. There may also be real VAT savings, depending on the nature of the activities carried out by the members of the VAT group. This would need to be weighed up against any adverse impact on VAT recovery where the VAT group includes a member that carries out VAT-exempt or non-business activities. Finally, ensure that all members are satisfied with the joint and several liability provisions which arise for each of the members.

VAT Deregistration

There are many reasons why a person may deregister for VAT. The person's turnover level may drop below the relevant threshold or they may be ceasing to trade entirely. In other cases, companies may go into liquidation and partnerships or co-ownerships may dissolve. A person

in the three-year period prior to deregistration taking effect.

Care should be taken to ensure that deregistration is not applied for if the person will be incurring costs after deregistration which would otherwise be recoverable. Obviously, once a VAT registration has been cancelled, it will be more difficult to reclaim the VAT incurred after that date, even where the costs relate to the period when the person was registered for VAT. It is also important to remember that where a person's turnover has dropped below the relevant threshold, it may not be possible to deregister if the person is continuing to receive 'reverse-charge' goods or services in Ireland.

Conclusion

As VAT is a tax on the value of transactions rather than on profit, it needs to be considered whenever business transactions are carried out; VAT errors can quickly accumulate and become costly. While, for VAT purposes, the concept of acting 'in business' is broadly interpreted, if an entity is not acting in a business capacity, and is not deemed to be so acting in a business capacity under the legislation, then it should not be obliged to apply VAT to its transactions.

We will see in **Chapter 9** that VAT is based on EU law and that therefore the Irish VAT system must operate within the confines of EU law. Consequently, advisors need to keep up to date with relevant legislation and CJEU case law.

In this chapter, we have looked at the main circumstances in which traders become obliged to register for VAT in Ireland and also the procedure for filing VAT returns and issuing invoices. We have also seen that although the general rule is that the supplier is liable to account for any VAT arising on a transaction, in certain cases the obligation is reversed and instead the customer is obliged to 'self-account' for any VAT arising on the 'reverse-charge' basis.

Another key point to remember is that for VAT purposes transactions are categorised as either a supply of goods or a supply of services. This categorisation is critical as it is the driver for decisions such as identifying the VAT rate applicable, the party that is obliged to account for VAT and even the country that has the right to tax the transaction for VAT purposes. In order to approach this categorisation in a methodical manner, in this guide we will first consider the VAT rules applicable to goods and then progress to the VAT rules applicable to services.

In the next chapter, we will look in more detail at what constitutes a supply of goods for VAT purposes and also introduce the 'place of supply' rules that determine the country where a supply of goods is deemed to take place for VAT purposes.

Appendix 1.1 – Form TR2

	TAX REGISTRATION	TR2

This form can be used to register a limited company and other bodies such as those listed at 5 below, for Corporation Tax, for PAYE/PRSI (as an employer), for VAT and/or Relevant Contracts Tax (RCT).

Persons, other than companies and bodies listed at 5 below, requiring to register should complete **Form TR1** or **PAYE employees** taking up their first employment should complete **Form 12A.**

ALL companies are required to make p...

Phone (inc. area code)   Website

Mobile No.   E-Mail

4. Registered Office Address *

Phone (inc. area code)   Website

5. Legal Format   (Tick ☑ appropriate box)

☐ Co-Operative Society   ☐ Private Unlimited Company   ☐ Statutory Body

☐ Public Limited Company   ☐ Private Limited Company   ☐ Branch of Foreign Company

☐ Other   (specify)

6. Date company was registered *(Irish registered companies)**   D D M M Y Y Y Y

7. Companies Registration Office (CRO) number *(Irish registered companies)**

8. When did the business or activity commence?*   D D M M Y Y Y Y

9. To what date will annual accounts be made up?*   D D M M Y Y Y Y

10. If you want your tax affairs to be dealt with in Irish, tick ☑ the box   ☐

11. If the company was registered for any tax in this country previously what reference numbers did it hold?

Corporation Tax

Employer (PAYE/PRSI)

Value Added Tax

Relevant Contracts Tax (RCT)

12. Type of Business*

(a) Is the business   ☐ mainly retail   ☐ mainly wholesale   ☐ mainly manufacturing

☐ building & construction   ☐ forestry/meat processing   ☐ service and other

(b) Describe the business conducted in as much detail as possible. Give a precise description such as 'newsagent', 'dairy farmer', 'textile manufacturer', 'property letting', 'investment income', etc. **Do not** use general terms such as 'shopkeeper', 'manufacturer', 'computers', 'consultant', etc. If the application is a property related activity you may also need to complete Panel 26, page 3.

(c) State the company's expected turnover in the next 12 months   €

31

Part A continued   **General Details**

13. **If the business will supply plastic bags to its customers tick ☑ the box** ▢

14. **Directors,** give the following information in relation to each director. If necessary, continue on a separate sheet. A minimum of two directors are required.

Name	Private Address	Shareholding	PPSN
		. %	
		. %	
		. %	

15. **Company Secretary,** if this is one of the directors above the name will suffice.*

Give the following information in respect of all partners, trustees or other officers. Under 'Capacity', state whether acting precedent partner, partner, trustee, treasurer, etc. If necessary continue on a separate sheet.

Name	Private Address	PPSN

16. **Shareholders,** give the details of any shareholder (other than a director whose details are shown above) who has 30% or more beneficial interest in the issued capital.

Name	Private Address	Shareholding	PPSN
		. %	

17. **Adviser Details,** give the following details of the company's accountant or tax adviser, if any, who will prepare the accounts and tax returns of the company.

Name

Address

Phone (inc. area code)   E-Mail

Contact name for Advisor

Tax Adviser Identification Number (TAIN)   Mobile No.

Client's Reference

If correspondence relating to the following is being dealt with by the accountant or tax adviser tick ☑ relevant box

VAT (i.e. VAT3's) ▢   RCT ▢   Employer PAYE/PRSI ▢

18. **If the business premises is rented, state:**
    (i) The name and private address of the landlord (not an estate agent or rent collector)
    (ii) The amount of rent paid per: week ▢ month ▢ or year ▢ (Tick ☑ frequency) €
    (iii) The date on which the company started paying the rent   D D M M Y Y Y Y
    (iv) The length of the agreed rental/lease period

19. **If you acquired the business from a previous owner, state**
    (i) The name and current address of the person from whom it was acquired
    (ii) The VAT/registered number of that person

1. REGISTRATION AND ADMINISTRATION

Part B — Registration for Corporation Tax (CT)

20. If the company is registering for Corporation Tax tick ☑ the box ☐

Part C — Registration for VAT

21. If the company is registering for VAT tick ☑ box and complete this part ☐

22. Registration

(a) State the date from which the company requires to register for VAT * `D D M M Y Y Y Y`

for goods and services? (tick ☑ the relevant box) Yes ☐ No ☐

If your answer is 'Yes', is this because

    (a) expected annual turn over will be less than €2,000,000 (net of VAT)? (a) ☐ Tick ☑ either (a) or (b) as appropriate

  or (b) at least 90% of your expected annual turn over will come from supplying goods and services to persons who are not registered, e.g. hospitals, schools or the general public? (b) ☐

24. State the expected annual turnover from supplies of taxable goods or services within the State * € ☐

25. State your bank or building society account to which refunds can be made

Bank/Building Society	
Branch Address	
IBAN (Max. 34 characters)	
BIC (Max. 11 characters)	

26. Developer/Landlord - Property details for VAT purposes

  (a) Address of the property

  (b) Date purchased or when development commenced `D D M M Y Y Y Y`

  (c) Planning permission reference number, if applicable

  (d) Attach a copy of the minutes of the meeting or signed statement*, where it was resolved that the property in question would be purchased and/or developed and would be disposed of or used in a manner which would give rise to a VAT liability, e.g. by sale of the property or by exercising the Landlord's 'option to tax'.

    *The minutes should show the date of the meeting, the names of all those present at the meeting and should be signed by the company secretary or precedent acting partner in the case of a partnership. The statement should be signed by the company secretary or director.

Part D — Registration as an Employer for PAYE/PRSI

27. If the company is registering as an employer for PAYE/PRSI tick ☑ box and complete this part ☐

28. Persons Engaged

  (a) How many **employees** are: **Full time** - usually working 30 hours or more per week? ☐

                      Part time - usually working less than 30 hours per week? ☐

  (b) State the date your first employee commenced or will commence in your employment * `D D M M Y Y Y Y`

Part D (continued) — Registration as an Employer for PAYE/PRSI

29. What payroll and PAYE/PRSI record system will you use? (Tick ☑ the relevant box)

(a) Computer System ☐ If you are using a computerised payroll package you should register for the Revenue On-Line Service (ROS) at **www.revenue.ie** to receive electronic copies of Tax Credit Certificates and to file your P35 End of Year Return on-line.

(b) Other Manual System ☐ Wages books are available from Office Suppliers/Stationery Bookstores.

30. Correspondence on PAYE/PRSI

If correspondence relating to PAYE/PRSI is being dealt with by an agent, tick ☑ this box and give the following details, if different from Panel 17 page 2. ☐

Name _____

Address _____

Phone (inc. area code) _____ E-Mail _____

Tax Adviser Identification Number (TAIN) _____ Mobile No _____

Client's Reference _____

Part E — Registration for Relevant Contracts Tax (RCT)

Note that Principal Contractors are obliged to use Revenue's Online Service to fulfill their RCT obligations. Principal Contractors are obliged to register and account for VAT in relation to Construction Services under the VAT Reverse Charge rules. Please refer to Part C of this form, Registration for VAT). Detailed information on RCT and VAT, including guides on Principal Contractor obligations, is available on the Revenue website www.revenue.ie

31. Are you applying to register as a (tick ☑ the relevant box) *

(a) Principal only ☐   (b) Principal & Subcontractor ☐   (c) Subcontractor only ☐

If (a) or (b) applies, please provide the number of subcontractors engaged. ☐

32. Date of Commencement for RCT * D D M M Y Y Y Y

33. If you are a Principal Contractor have you registered for ROS, or have you an agent willing to carry out all RCT functions who is registered for ROS? State the Tax Advisor Identification Number (TAIN) of your agent, if applicable Yes ☐ No ☐

34. Have you previously registered with Revenue as a Principal? Yes ☐ No ☐

35. If so, state the date you last ceased to be a Principal D D M M Y Y Y Y

Additional Information

The following leaflets will provide additional information on the taxation aspects of running a business. They are available at **www.revenue.ie**

Guide to Value Added Tax
Employer's Guide to PAYE
Employers Guide to Benefit-in-kind
Code of Practice for Determining Employment or Self-Employment Status of Individuals

If you require further information please contact your local Revenue office or Employer Helpline at **LoCall 1890 25 45 65.**

If you want information on payment options, including **Direct Debit,** contact the **Collector-General at LoCall 1890 20 30 70.**

You can access ROS and get more information at **www.revenue.ie**

Declaration — This must be made in every case before the company can be registered for tax

I declare that the particulars supplied by me in this application are true in every respect

Name (in BLOCK LETTERS)* _____

Signature* _____

Capacity of Signatory* _____ DATE* D D M M Y Y Y Y

(To be signed by the company secretary or other authorised officer)

- Introduction
- Supplies of Goods
- VAT Registration Threshold
- Deemed Non-supplies of Goods
- Place where Goods are Supplied
- Intra-Community Supplies
- Exports of Goods to non-EU Countries
- Distance Sales
- Supply and Installation of Goods
- Intra-Community Acquisitions
- Triangulation
- Statistical Obligations in Relation to EU Transactions
- Imports of Goods from Outside the EU
- VAT56 Authorisation
- Summary of VAT Issues Impacting on Irish Businesses operating in an International Context
- Conclusion

Introduction

Although certain transactions are effectively disregarded for VAT purposes, e.g. where they are specifically deemed to be 'outside the scope' of VAT legislation (see below), the general rule is that all business transactions fall in principle within the VAT regime and need to be

respective legislation of two EU Member States. They also ensure that a transaction is not subjected to double taxation within the EU, i.e. avoiding a scenario where the tax authorities in two EU Member States take the view that the same transaction falls to be taxed under their legislation.

This chapter outlines the main VAT rules governing the domestic supply of goods and also scenarios where goods are disposed of in cross-border transactions.

Supplies of Goods

Section 2 of the Value-Added Tax Consolidation Act 2010 (VATCA 2010) defines goods as "all movable and immovable objects", e.g. tangible property, whether new or used. The legislation goes on to provide that for VAT purposes, goods include the provision of certain energy products (such as power, gas, heat and electricity) but exclude "things in action" and money.

The legislation specifically lists transactions that are deemed to be supplies of goods for VAT purposes and transactions that are effectively to be disregarded for VAT purposes (sections 19 to 22 VATCA 2010). Examples of transactions that are deemed to be supplies of goods are as follows:
1. The transfer of ownership of goods by agreement, e.g. where a vendor agrees to sell equipment to a purchaser. This is typically the most common type of transaction involving goods.

> **Tax Tip** Regardless of whether you are advising the supplier or customer in a particular transaction, it is clearly important to review carefully any clauses in the transaction agreements that deal with VAT, as these may be aimed at contractually 'shifting' the ultimate burden of any VAT liability in a particular manner between the parties (notwithstanding the position that would normally arise vis-à-vis the relevant tax authorities under VAT legislation). For example, a supplier of goods may be liable to pay a VAT liability to Revenue arising from the sale of goods and the supplier will want to ensure that the customer will pay the VAT to him. However, the customer may not want to pay the VAT and if it is not clear in the agreement that he is obliged to do so, then he may refuse to pay the VAT. It is therefore common in respect of larger transactions for there to be written agreement/contracts or provisions of same that govern the VAT treatment of the transaction (as well as other legal and commercial matters).

2. The handing over of goods by a vendor (or finance company as the case may be) at the commencement of a hire-purchase agreement. As this is deemed to be an 'upfront' supply of the goods, no VAT arises on the hire-purchase rentals and, as outlined below, the eventual transfer of legal ownership of the goods to the customer (e.g. when the last payment has been made) is deemed to be a 'non-supply' that is effectively disregarded for VAT purposes (as the initial handing over of the goods to the customer at the beginning is treated as the supply).

> **Tax Tip** The VAT issues surrounding hire-purchase transactions can be complex and further detail on relevant issues can be found in regulation 10 of the Value-added Tax Regulations 2010 (S.I. No. 639 of 2010) (the '2010 VAT Regulations') as well as Revenue's *Hire Purchase Transactions* leaflet (November 2013).[1]

3. The sale of movable goods through an undisclosed agent, i.e. where someone is acting on commission and concludes the sale in their own name but in fact is acting on the instructions of, and for the account of, someone else. For example, Company A owns a machine, which it wants to sell. Company C wants to buy a machine but, for commercial reasons, it will not deal with Company A and

---

[1] See www.revenue.ie/en/tax/vat/leaflets/hire-purchase-transactions.html (accessed June 2016).

is unaware that Company A is selling the machine. Company A appoints Company B as its agent in order to sell the machine and pays Company B a commission. Company B tells Company C that it has a machine which it will sell to Company C and Company C agrees to buy the machine from Company B. For VAT purposes, the machine has been sold by Company A to Company B and then

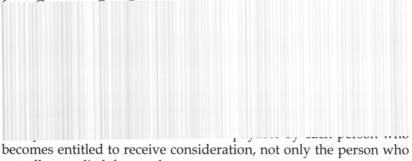

becomes entitled to receive consideration, not only the person who actually supplied the goods.

5. The transfer of goods to the State or a local authority under a compulsory purchase order (CPO) or goods that have been seized by someone acting under statutory authority.

> **Tax Tip** There is typically minimal (if any) scope for negotiation with respect to VAT liabilities in the context of a CPO or statutory seizure of goods, but nevertheless it is necessary to remember that they are deemed to be a supply of goods in question for VAT purposes, and so the owner of the goods may be left with an unwelcome VAT liability on the deemed 'supply'.

6. The application of movable goods on which any input credit has been claimed, to a non-business, non-taxable or VAT-exempt use. This is commonly referred to as a 'self-supply' of the goods and includes disposals of goods free of charge (gifts). The following example illustrates the point.

EXAMPLE 2.1: SELF-SUPPLY OF MOVABLE GOODS

A VAT-registered sole trader provides VATable consultancy services in one premises and also provides VAT-exempt educational services in another premises. The trader buys furniture for use in the consultancy trade premises (and reclaims the VAT arising on the purchase accordingly) but then a short time later decides to use the furniture for the VAT-exempt educational activities, so he moves the furniture. As the goods have been applied to a VAT-exempt use, a VAT charge arises for the sole trader on the transfer that effectively 'claws back' the VAT recovery previously taken.

If the trader instead decided to use the furniture for private use or to give it away for free, a VAT charge also arises in this instance as the trader has effectively diverted the furniture from a business use.

Tax Tip The VAT charge on gifts is avoided if the gift is made for business purposes and either the total VAT-exclusive cost of the item (or items, in the case of a series of gifts) to the disposer does not exceed €20, or where the gift is a commercial sample (i.e. not in a form normally available for sale) that is given to an actual, or potential, customer.

Tax Tip With respect to the €20 relief, you should note that this is an 'all in or all out' provision so that, for example, a business gift costing €20.01 does not qualify for any relief.

Tax Tip Goods replaced under warranty are normally not considered to be a 'gift' for VAT purposes.

Tax Tip Special offers such as 'two for the price of one' or 'buy one, get one free' are not typically seen as gifts. Rather, they are generally considered to be simply a reduction in price for the relevant items, and regular VAT rules therefore apply to such supplies.

Tax Tip In an audit situation, with respect to a self-supplied good, it would be worth considering if an argument can be made that VAT should arise on the value of the good in question at the time the self-supply was made rather than on its original cost. For example, Peter purchased a new laptop for use in his trade and he recovered the VAT accordingly. The laptop cost approximately €2,000 and the VAT reclaimed was approximately €500. Five years later, the laptop was worth €100 so he gave it to his sister for free and purchased a new one. Technically, Peter has a VAT liability of €500 arising from the gift to his sister as that is the amount he reclaimed when he bought it. However, Revenue may accept that the VAT liability should be based on the value of the laptop at the time it was given away (i.e. VAT included in the €100).

below.

8. For VAT purposes, a supply of immovable goods (land and build-ings) is regarded as including the transfer in substance of the right to dispose of the goods (e.g. as owner). An example of this is where a vendor sells a 999-year 'lease' in an apartment for an upfront mar-ket value price. Although this is not legally a freehold sale, for VAT purposes it would be treated as a supply of the goods in light of the substance of the transaction. Some of the main aspects of the VAT on property rules are outlined in **Chapter 4**.

VAT Registration Threshold

As outlined in **Chapter 1**, Irish VAT law provides that where an Irish-established trader makes taxable supplies in Ireland, then unless the trader elects to VAT register in Ireland, the trader will not actually be required to VAT-register with respect to those sales until it exceeds or is likely to exceed the relevant VAT registration threshold.

Where at least 90% of an Irish established trader's turnover is derived from the supply of goods, the relevant threshold is €75,000 (referred to as the 'goods threshold'); otherwise, the threshold is €37,500 (referred to as the 'services threshold'). In each case, the thresholds are applied by looking at continuous periods of 12 months. However, for non-Irish established traders, there is a 'nil' VAT-registration threshold, which means that unless another provision of VAT law expressly relieves the supplier from doing so, the supplier will be required to VAT-register and account for any VAT arising on even very low-value sales of goods in Ireland.

As there is a potential for the Exchequer to be left at a loss if a supplier simply fails to remit the VAT arising, Revenue is permitted by law to require VAT-registered persons supplying taxable goods or services to provide security for the VAT that becomes due as a result of sales made in Ireland, e.g. by way of a bond. Also, Irish 'premises providers' (i.e. anyone who allows another person on to their property to trade) can be made jointly and severally liable for outstanding VAT due on the sale of goods in their premises by certain mobile (non-established) traders, unless the premises provider gives certain information to Revenue on the traders in advance of the traders using the premises.

The VAT legislation also sets out the procedures to be followed where goods are disposed of by way of a forced sale, e.g. by a receiver or mortgagee in possession. These are outlined in **Chapter 8**.

Deemed Non-supplies of Goods

As can be seen from the above, a 'supply' of goods is deemed to take place in a broad range of situations. Conversely, section 20 VATCA 2010 deems a number of transactions to be 'non-supplies' so that they are effectively disregarded for VAT purposes:

- In a hire-purchase agreement we have seen that the initial handing over of goods to the customer is treated as a supply of goods for VAT purposes. At the end of the hire-purchase agreement, in order to avoid double taxation, the transfer of legal ownership is deemed not to be a supply of goods for VAT purposes when the ownership of the goods is transferred.
- Where the legal ownership of goods is handed over as security for a loan (e.g. for a mortgage), the transfer is deemed not to be a supply. Similarly, the legal transfer back of the goods by the bank (when the loan has been repaid) is considered a non-supply.
- The transfer of assets that form part of a business (and can themselves be operated as an independent business undertaking) is deemed not to be a supply of goods for VAT purposes in certain circumstances. This is commonly referred to as VAT 'transfer of business relief'. In order for transfer of business relief to apply to the sale of goods, the transferee must be an 'accountable person', i.e. Irish VAT-registered or required to be VAT-registered. Typically, relief would not apply to the 'standalone' sale of stock-in-trade or the once-off sale of business assets. As practitioners commonly have to consider whether this relief applies, we have provided in **Appendix B** to this book the relevant Revenue guidance which outlines circumstances where transfer of business relief may apply.

- Where an insurance company disposes of assets that it accepts from an insured person as part of the settlement of a claim, then that disposal is deemed not to be a supply for VAT purposes if the insured party paid VAT on acquiring the goods and was not entitled to reclaim any of that VAT.

The relevant detailed provisions regarding the place of supply of goods can be found in sections 29 to 31 VATCA 2010. Some key aspects of these rules are as follows.

1. In the case of goods that are not dispatched or transported, the place of supply is where the goods are physically located at the time of supply.

EXAMPLE 2.2: GOODS THAT ARE NOT DISPATCHED OR TRANSPORTED

If a French supplier agrees with an Italian business to sell goods located in Cork, the place of supply of the transaction is Ireland and therefore Irish VAT rules apply, regardless of the nationalities of the parties involved.

It will be apparent from **Example 2.2** that if goods are located outside Ireland at the time of supply, the sale is 'outside the scope' of Irish VAT and instead the relevant foreign rules will need to be identified and respected.

Tax Tip Particular care should be taken where goods are sold in non-EU countries as any number of local (non-EU) taxes and compliance obligations may be relevant, and depending on the circumstances these taxes may prove to be an absolute cost for either the vendor or customer.

2. In the case of goods that are dispatched or transported (but excluding 'distance sales' which are outlined below), the place of supply is where the transportation begins.

EXAMPLE 2.3: GOODS THAT ARE DISPATCHED OR TRANSPORTED

If a vendor sells goods that are dispatched from Galway to Oslo, the place of supply is Ireland. Conversely, if the goods sold by the vendor were dispatched to Galway from Oslo, the place of supply would be Norway.

At this point it is worth noting that where Ireland is the place of supply, then even though the goods in question may normally attract VAT at a positive rate (e.g. 23%), it may be possible for the vendor to apply 0% Irish VAT ('zero-rating') to the goods on the basis that they are being dispatched abroad.

Intra-Community Supplies

For cross-border EU dispatches, in order to support zero-rating of goods that would normally attract a higher rate of VAT, it is necessary that the vendor can demonstrate that the goods are being physically dispatched from Ireland to a VAT-registered customer in another EU Member State within three months of the supply.

These zero-rated transactions are commonly referred to as 'intra-Community supplies' of goods. Evidence of the transport and the customer's VAT number should be retained as part of the vendor's VAT records, and certain VAT invoicing formalities must be observed (see below). For the purposes of zero-rating the supply, it is not necessary that the EU country of the customer's VAT number and the EU country where the goods arrive are the same.

However, it is vital that the supplier is satisfied that the conditions for zero-rating are met (or will be met) before making a sale without charging VAT. If the necessary conditions are not met, the vendor may be liable to VAT on the sale at the rate that would normally be applicable to the goods in Ireland, e.g. 23%.

Effectively, as a 'quid pro quo' for the vendor applying 0% VAT on an intra-Community supply of goods, the customer is normally regarded as making an 'intra-Community acquisition' of the goods on which the customer is required to self-assess for local VAT in the other EU country on the reverse-charge basis. This is discussed in further detail below.

EU Commission's VAT Information Exchange System ('VIES') website.[2]

Exports of Goods to non-EU Countries

For exports of goods that are dispatched by the vendor from Ireland to non-EU countries, the place of supply is Ireland and the 0% VAT rate can be applied where the vendor can show evidence that an export to a non-EU country has in fact taken place.

Tax Tip In the case of an export of goods where the purchaser is dealing with transport, in order to apply the 0% VAT rate (instead of the normal applicable VAT rate) the vendor must satisfy itself that the purchaser is not established in Ireland.

Tax Tip To ensure the VAT treatment applied to the sale of goods is correct, it is important to know which countries are regarded as being within the EU for VAT purposes. At the time of writing, the 28 EU Member States are: Austria, Belgium, Bulgaria, Croatia, Cyprus, Czech Republic, Denmark, Estonia, Finland, France, Germany, Greece, Hungary, Ireland, Italy, Latvia, Lithuania, Luxembourg, Malta, Netherlands, Poland, Portugal, Romania, Slovakia, Slovenia, Spain, Sweden and the United Kingdom.

[2] See http://ec.europa.eu/taxation_customs/vies/ (accessed January 2016).

> **Tax Tip** It is also important to be aware of the countries and territories that are excluded from the VAT territory of the EU. Examples of these areas include: Jersey, Gibraltar, the Åland Islands, Livigno, Campione d'Italia and the Italian waters of Lake Lugano, the Canary Islands, Ceuta and Melilla, Andorra, the Faroe Islands, Greenland, the French Overseas territories (DOM), the Netherlands Antilles, San Marino and Vatican City.

Distance Sales

In the case of a 'distance sale' of goods (being goods dispatched from Ireland by or on behalf of the vendor to a non-VAT registered customer in another EU Member State, or goods dispatched by or on behalf of a vendor in another EU Member State to an unregistered customer in Ireland) instead of the place of supply being where transportation begins, the place of supply is where the transportation ends. Distance sales rules do not apply to new means of transport (e.g. a new motor car). A common example of distance sales is a mail-order sale of goods to a private individual. For example, if an Irish company created a website selling leprechaun figurines and orders were received from German and French private customers, such sales would be considered 'distance sales'. The VAT liability on the sale of the goods to those customers would be due in Germany and France.

The distance sales place of supply rule can trigger multiple VAT registration requirements and ongoing compliance obligations for a mail-order company selling to customers in other EU countries. This can cause a number of difficulties for the supplier, not least when a supplier would prefer to apply universal pricing for the goods in question (as the VAT rate applicable in the relevant countries can differ).

However, provided the goods are not subject to excise duty, this distance sale place of supply rule may be ignored (so that the place of supply continues to be the country where transportation begins) where the value of the sales is below the relevant threshold for the EU 'destination' country in question. The threshold is typically the equivalent of €35,000 or €100,000, depending on the country and the local currency. For EU businesses making distance sales of goods into Ireland, the Irish threshold is breached when the business either exceeds or is likely to exceed €35,000 of distance sales into Ireland per calendar year.

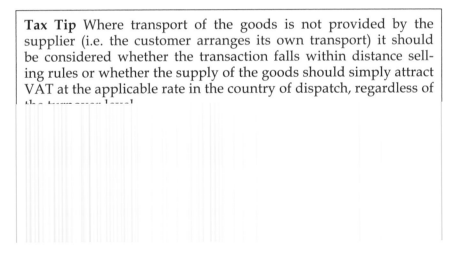

Tax Tip Where transport of the goods is not provided by the supplier (i.e. the customer arranges its own transport) it should be considered whether the transaction falls within distance selling rules or whether the supply of the goods should simply attract VAT at the applicable rate in the country of dispatch, regardless of the turnover level.

Supply and Installation of Goods

Supplies of goods that are installed or assembled by the supplier are deemed to be supplied where the installation or assembly takes place.

EXAMPLE 2.4: GOODS THAT ARE INSTALLED OR ASSEMBLED BY THE SUPPLIER

An Austrian business supplies and installs goods in Ireland. The place of supply for VAT purposes is Ireland. As previously discussed, because there is a 'nil' VAT registration threshold in Ireland for non-Irish established suppliers, it could be expected that the Austrian supplier would automatically be obliged to VAT register here.

However, where the customer carries on a business in Ireland or is a public body (such as a local authority), a reverse-charge procedure applies so that the customer must self-assess for any VAT arising on the supply of the goods (section 10(2) VATCA 2010). This can result in non-Irish established suppliers being freed of any obligation to VAT register here, i.e. if they are only carrying out 'reverse-charge' contracts in Ireland. The supplier may of course be obliged to VAT register in Ireland due to other transactions it carries out.

Goods Sold Onboard Journeys within the European Union

Where goods are sold onboard aircraft, trains, or vessels that have a departure and destination within the EU, then the place of supply is the country where the journey commenced.

Intra-Community Acquisitions (ICAs)

Detailed rules for intra-Community acquisitions of goods (ICAs) are set out in sections 3, 9, 14, 24, 32 and 92 VATCA 2010 as well as the 2010 VAT Regulations.

Broadly, ICAs occur when a business or public body acquire goods that are dispatched from another EU Member State. If a party making an ICA in Ireland is either already Irish VAT-registered or else is not Irish VAT-registered (e.g. a business carrying out VAT-exempt sales) but the value of its ICA in Ireland exceeds (or is likely to exceed) €41,000 in a 12-month period, then the party must self-account for VAT on the ICA on the reverse-charge basis.

Tax Tip The €41,000 threshold does not apply to ICAs of 'new means of transport' (see below and the definition in section 2 VATCA 2010) or to goods that are subject to excise duty. Special VAT rules also apply to certain transactions involving alcohol products, to align the VAT and excise duty treatment. (More can be found on these rules in section 92 VATCA 2010.)

The reverse charge rule for ICAs of goods often results in businesses and public bodies triggering an obligation to VAT register and remit VAT to Revenue, even though their ongoing sales are not subject to VAT. For purchasers that have full VAT recovery, however, there may be a silver lining. When such purchasers self-account for VAT (i.e. include the VAT amount in the 'Box T1' sales figures and also in the 'Box T2' purchases figures in the same VAT return (see **Chapter 1**)) the transaction should be cash-flow neutral from an Irish VAT perspective as the entries in the VAT return are effectively self-cancelling.

Tax Tip Interestingly, there may be a slight cash-flow advantage for a business that purchases goods from outside the State compared to making purchases from an Irish supplier (where VAT would generally need to be paid to the supplier and then reclaimed from Revenue).

ICAs are also considered to occur where anyone (even a private individual) acquires a 'new means of transport' from another EU Member State. For example, in the case of a car, the person normally remits VAT on the acquisition into Ireland at the same time as paying vehicle registration tax (VRT).

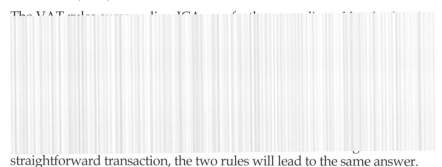

straightforward transaction, the two rules will lead to the same answer.

Example 2.5: Intra-Community Acquisition of Goods in One EU Country

If an Irish VAT-registered company in Kilkenny purchases goods that are dispatched to Ireland from a supplier in the UK and gives its Irish VAT number to the UK company, then the place of the ICA will be Ireland under both of the rules outlined above. This is on the basis that the goods will arrive in Ireland and the Kilkenny purchaser is registered for VAT in Ireland. The Kilkenny company will then self-account for Irish VAT on the ICA on the reverse-charge basis.

However, in other cases, it is possible that VAT could arise in other jurisdictions, as shown in **Example 2.6** below.

Example 2.6: Possible Intra-Community Acquisitions of Goods in Two EU Countries

If an Irish VAT-registered company purchases goods from a UK supplier and asks the UK supplier to deliver the goods to a branch of the Irish company in Slovakia, there would typically be an ICA in Slovakia as the goods are transported there. Subject to Slovakian

VAT law (and also the availability of 'triangulation relief' – discussed below), it is possible that the Irish company would have obligations to deal with the ICA in Slovakia and also remit Slovakian VAT on any subsequent sales of the goods in Slovakia. In addition, and as already outlined above, if the Irish company provides its Irish VAT number to the UK supplier in order for the supplier to zero rate the supply, the Irish company would also be deemed to have made an intra-Community acquisition in Ireland. Consequently, it is necessary to consider whether triangulation relief can be applied in order to simplify the VAT implications and remove VAT liabilities in multiple countries.

Triangulation

As outlined in the example above, VAT legislation deems the place where an ICA takes place to be the country where the transportation in relation to the supply ends. However, it also deems the place of the ICA to be where the purchaser is registered for VAT. The combination of these two rules could lead to difficulty.

Triangulation relief is a simplification measure designed to prevent traders being obliged to register for VAT in multiple EU countries in relation to transactions involving the same goods. It only applies where there are three parties in a chain of transactions, each located in three separate EU Member States. An example is the best way to explain this.

EXAMPLE 2.7: TRIANGULATION RELIEF IN CHAIN TRANSACTIONS

IreCo (based in County Kerry) intends to sell goods to UKCo (based in London) who in turn will sell the goods to SwedishCo in Stockholm. The goods will move directly from Kerry to Stockholm. IreCo will 'zero rate' the sale to UKCo as the latter is UK VAT-registered and the goods are being delivered from Ireland to another EU Member State within three months of the supply. Under general EU VAT principles (and subject to any nuances in local legislation) UKCo will be obliged to self-account for VAT in the UK (where it is VAT registered) and it will also be obliged to self-account for VAT in Sweden as this is the place where the transportation ends. To prevent situations like this, triangulation relief was formulated.

Where the conditions for triangulation relief are met, instead of UKCo (the 'middle trader' in the triangular arrangements) being

further below); and

- SwedishCo self-accounts for VAT on the goods at the appropriate rate in Sweden.

Triangulation relief effectively allows the 'middle trader' in the triangle to disregard the rule that imposes an obligation on a person to record an ICA in their own country of VAT registration as well as the country where the goods arrive (assuming various conditions are satisfied).

Tax Tip Different EU Members States have varying conditions and procedures with respect to triangulation relief. For example, it may be the case that the local tax authorities must be notified in advance of the transaction in order for the relief to apply. Consequently, always make sure to check the position in the relevant countries to ensure that the local requirements are being met.

Tax Tip If Ireland is the place where the goods arrive and the middle trader is not established in Ireland, then, provided the middle trader is selling the goods to an accountable person (i.e. someone who is Irish VAT-registered or required to be registered), section 23 VATCA 2010 allows the middle trader to avoid registering for Irish VAT and instead obliges the Irish customer to self-account on the goods.

Statistical Obligations in Relation to EU Transactions

There are a number of statistical VAT requirements to be met when goods are sold cross-border within the EU. Penalties can apply where these obligations are not satisfied.

- The Irish VAT return ('VAT3 return') contains Boxes E1 and E2, which respectively record the VAT exclusive value of dispatches of goods from Ireland and arrivals of goods into Ireland (see **Chapter 1**).
- In addition, suppliers making any 'zero-rated' intra-Community supplies of goods from Ireland to VAT-registered customers in other EU Member States must file electronic VIES statements that record the value of the supplies being made and the VAT-registration numbers of the customers. These statements are filed on the Revenue On-Line Service (ROS) on a quarterly basis, unless the VAT-exclusive value of the intra-Community supplies exceeds €50,000 per calendar quarter (or in any one of the past four quarters), in which case the statements must be filed on a monthly basis. VIES returns also apply to supplies of services.
- INTRASTAT returns also need to be filed if either the value of goods dispatched from Ireland to other EU countries exceeds €635,000 annually or if the value of goods acquired into Ireland from other EU countries exceeds €500,000 annually (the arrivals return threshold was €191,000 prior to 1 January 2016). These are detailed electronic returns that record details such as the value and quantity of the goods as well as their commodity code. INTRASTAT returns only applies to goods.

Tax Tip INTRASTAT returns and VIES statements are administered by the VIMA (VIES, IntraStat, Mutual Assistance) Office in Dundalk, County Louth. Refer to the 'VIES and INTRASTAT Traders Manual' (available on www.revenue.ie) for more details on these returns.

Imports of Goods from Outside the European Union

When goods are imported from outside the EU, generally VAT must be paid at the point of entry (i.e. at the same time as any customs duty). The rate of VAT payable on importation into Ireland should be the same as the rate that applies to sales of the same product in Ireland. For example, if an Irish supermarket imports apples into Ireland from

South America, the VAT rate applying on importation would be 0% because apples are subject to VAT at 0% in Ireland.

It may be possible to defer payment of VAT on importation by obtaining authorisation from Revenue, although this can generally only be obtained when the trader is known to Revenue and has provided a bank guarantee to Revenue. In addition, it may be possible to ~~~ ~~~

~~import VAT is then~~ reclaimed in the normal manner by taking an input credit in the relevant VAT3 return (i.e. it is included as purchases VAT in Box T2).

Tax Tip Although this book only addresses VAT, it is clearly important for anyone importing goods into Ireland to also identify any customs duty implications and liabilities. Businesses commonly use customs clearance agents to assist with these.

VAT56 Authorisation

Irish VAT legislation contains a cash-flow relieving procedure whereby traders may be authorised by Revenue to purchase or import most goods and services at the 0% VAT rate, provided various conditions are met. The detailed rules are contained in section 56 VATCA 2010, but a key requirement of the application is that the trader can show that at least 75% of its turnover derives from one or more of the following:

- zero-rated intra-Community dispatches of goods from Ireland to VAT-registered customers in other EU countries;
- exports of goods from Ireland to non-EU countries; or
- contract work on goods that are returned to customers outside of Ireland.

When the authorisation is obtained, the business provides a copy of the authorisation (which generally lasts for one to two years) to its suppliers, who then quote the relevant authorisation number on their invoices (and do not charge VAT on the invoices). Penalties can be imposed where the authorised person fails to notify Revenue that it has ceased to qualify for the relief. The authorisation cannot be used for expenditure such as the purchase or hire of passenger motor vehicles, petrol, food, drink, most accommodation, entertainment or other personal services. Instead, VAT is applied as normal on these. Also, if an authorised person uses the authorisation to make a purchase at the 0% rate but applies the purchase to a VAT-exempt or non-business purpose, the authorised person normally triggers a VAT liability on the purchase, i.e. in order to leave it in the same position as any other trader that makes a 'self-supply' of goods.

> **Tax Tip** Suppliers that are applying the 0% VAT rate on sales in reliance on a section 56 authorisation provided by a customer should ensure that they keep track of the expiry date on the authorisation. Otherwise, the supplier may be liable for VAT on the sale in the normal manner.

Summary of VAT Issues Impacting on Irish Businesses operating in an International Context

Though this book does not cover all aspects of VAT legislation in relation to cross-border and international trade, the following summarises the Irish VAT treatment covering common types of cross-border transactions involving the sale of goods in which a trader will be involved.

- If goods are sold within Ireland, the place of supply is Ireland, and Irish VAT should normally be charged at the appropriate rate. Where the supplier is not established in Ireland, the reverse charge procedure may apply to the sale in supply-and-install or triangulation relief scenarios, subject to meeting the necessary conditions. A reverse charge also applies to certain sales of scrap metal between businesses and (with effect from 1 January 2016) to certain wholesale supplies of gas and electricity and also gas and electricity certificates in Ireland (even where both parties are established in Ireland).
- If goods are sold from Ireland and dispatched to a VAT-registered customer in another EU Member State, then the vendor should zero-rate the supply and should quote the customer's VAT number on the invoice (assuming the various conditions are satisfied).
- If goods are sold and dispatched by the vendor from Ireland to an unregistered person in another EU Member State, then Irish VAT should be charged. However, if the value of sales made exceeds

the distance-selling threshold in the other country, then there may be an obligation to account for local VAT in that other country; as already noted, each country has its own threshold, but they are typically either €35,000 or €100,000, depending on the size of the country. The vendor can normally elect to account for local VAT even if the relevant threshold is not met, in which case the relevant procedural

acquisition (ICA) of goods in Ireland, they must self-account for VAT at the appropriate rate. This generally is a VAT cash-flow neutral transaction, provided the trader has full VAT recovery entitlement.

- If a taxable person (as well as public bodies and local authorities, etc.) makes an intra-Community acquisition of goods into Ireland, then even if they normally have no other reason to be VAT-registered, they must self-account for the VAT arising if the value exceeds €41,000 in a continuous 12-month period.
- Anyone who imports goods into Ireland from outside the EU must pay VAT at the point of entry at the appropriate rate of VAT, unless a deferral is agreed with Revenue. If there is VAT recovery entitlement, the importer should ensure that appropriate documentation is obtained in order to support taking an input credit on the import.
- If goods are sold outside Ireland (and particularly in a non-EU country), it is important to confirm the applicable local rules, especially as certain local taxes may not be reclaimable.
- Businesses engaged in cross-border trade need to ensure that their systems are equipped to satisfy relevant VAT invoicing and compliance requirements, including any obligation to file statistical returns.

Conclusion

As we have seen in **Chapter 1**, for VAT purposes, transactions are generally categorised as being supplies of goods or supplies of services. This chapter examined the more important VAT rules governing supplies of goods in Ireland and in an international context. We will now move on to the rules that apply to supplies of services.

- Introduction

- How to Determine if 'Services' are being Supplied

- Intangible Assets and Transfer of Business Relief

- Self-supplies of Services and Services Supplied through Agents

- Place where Services are Supplied

- Exceptions to the General Place of Supply Rules

- Use and Enjoyment Rules

- Mini One Stop Shop ('MOSS')

- VAT Recovery

- Conclusion

Introduction

Having, in the previous chapter, examined the VAT rules that apply to supplies of goods, we now turn our attention to the rules that apply to supplies of services. This chapter outlines when a supply of services is considered to occur for VAT purposes and also how cross-border sup-

all transactions that are not supplies of goods. Key provisions of the VAT legislation dealing with supplies of services are contained in sections 25 to 28 of the Value-added Tax Consolidation Act 2010 (VATCA 2010).

Examples of 'services' for VAT purposes include:
- provision of most food and drink in the course of running a restaurant/café, etc., or from a vending machine;
- supplies of intangible assets such as goodwill, know-how and other intellectual property;
- provision of loans and supplies of insurance;
- supplies of software licences and downloads, e.g. music, images;
- provision of staff (e.g. hire of personnel);
- leasing goods (with respect to immovable goods, this is subject to the specific VAT on property rules (see **Chapter 4**));
- agreeing to perform an act, or agreeing to omit to perform an act, e.g. agreeing not to compete with a business in a particular geographical area for a fee.

In addition, VAT law specifically states that the 'toleration of a situation' is the supply of a service. For example, Revenue has stated in its guidance that it views the granting of rights-of-way over land as a service for VAT purposes.

Tax Tip The starting position for a practitioner who is considering the VAT treatment of transactions is to remember that services are broadly defined for VAT purposes. This means that unless a transaction is either (i) regarded as a supply of goods or (ii) outside the scope of VAT entirely (e.g. certain non-business transactions), a practitioner's starting point should generally be that supply of services is taking place.

59

Generally, it is apparent in a services transaction who is receiving the services in question as this will usually coincide with who is engaging and instructing the work.

In certain cases, however, VAT law deems services to be provided to a particular party to the transaction. Examples of this include services provided through an agent (which are considered in more detail below) and also the legal services of barristers and solicitors where insurance claims are being resolved. In the latter case, and despite the insurance company appointing the legal services in question, VAT law deems the legal services to be supplied to the insured person (consequently enabling the insured party to reclaim VAT on the services in line with their normal entitlement).

Intangible Assets and Transfer of Business Relief

Although services are construed broadly, VAT law specifies that the transfer of intangible business assets (e.g. goodwill, intellectual property rights, etc.) in connection with the transfer of a business should effectively be disregarded for VAT purposes where certain conditions in section 26 VATCA 2010 are met. This is the corollary of the transfer of business relief available for goods (see section 20(2)(c) VATCA 2010) as outlined in **Chapter 2** and the associated Revenue VAT information leaflet, the text of which is reproduced at **Appendix B**.

Self-supplies of Services and Services Supplied through Agents

There are special VAT rules dealing with self-supplies of services and services supplied through agents or intermediaries.

In **Chapter 2**, we considered VAT liabilities that can arise on 'self-supplies' in the context of goods. 'Self-supplies' are more limited in respect of services and currently include catering supplies made entirely free of charge by employers to employees, as well as the usage of certain immovable goods (land and buildings) that form part of the assets of a business that were acquired or developed before January 2011 for private or non-business use (see section 27 VATCA 2010). Self-supplies of properties (e.g. the private use of a property acquired for a VATable business purpose) are dealt with under the Capital Goods Scheme (see **Chapter 4**). Where a self-supply of services occurs, an absolute VAT cost arises, i.e. it is not recoverable.

Where services are supplied using an agent, it is necessary to consider if the agency arrangement is disclosed or undisclosed (see **Chapter 1**). In practice, there can be significant variations and permutations in how agency arrangements are structured, so care should always be taken in this area, as the VAT implications may differ. However, some general VAT rules to be aware of are as follows:

they are dealing with the agent. This would be because the undisclosed agent is concluding contracts and purporting to act in its own name, but is in fact acting under the instructions of and for the account of the principal. In an undisclosed agency scenario, two supplies of services are deemed to occur simultaneously for VAT purposes. The principal is viewed as supplying the services in question to the agent (and issues a VAT invoice to the agent for the services) and the agent in turn is viewed as onwards supplying the services to the purchaser. Consequently, the agent invoices the purchaser for the services and as the invoice includes margin/commission, this follows the same VAT treatment (e.g. VAT rate) as the service in question.

Tax Tip Care should always be taken in relation to sales of services through agents or intermediaries as the VAT treatment and invoicing requirements can differ significantly depending on the specific arrangements.

Place where Services are Supplied

As with supplies of goods, there are specific 'place of supply' rules to determine where services are treated as occurring for VAT purposes. The current key provisions are contained in the Council Implementing Regulation (EU) No. 282/2011 (the '2011 Implementing Regulation') and also sections 33 to 35 VATCA 2010, which set out general place of supply rules, followed by a number of exceptions.

The general place of supply rules depend on whether the customer is a 'taxable person' (i.e. a person involved in business) or a consumer. Supplies to business customers are known as 'business to business' (B2B) supplies, while supplies to consumers are known as 'business to consumer' (B2C) supplies. A supplier trying to establish in good faith whether the customer is 'in business' for these purposes can typically use any commercial information available about the customer, or else can rely on the fact that the customer has provided an EU VAT registration number.

Tax Tip It is good practice to verify VAT numbers using the EU Commission's VIES website (http://ec.europa.eu/taxation_customs/vies) and to keep evidence (as part of the business's VAT records) that checks are carried out periodically in respect of customer VAT numbers.

Business-to-Business (B2B) Supplies of Services – General Rule (section 34(a) VATCA 2010)

For B2B supplies, the basic aim is to treat the services as being supplied where they are received. Therefore, the general place of supply rule is that if services are supplied to a 'taxable person' (i.e. a business) acting as such, the services are treated as taking place in the country where the business customer is established/located. If the services are being provided to an establishment of the customer in some other country, the services are treated as taking place there. If the business customer does not have a place of business or such an establishment, the place of supply is where the person receiving the service has their permanent address or usual place of residence. (We consider the meaning of 'establishment' further below.)

Once the place of supply has been identified, the next question is: which party to the transaction is required to remit any VAT arising in that country on the services?

Where the supplier itself has its place of business or establishment in the country where the services are regarded as taking place, the supplier may be obliged to charge local VAT. However, where the supplier is not established in that country, then instead of the supplier being required to charge VAT to the customer on the services in that country, generally the business customer is required to 'self-account' for any VAT arising on the services in that country, i.e. the 'reverse charge' procedure applies, as outlined in **Chapter 1**. The following example illustrates the point.

EXAMPLE 3.1: REVERSE-CHARGE PROCEDURE

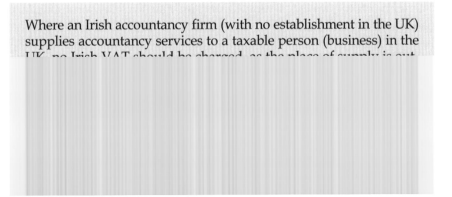

Where an Irish accountancy firm (with no establishment in the UK) supplies accountancy services to a taxable person (business) in the UK, no Irish VAT should be charged, as the place of supply is out...

Instead of the supplier invoicing with a VAT charge, the Irish business customer in the example above self-accounts for Irish VAT at the standard rate on the services (if the customer is not already Irish VAT-registered, a 'nil' VAT registration threshold applies (see below)) and may take VAT recovery on the services in the same return under normal VAT recovery rules. This means that the receipt of the services may well be VAT cash-flow neutral in Ireland for the customer (i.e. where the customer has full VAT recovery entitlement) or, conversely, if the customer does not have full VAT recovery, a net VAT liability may arise and be payable by the customer to the Irish Revenue Commissioners.

> **Tax Tip** The reverse-charge mechanism for general B2B services is often referred to as the 'Fourth Schedule service' rules. This is because in the VAT legislation preceding VATCA 2010 (i.e. Value-added Tax Act 1972, as amended) there was a reverse-charge rule when certain conditions were met for a list of services specified in the Fourth Schedule of that Act.

The Concepts of 'Establishment' and 'Place of Business' At this point, it is worth considering what the concepts 'establishment' and 'place of business' mean for VAT purposes.

Establishment Typically, the place where a business is regarded as being located is where the functions of the business's central administration are carried out. Relevant factors to consider in this context include identifying where decisions concerning the general management of the business are taken, where the registered office of the business is located and where management meets (not merely the presence of a postal address).

The term 'establishment' is not defined in Irish VAT law and does not necessarily have the same meaning as the term 'permanent establishment' (which is used in direct tax rules and double taxation treaties). The Court of Justice of the European Union (CJEU) has decided that for VAT purposes, in order for a business to have an establishment in a country, there must be the permanent presence of human and technical resources necessary to supply the services in question.[1] For example, in different cases, it was confirmed that the mere presence of either a fleet of cars or gaming machines on a ferry did not in themselves constitute VAT establishments.

The 2011 Implementing Regulation subsequently sets out a legislative definition of establishment in the context of the place of supply rules and broadly reiterated the permanent presence of human and technical resources criteria. Having a VAT number in another EU Member State would not in itself automatically mean that the business has a VAT establishment there but if, for example, the business has an agent working on its behalf in another country, it would be advisable to consider whether this would constitute an establishment there, especially if the agent is negotiating or concluding any contracts, or playing a role in the delivery of the services to the customer.

Tax Tip Care should always be taken when considering whether an establishment exists for VAT purposes. This can be a contentious area and will depend on the specific facts of the case. Practitioners should also always refer to the detailed rules in the 2011 Implementing Regulation when undertaking any analysis. In addition, it should, of course, be remembered that the concept of establishment is effectively a rolling concept, i.e. businesses should continue to monitor their presence in other jurisdictions in case any change in activities or other developments alter the analysis

---

Invoicing and Statistical Filings for Supplies of Services falling under the B2B General Rule As already discussed, under the general B2B place of supply rules, the supplier does not charge VAT to foreign business customers and instead the business customer self-accounts for any local VAT under the reverse-charge basis. Despite not being liable for Irish VAT on the services, an Irish supplier providing such services

---

[1] See *ARO Lease BV v. Inspecteur van de Belastingdienst Grote Ondernemingen te Amsterdam* [Case C-190/95] and also *Gunter Berkholz v. Finanzamt Hamburg–Mitte–Altstadt* [Case C-168/84].

to customers in other EU countries is nevertheless obliged to respect certain VAT invoicing and statistical filings requirements:

- Regarding invoicing, the Irish supplier must issue a VAT invoice for B2B supplies to EU (non-Irish) customers which (i) states the customer's EU VAT number and (ii) indicates on the face of the invoice that a reverse-charge rule applies.

outside Ireland but in the EU, then the supplier will have to comply with the rules regarding invoicing, include the relevant amount in the statistical part of the VAT return (Box ES1) and also complete VIES returns. However, if the customer is established outside of the EU, then these obligations should not arise.

VAT Registration and Statistical Filings where Services falling under the B2B General rule are Received in Ireland Where reverse-charge services that fall under the B2B general rule are received in Ireland from a supplier (either in another EU country or from a non-EU country) by an Irish VAT-registered person or a 'taxable person' acting as such and carrying on a business in Ireland, the customer is generally obliged to self-account for any VAT arising (section 12 VATCA 2010). A 'nil' VAT registration threshold applies in Ireland in this context, so that an Irish business that receives VATable reverse-charge services in Ireland but whose supplies are all VAT exempt would still be required to Irish VAT register.

The customer is also required to record the VAT exclusive value of any such taxable reverse-charge services received in Ireland from non-Irish EU businesses in Box ES2 of its VAT return(s). The following example illustrates the point.

EXAMPLE 3.2: REVERSE-CHARGE MECHANISM – VAT-EXEMPT BUSINESS

Aoife is a sole trader and operates a bookmaker business through a shop in Dundalk (she's a 'bookie'). The activities of bookmakers are exempt from VAT in Ireland and Aoife is not registered for VAT. In order to grow the business, Aoife engages the consultancy services of a retail specialist who is based in Belfast. The retail specialist provides consultancy services to Aoife and a fee of €5,000 is agreed. As a result, Aoife is obliged to register for VAT and to self-account for VAT on the service received (€5,000 @ 23% = €1,150). Aoife will need to include the €1,150 of VAT as sales VAT (Box T1) in her VAT return as well as the value of the service received (€5,000) in Box ES2 of the return. Aoife will not be able to recover the VAT as she is involved in a VAT-exempt activity and the cost relates to this activity.

Tax Tip In relation to reverse-charge transactions involving services, if a business is receiving reverse-charge taxable services in Ireland from either non-Irish EU suppliers or non-EU suppliers, the reverse charge is recorded by reflecting a VAT liability on the services (at the VAT rate applicable to the services in Ireland, e.g. 23% if the service is a standard-rated service) in Box T1 of the relevant VAT3 return. The customer then reflects a VAT input credit in Box T2 of the same VAT3 return, to the extent that the customer has VAT recovery entitlement. If the services in question are being received from a supplier in another EU country, the customer also reflects the VAT-exclusive value of the services in Box ES2 of the VAT return.

Tax Tip Given the prevalence of the reverse-charge mechanism for B2B services (and subject to the exceptions outlined below), Irish business customers should generally query situations where foreign VAT is being charged to them by suppliers. It may be appropriate to request the supplier to issue a credit note and revised invoice (without a foreign VAT charge). It can be very difficult for an Irish business to obtain a refund of foreign VAT which has been charged to it in error.

Business-to-Consumer (B2C) Supplies of Services – General Rule (section 34(b) VATCA 2010)

With respect to B2C services, the general place of supply rule is that the services are treated as being provided where the supplier's business is established/located. If the supplier is providing the services from an establishment in another country, the services are treated as being supplied there. If the supplier has no such place of business or establishment, the place of supply is where the supplier's permanent address or usual place of residence is located.

EXAMPLE 3.3: B2C SUPPLIES OF SERVICES – GENERAL RULE

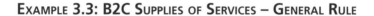

where the supplier is located is where the customer (a non-taxable person) is outside the EU and the services in question fall within a specified list (see section 33(5) VATCA 2010). Examples of such services include advertising, consultancy services, the provision of staff, data processing, etc. In such a case, the supplier is not liable to charge Irish VAT as the services are instead regarded as being supplied outside the EU, as illustrated in the following example.

EXAMPLE 3.4: B2C SUPPLIES OF SERVICES TO A NON-EU CUSTOMER

If an Irish supplier provides general advisory services to a private individual in Japan, no Irish VAT arises as the services are regarded as being supplied in Japan; however, local Japanese tax obligations should be checked.

Summary of the Supplies of Services Rules

Table 3.1 below summarises the general Irish VAT position for B2C and B2B services (falling under section 34(a) and (b) VATCA 2010). This assumes that the services in question are ordinarily subject to VAT when provided in Ireland, i.e. not VAT-exempt services such as lending/insurance, etc.

TABLE 3.1 SUPPLIES OF SERVICES – GENERAL RULES: SUMMARY OF IRISH VAT POSITION

Supplier of Service	Recipient of Service	Irish VAT Charged?	Party Liable for Irish VAT
Irish	Irish business	Yes	Supplier
Irish	Irish private	Yes	Supplier
Irish	Foreign EU business	No	N/A (likely foreign reverse-charge VAT)
Irish	Foreign EU private	Yes	Supplier
Irish	Non-EU business	No	N/A (local taxes may arise)
Irish	Non-EU private	Yes	Supplier
Irish	Non-EU private (section 33(5) and 33(m) VATCA 2010)	No	N/A (local taxes may arise)

Exceptions to the General Place of Supply Rules

As already mentioned, sections 33 to 35 VATCA 2010 contain a number of exceptions to the general place of supply rules that we have looked at for B2B and B2C services. Further details on the parameters and application of the exceptions can also be found in the 2011 Implementing Regulation.

Examples of current exceptions to the general rules can be broadly summarised as follows:

Services	Place of Supply	Comments
Passenger transport	Where transport takes place	An 'apportionment' of the services may be needed for VAT purposes where the journey crosses borders.
Services in connection with immovable goods (land and buildings, often referred to as 'land-related' services)	Where the immovable goods are located	Instead of the supplier charging VAT, a reverse charge may apply to certain 'land-related' services (e.g. services of experts and estate agents) that are supplied by a non-Irish established supplier in respect of Irish located property, where the recipient is a business in Ireland or a public body. The conditions for this reverse-charge rule are set out in section 12(2) VATCA 2010.

Intra-Community transport of goods	Place of departure	This exception only applies if supplied to a consumer.
Admissions to cultural takes place	Where the event takes place	Examples include admission to trade fairs, exhibitions, etc.
or similar services		
Valuing or working on movable goods	Where the services are physically carried out	This exception only applies if supplied B2C.
Restaurant or catering services	Where the services are physically carried out	However, where certain conditions are met and the services are provided onboard of trains, ships and planes within the EU, the place of supply is the country of departure of the train, ship or plane (section 34(k) VATCA 2010).
Short-term hiring of means of transport (e.g. cars, boats, planes)	Where the means of transport is put at the disposal of the customer	Short-term hire is defined as having the continuous possession or use of a means of transport throughout a period of not more than 30 days (or 90 days with respect to a vessel).
Long-term hiring of means of transport	Where the customer is established, has a permanent address or usually resides	This exception only applies if supplied B2C. However, if the means of transport is a pleasure boat, the B2C long-term hire services are regarded as supplied where the pleasure boat is put at the disposal of the customer if the services are being provided by the supplier from its place of business or a fixed establishment (section 34(kb) VATCA 2010).

Electronic services (e.g. downloadable software, web hosting, digital goods) telecommunications services and radio/ TV broadcasting	Where the customer is established, has a permanent address or usually resides	This exception only applies if supplied B2C. The Mini One Stop Shop ('MOSS') scheme may potentially be availed of in order to simplify VAT accounting obligations on these services (see below).
Services of 'disclosed' intermediaries (i.e. acting in the name and on behalf of another person)	Where the underlying transaction is regarded as being supplied	This exception only applies if supplied to consumers. Examples of VAT issues to consider in respect of services supplied through agents are outlined above.
Services falling within specified 'use and enjoyment' rules	Where the services are used and enjoyed	These services are specified in section 35 VATCA 2010 and are outlined further below.
Services falling within sections 33(5) and 34(m) VATCA 2010, and provided to non-EU customers	Where the customer is established, i.e. outside the EU	This exception only applies if supplied B2C (as outlined above).

Tax Tip Clearly, if a business is providing services that have a foreign country as their place of supply, then unless a reverse-charge rule applies, whereby the customer will self-assess for VAT arising there, the business will need to consider whether it is triggering foreign VAT obligations, e.g. foreign VAT-registration requirements, obligations to remit VAT and make VAT filings.

Use and Enjoyment Rules

Irish VAT law contains specific 'use and enjoyment' rules that are aimed at avoiding distortion of competition, double taxation (i.e. where services would normally be regarded under the place of supply rules as being provided in the State but are in fact effectively used and enjoyed

- hiring-out of means of transport that are used and enjoyed outside the EU (where the place of supply would otherwise normally be in Ireland and subject to Irish VAT);
- telecommunications services, telephone cards, radio or television broadcasting services that are supplied to non-EU private individuals but are in effect used and enjoyed in Ireland;
- certain banking, financial and insurance services, including reinsurance and financial fund management (but excluding the provision of safe deposit facilities) supplied to private individuals; and
- certain intermediary services in relation to money transfer services.

Tax Tip Given the complexity of the place of supply rules for services, rather than assuming that the general rules apply to a particular transaction, it is important that practitioners refer to the various exceptions (as outlined above) in the legislation and check that none of these are relevant.

Mini One Stop Shop ('MOSS')

In the normal course, a business can only remit Irish VAT in its Irish VAT returns and will need to register in other countries in order to remit VAT due to the tax authorities there. B2C supplies of electronic services, telecommunications and radio and television broadcasting services are currently regarded as supplied where the customer is established. This would normally trigger multiple foreign VAT registration obligations for businesses selling these services to non-taxable (private) customers throughout the EU.

71

However, with effect from 1 January 2015, a business making such sup-plies can instead opt to remit any foreign EU VAT due on these sales through a single VAT registration. For EU businesses, this is in the EU Member State where the supplier's business is established. For non-EU businesses making such supplies, the MOSS VAT registration can be made in the supplier's choice of Member State (or if the supplier is already established in one or more EU Member States, in any one of these Member States). This is referred to as the Mini One Stop Shop ('MOSS') scheme.

Suppliers availing of MOSS in Ireland use the Revenue On-Line Service (ROS) to file and pay quarterly VAT returns electronically for the rel-evant supplies. The Revenue Commissioners then distribute the VAT due in each Member State on the services to the relevant tax authori-ties. However, the EU Member State of MOSS registration retains a per-centage of the VAT collected on the MOSS supplies. The percentage retained is 30% during 2015/2016 and 15% during 2017/2018.

The MOSS scheme is limited to B2C supplies of electronic services, telecommunications services and radio and television broadcasting services, and also cannot be used to reclaim foreign VAT (we consider procedures for reclaiming foreign VAT further below).

More detail on the MOSS scheme (which is entirely optional but is sub-ject to meeting a number of conditions) can be found in sections 91A to 91F VATCA 2010 and also on the Revenue website (www.revenue.ie).

Tax Tip It is advisable that any supplier engaged in cross-border supplies of services should obtain local VAT/sales tax advice to ensure that it is meeting any relevant foreign tax obligations.

VAT Recovery

As already noted, the general rule for B2B services is that instead of the business customer being charged VAT, a reverse-charge rule applies. However, there will be cases where foreign VAT is being charged cor-rectly, so the question of how a business customer can seek to recover this arises.

It is not possible to reclaim any foreign input VAT through an Irish VAT registration. Consequently, if foreign VAT is being (correctly) incurred on services received, it will be necessary for the customer to identify if it has a foreign VAT registration that can be used in the relevant country to reclaim the VAT. Otherwise, if the customer is an

EU business and the VAT has been incurred within the EU, it may consider seeking to reclaim the foreign VAT through an Electronic VAT Reclaim (EVR). Further detail on EVR reclaims of Irish VAT can be found in section 101 VATCA 2010. Non-EU traders may be able to reclaim the VAT through what is commonly referred to as the '13th Directive reclaim' procedure (in Ireland, these claims are submit-

---

Tax Tip If a business incurs non-EU VAT or sales tax, the scope and conditions for recovery may vary significantly from country to country (or even at a more granular level, such as from province to province); indeed, there may be no ability to recover the tax suffered. Therefore, it would be necessary to confirm the specific rules in place for the relevant jurisdiction. In our experience, it can be extremely difficult for Irish businesses to reclaim VAT (or other equivalent indirect taxes such as goods and services tax (GST)) incurred outside the EU.

Conclusion

As can be seen from the above, the rules regarding services can be quite tricky to follow. There are a number of basic rules in relation to supplies made to business customers and other rules that apply to supplies made to consumers. There are also a significant number of exceptions to these basic rules and businesses need to be aware of these in order to apply VAT correctly to transactions, particularly transactions which involve a cross-border element.

In the next chapter, we will focus on the VAT rules that apply to transactions involving immovable goods (properties) located in Ireland. As we will see, while a number of the basic rules that apply to sales of goods and services equally apply to property transactions, there is a range of specific provisions of which businesses and their advisors need to be aware.

- Introduction
- The Old VAT on Property Rules (Pre-1 July 2008)
- The New VAT on Property Rules (Post-1 July 2008)
- The 'Transitional' VAT on Property Rules
- The Capital Goods Scheme
- Common VAT Issues to Watch for in Property Transactions
- Conclusion

Introduction

In the previous two chapters, we have considered the VAT treatment of supplies of goods and supplies of services generally. This chapter focuses on key issues that arise for those involved in property transactions (which

rules of the country where the property

As such, this chapter only deals with transactions involving property located in Ireland. If a property in Northern Ireland, for example, is sold or leased, UK VAT on property rules would be relevant.

It is also worth noting at the outset that the current Irish VAT and property rules focus on the *substance* of property transactions rather than just their legal form or how they are described. This means that each transaction needs to be considered on its own facts. For example, very long leases can be treated the same as outright sales of property for VAT purposes.

It is useful to briefly summarise the three sets of rules which one needs to be aware of when advising on Irish property transactions:
A. **The 'old' rules** – the VAT provisions for property transactions that took place before 1 July 2008.
B. **The 'new' rules** – the 'new' VAT regime for property transactions taking place from 1 July 2008 (this new regime was introduced in order to update and simplify the VAT on property rules).
C. **The 'transitional' rules** – the set of VAT rules for certain property interests owned before 1 July 2008 and being disposed of after that date.

THE 'OLD' VAT ON PROPERTY RULES (PRE-1 JULY 2008)

Although the 'old' VAT on property rules are no longer in force, they are still of practical importance rather than just academic interest. It can be necessary to refer to these old rules when trying to piece together the VAT history of a property that is now being sold or leased by a business, especially where the business only has limited VAT records available on the property. Furthermore, many leases granted under these rules are still in place, so that the VAT treatment of the lease rentals is dependent on the old provisions and a landlord's entitlement to reclaim VAT on ongoing letting expenses may depend on how the lease was treated under the old rules. It will also become apparent as we proceed in this chapter that certain key terminology in the old rules has been carried forward into the current system.

Supplies of Immovable Goods (Land and Buildings)

Supplies of 'immovable goods' (land and buildings) were subject to VAT at the reduced rate (currently 13.5%) before 1 July 2008. A supply not only included the sale of a property but also the creation or disposal of an interest of 10 years or more (commonly called 'long leases' or 'legacy leases') in the property.

Examples of supplies of immovable goods under the old VAT on property rules were as follows:
• sale of a freehold interest;
• grant of a 999-year interest;
• assignment of the unexpired portion of a 25-year lease; and
• surrender of the unexpired portion of a 10-year lease.

Tax Tip Remember that for VAT purposes lease 'surrenders' generally include the abandonment or forfeiture of a lease by the tenant.

Requirements for VAT to Arise

Under the old VAT on property rules, leases of less than 10 years were considered to constitute the supply of a service (not a supply of goods) and therefore an entirely separate set of rules, i.e. as pertaining to supply of services, applied to such transactions. These leases were commonly known as 'short leases', as outlined below.

In order for the supply of immovable goods to be taxable under the old VAT rules, all of the following five conditions had to be satisfied (section 4 of the Value-added Tax Act 1972 (VATA 1972)), hereinafter referred to as the 'five conditions':
1. The property must have been 'developed' on or after 1 November 1972. In this context, 'development' means the construction of a new building, the substantial reconstruction of an existing building or

the demolition, extension or alteration of an existing building. It also includes engineering works to materially adapt land, e.g. preparing a previously 'greenfield' site for construction work by laying sewer pipes in the ground.

2. The person making the property disposal must have disposed of a 'taxable interest' i.e. the freehold or a leasehold interest of 10 years

place in connection with a development agreement.

4. The person making the supply must have been entitled to an input credit on the acquisition of the property or on any subsequent 'development' of the property. The key point here was to identify if there was any VAT-recovery entitlement, even if this was small. For example, a bank could use a property mainly for VAT-exempt lending and partly for VATable leasing activities, so that there would be some level of VAT recovery entitlement.

5. In the case of 'long' leases, the 'economic value test' (EVT) must also have been satisfied (from 25 March 2002). This test did not apply to short leases or to freehold interests. The EVT test ensured that any transaction involving 'long' leases (including assignments and surrenders of such leases) would be VAT exempt if the value ascribed to the long lease for VAT purposes was less than a specified formula in VAT law (section 4(3A) VATA 1972). This was the case even if the other four of the five conditions for VAT to apply were satisfied. (The methods for valuing a long lease are outlined below.) The EVT commonly resulted in landlords opting to apply the highest valuation method available for valuing the long lease (especially if the tenant had full VAT recovery on taking the lease) in order to ensure that the EVT was satisfied, as otherwise the lease would be VAT exempt and the landlord could suffer a VAT clawback on the property.

Transactions involving 'Long Leases'

Transactions involving long leases (also commonly known as 'legacy leases') were considered to be supplies of goods and the five conditions outlined above also applied to such transactions in order for VAT to apply on the leases. Where a long lease was created, the landlord generally retained an interest in the property, referred to as a 'reversion', i.e. the property would effectively 'revert' to the landlord once the long lease expired.

Under the old VAT on property rules, long leases were defined as leases for 10 or more years when they were first created. Long leases also included leases that, though at face value appearing to be for a period of less than 10 years, contained an option for the tenant to extend the lease beyond 10 years. Certain complexities and potential VAT issues (e.g. a potential irrecoverable VAT cost) arose for landlords where leases of between 10 and under 20 years were created, so it was not uncommon to see leases that contained options for tenants to extend the lease beyond a period of 20 years or a break clause in leases with lease terms exceeding 20 years' duration to permit the tenant to exit the lease at an earlier stage.

> **Tax Tip** When looking at leases granted under the 'old VAT on property rules' and trying to identify the likely VAT treatment applied, it is important to identify if the leases contained any extension or break options.

As long leases were treated as supplies of goods, once the five conditions were met, VAT arose upfront on a notional 'capitalised value' (which was intended to reflect what the lease would fetch on the open market) and VAT was not charged on the ongoing rents.

For example, if a person granted a 20-year lease over a property to a tenant, that 20-year lease was given a capitalised value for VAT purposes. The value was based on the annual unencumbered rent and the length of the lease. The landlord could obtain a valuation of the lease from a competent valuer or else the landlord could choose from the following two methods:
- the 'formula method', i.e. multiplying 75% of the annual rent by the number of full years in the lease; or
- the 'multiplier method', i.e. applying a multiplier that was published periodically by the Revenue Commissioners to the annual rent. The multiplier was based on the most recent national loan redemption yields.

When a tenant assigned (to a new tenant) or surrendered (to the landlord) a long lease, the same valuation methods could be used to identify the 'capitalised value' of the transaction, i.e. based on the annual rent and the number of full years remaining on the lease that was being assigned or surrendered.

Accounting for VAT on Long Leases

Under the old VAT on property rules, the procedures for accounting for VAT on transactions involving long (legacy) leases differed depending on whether a new long lease was being granted by a landlord, or a tenant who already held a long lease was assigning or surrendering that long

Where the tenant was entitled to a full input credit for the VAT charged and a joint application was made to the Revenue by the landlord and tenant, the landlord was freed from the obligation to charge VAT on the capitalised value of the lease and instead the tenant 'self-accounted' for the VAT. This meant, in effect, that the tenant recorded a simultaneous VAT charge and credit for the same amount of VAT in the same VAT return, which cancelled each other out in a VAT cash-flow neutral manner. Consequently, this procedure usually involved significant cash-flow savings for the tenant, as the tenant did not have to pay VAT to the landlord (or seek a VAT reclaim from Revenue) on the grant of the lease. The procedure was commonly referred to as the 'VAT4A' procedure (after the provision in section 4A VATA 1972) or the 'VAT4B' procedure (due to the name of the authorisation form that Revenue issued to the landlord and tenant when the application was processed).

A key point to note about the VAT4A procedure is that although the application of VAT to the lease was not readily visible (as the landlord did not actually charge and collect VAT), the transaction was taxed for VAT purposes and the tenant was treated as taking a full input credit on the lease.

Tax Tip Remember that the VAT4A procedure did not apply to sales of property. The procedure was only available for the granting of new leases of 10 years or more (including the grant of new, very long leases such as new 999-year leases).

2. Where a tenant assigned or surrendered an existing long lease and VAT applied to the transaction, the 'exiting' tenant was required

to charge VAT unless the transferee (e.g. the landlord in the case of a surrender, or the new tenant in the case of an assignment) fell within categories set out in section 4(8) VATA 1972. These categories included VAT-registered businesses and certain public bodies (e.g. a department of State, a local authority, etc.). If the transferee fell within one of these categories, the exiting tenant was freed from the obligation to charge VAT and instead the transferee (e.g. the landlord or the new tenant) self-accounted for the VAT, i.e. the 'reverse-charge' procedure applied.

Tax Tip At first glance, it may appear that under the old VAT on property rules, an assignment or surrender was not subject to VAT because no VAT changed hands between the parties. However, the 'reverse-charge' procedure was relatively common with respect to assignments and surrenders of long leases and there was no need to apply to Revenue (unlike the VAT4A procedure).

Long Leases: VAT Treatment of Landlords' Expenses

When advising on the VAT implications of being a landlord in respect of a long lease (legacy lease) granted under the old rules, it should be noted that VAT recovery is generally not available on costs relating to the sale or purchase of properties that are let on long (legacy) leases. Furthermore, a landlord is only permitted to reclaim VAT on a limited category of letting expenses (see below) in relation to long leases that were created before 1 July 2008. The first hurdle for taking VAT recovery is that the long lease in question was subject to VAT (including long leases to which the VAT4A procedure applied).

Deductible expenses (listed in section 4(10) VATA 1972 and now listed in section 93(3) VATCA 2010) for VATable long leases comprise:
* rent collection expenses;
* rent review expenses;
* a landlord's expenses in exercising an option to extend the lease or a break clause in the lease; and
* a landlord's costs in carrying out services that the landlord is required to provide under the lease (but only if the value of these is reflected in the rent and the capitalised value of the lease).

By concession, Revenue extend this last category of 'required costs' to include the supply of electricity, gas, power, heat, refrigeration and ventilation, but again, only if the value of these were reflected in the rent and capitalised value of the lease.

Revenue also concessionally permit VAT recovery for VATable long leases on a landlord's routine general overheads, such as office expenses and audit fees.

> **Tax Tip** If a landlord's letting portfolio includes leases with differ-

respect of long leases, under the old VAT on property rules if the landlord is being reimbursed by the tenants for services that the landlord agreed to receive on their behalf, the landlord can utilise the 'landlord's concession', a Revenue concession for shared services involving the tenant paying the landlord throughout the year (as agreed under the lease) and the landlord then issuing an invoice to each tenant once a year, charging VAT on the relevant services. Once a year, the landlord can take VAT recovery on the costs incurred and the tenant is permitted to take VAT recovery on the annual invoice (in line with the tenant's normal VAT recovery position for the leased property). The landlord remits the VAT charged to the tenant on the annual invoice in its VAT return.

> **Tax Tip** Care is needed when dealing with the VAT implications of service charges in respect of leases as this can be a tricky area where confusion can arise, especially as there are a range of ways that service charges are operated in practice.

Transactions involving 'Short Leases' and the 'Waiver of Exemption'

As noted above, under the old VAT on property rules a lease of less than 10 years' duration was known as a 'short' or 'short-term' lease for VAT purposes. Such leases were deemed to be a supply of a service and not a supply of goods. Consequently, there was a major distinction between the VAT treatment of long and short leases under the rules that existed prior to 1 July 2008. Short-term leases were exempt from VAT (paragraph 11 Schedule 1 VATA 1972); however, this had very serious implications. Where an exempt letting was created, the landlord would not have been entitled to reclaim any VAT on costs associated with acquiring or developing the property (or on ongoing letting expenses); if VAT had previously been recovered, then the landlord would have been obliged to repay all or part of this VAT to Revenue.

To avoid this, a landlord could apply to Revenue for a 'waiver of exemption'. This was done either by way of ticking the box on the tax registration form (i.e. Form TR2, see **Appendix 1.1** in **Chapter 1**) or by making a written application to Revenue. Once this waiver was in place, VAT at the standard rate was charged on the rents received under section 7 VATA 1972. This entitled the landlord to recover VAT on acquiring or developing the property, as well as ongoing costs associated with the property, such as maintenance costs, rent collection costs, etc. The landlord would also have been required to issue VAT invoices for the rent where the tenant was normally entitled to receive these.

> **Tax Tip** Remember: if a long lease was subject to VAT, then VAT arose upfront on the capitalised value, and so VAT should not be applied on the ongoing rents under such a lease. By contrast, if a short lease was granted, the lease is either VAT exempt (with no VAT recovery for the landlord on related costs) or else VAT is charged at the standard VAT rate on the ongoing rents.

The waiver of exemption applied to all short-term rents received by the landlord. Therefore, when deciding whether to apply for a waiver of exemption, care needed to be taken whether a liability to charge VAT would be triggered on other properties leased by the landlord. While the waiver of exemption was in place, a landlord was entitled to recover VAT on all costs relating to the let property. A landlord could (and can) also cancel a waiver of exemption in relation to short-term rents, e.g. a property developer could cancel a waiver after all of the units had been either sold or let on long leases. However, if the landlord recovered more VAT from Revenue than he or she has paid to Revenue when the waiver is cancelled, then the cancellation could trigger a balancing payment to Revenue (as per section 7(3) VATA 1972 and section 96 VATCA 2010).

Although the waiver originally applied globally to all short-term lettings, a number of restrictions were then placed on it as outlined below.
* Finance Act 2007 (FA 2007) introduced a restriction to disallow a waiver of exemption on residential properties that were acquired or developed since 2 April 2007. For the purposes of this restriction

in FA 2007, properties were viewed as being **acquired** when a binding contract was entered into for the acquisition of the property and were viewed as being **developed** when a planning permission application was received by the planning authority for the development of the property as a residential property.

~~It of the new~~ VAT on property rules introduced on 1 July

recovery entitlement on the let property (~~ ~~
VAT-exempt activities such as education, financial services, etc.), unless specified conditions in section 7B VATA 1972 and section 96 VATCA 2010 are met. These conditions include ensuring that a sufficient level of VAT is being paid to Revenue by the landlord on the lease rentals to meet a formula specified in the VAT provisions.

Tax Tip The waiver of exemption was typically ring-fenced to the taxpayer that applied for the waiver. For example, if a sole trader exercised the waiver individually, this would typically not extend to property held by his spouse/civil partner, or held by way of his company or a partnership of which he is a member.

THE NEW VAT ON PROPERTY RULES (POST-1 JULY 2008)

The 'old' VAT on property system, the key provisions of which we have discussed above, was overhauled with effect from 1 July 2008, with the aim of simplifying the rules. We will now consider key aspects of these new rules by examining the VAT treatment of sales of property and then leases.

Sales of Property – What is Regarded as a Sale?

Under the old VAT on property rules, we have seen that a supply of property (immovable goods) was regarded as taking place if the freehold was sold or the transaction involved a lease that was for a period of at least 10 years when it was first granted. By contrast, under the new VAT on property rules, effectively a 'substance' test is applied, by which a sale of property is regarded as taking place if either the freehold is sold or if, looking at the *substance* of the transaction, the transaction is *equivalent* to a disposal of ownership in the property (section 19(2) VATCA 2010). These are commonly referred to as 'freehold equivalent' sales.

Therefore, transactions taking place post-1 July 2008 need to be looked at on a case-by-case basis to see whether a lease granted by a landlord may be re-categorised as a freehold equivalent sale for VAT purposes. Examples of freehold equivalent sales would generally include very long leases (e.g. 200-year leases) that are being granted for a nominal rental and an upfront payment that equates to the market value of the property. Revenue guidance has indicated that as a "very general rule of thumb, leases of 75 years duration or longer are likely to be considered as 'freehold equivalent'."[1]

Regarding the time when a supply of property is deemed as taking place, Revenue guidance has also confirmed that, although a sale may be regarded for other tax heads as taking place (when, for example, an enforceable contract has been signed), for VAT purposes the question is normally whether there has been a *transfer in substance* of the right to dispose of the property as owner. Revenue generally regard this as taking place on the earlier of the closing of the sale or when the full consideration due under the contract has been paid (with deposits paid to the vendor prior to closing being subject to any VAT due on them, when the deposits are received).

When is a Sale of Property Subject to VAT?

We will see later in this chapter that property transfers can potentially be made free from a VAT charge if the property is transferred to an accountable person as part of an overall business transfer (this is referred to as 'transfer of business relief' as per section 20(2)(c) VATCA 2010). However, where a property transfer *does* not qualify for this treatment (e.g. a straightforward or standalone property sale), the relevant VAT rules are set out below.

For VAT to arise on the supply of a property (being a freehold sale or a freehold equivalent sale) under the 'new' rules, as provided for under

---

[1] See Q&A VAT on Property Rules (December 2008) at www.revenue.ie/en/tax/vat/property/vat-on-property.html (accessed June 2016).

section 94 VATCA 2010, there are generally three conditions that must be satisfied:

1. The property must have been 'developed' in the past 20 years (this is often referred to as the 'twenty-year rule'. As already seen, for VAT purposes, the definition of development is quite broad (as per section 2

[text obscured] works and operations that

[text obscured] development [text obscured]

3. The property must be considered new (for VAT purposes) at the time of the supply (see below).

If VAT arises on a sale as a result of the conditions above being met, the VAT rate applicable is the reduced rate (13.5% at time of writing) and there is a 'nil' VAT registration threshold for property sales so that VAT registration is required if a supply of property is made that meets the above conditions, regardless of the sales or transaction price (section 94(4) VATCA 2010). The taxable amount is the full consideration for the supply.

When will a Property be considered 'New'?

Whether a property will be regarded as 'new' for VAT purposes will largely depend on the level of development works (if any) that have been carried out in the five years prior to the sale. Assuming a property has been developed within the past 20 years, then the property will be regarded as new and a sale of the property will be subject to VAT, unless at the time of supply:

1. it is a completed property that was most recently completed more than five years ago and has not been developed since that date; or
2. it is a completed property that was most recently completed more than two years ago, and which since that completion date (a) has not been developed; and (b) has been sold subject to VAT at least once between parties who were not connected to each other; and (c) has been occupied for at least 24 months in aggregate; or
3. it is a building that was completed more than five years ago that has either not been developed since its completion or any subsequent development (by any party) has been only minor development; or

4. it is a building that was completed within the past five years, and which since that completion date (a) has been sold subject to VAT at least once between parties who were not connected to each other; (b) has been occupied for at least 24 months in aggregate; and (c) any development work carried out (by any party) since completion has been minor development.

The above are commonly referred to as the **'two- and five-year rules'**.

If a property is not regarded as new at the time of sale, the property is old and the supply will generally be VAT exempt. Later in this chapter we will consider an election that can be made by the vendor and purchaser to apply VAT to the sale (despite the property being old), but first we will examine the two- and five-year rules in more detail. To do so, it is clearly important to know what the various terms referred to above mean in order to apply the two- and five-year rules correctly.

'Buildings' (section 2 VATCA 2010)

For the purposes of the two- and five-year rules, a distinction is made between buildings and other properties (e.g. golf-courses, bridges, etc.). In particular, the concept of minor development (see below and section 94(2) VATCA 2010) only applies to buildings.

'Development' (section 2 VATCA 2010)

We have already seen with respect to the pre-1 July 2008 VAT on property rules that, for VAT purposes, 'development' is defined quite broadly. A property is regarded as developed when:
• a new building is constructed; or
• an existing building is extended, altered or reconstructed; or
• an existing building is demolished; or
• some engineering or other operation or work which adapts the land or building for materially altered use is carried out.

Work on land that is not designed to make a material alteration in the use to which the land is put is not considered as development. Therefore, if engineering works are carried out on agricultural lands for fencing, land drainage, laying of roads for agricultural purposes etc., these works are not regarded as development.

Work on maintaining or repairing a property generally does not constitute development, although the facts of each case need to be considered.

> **Tax Tip** The fact that planning permission has been obtained for development does not, of itself, mean that it constitutes development for VAT purposes.

that the cost of such development does not exceed 25% of the consideration for the (subsequent) supply of the property. An example would be development works carried out on a factory premises a year prior to sale. When the owner comes to sell the factory, assuming the use of the property has remained the same after the works, the works carried out would be regarded as minor development, provided the cost of the works (excluding VAT) are not greater than 25% of the (VAT exclusive) sales price.

'Completion' [of development] (section 94(1) VATCA 2010)

The concept of 'completion' under the new rules is a key concept for the purposes of determining whether a property will be regarded as new for VAT purposes. This is because the two- and five-year rules referred to above only apply once the property has been completed and, effectively, the clock starts from the date of completion.

Completion of development in the context of property means that the development of the property has reached the state where it can effectively be used for the purposes for which it was designed. The physical state that the property is in when completed, i.e. the degree of finishing and fitting that will have been carried out, will depend on its intended use and may vary from one type of building to another.

Finishing and fitting work that is normally carried out by the person who will use the property, whether as owner or tenant, does not itself have to be finished for the property to have reached the point

---

[2] See http://www.revenue.ie/en/tax/vat/leaflets/property-guide/

of being regarded as completed. In all cases, an essential requirement for completion is the connection of the utility services that will enable the property to be used for the purposes for which it was designed (if any required).

Tax Tip The supply of a partly completed property that has been developed in the past 20 years and that is made in the course of business is always subject to VAT, e.g. a half-constructed building. This is because **the two- and five-year rules only apply once the property has been completed.**

'Occupied' (section 94(1) VATCA 2010)

As outlined above, a building or property will not be regarded as new at the time of a sale if it has been completed more than two years ago and since that completion date has:
(a) been sold at least once to an unconnected purchaser;
(b) been occupied for at least 24 months in aggregate; and
(c) any development work carried out since the completion date has been minor development.

A property is regarded as occupied when it is fully in use following its completion, the use being the one for which planning permission for the development of the goods was granted. It is essential to note that Revenue regard this test as looking at whether there is a physical practical use, and not a purely economic or legal occupation.

It should also be noted that under the two-year rule, the question is whether there has been 24 months' occupation *in aggregate*, i.e. by all tenants/occupants, even where there have been breaks in occupation.

'Connected' (section 97(3) VATCA 10)

The two-year rule is only relevant if the building or property in question has previously been sold to an unconnected purchaser since the date of completion. In this context, 'connection' is defined broadly (see **Appendix 4.1** to this chapter).

The following examples illustrate the application of the two- and five-year rules in practice.

EXAMPLE 4.1: THE TWO- AND FIVE-YEAR RULES IN PRACTICE

Salt Limited obtains planning permission to build a commercial office block on a site, commences work and within six months of

liable for 13.5% VAT on the sale to Spice Limited.

Spice Limited occupies the property for a year and then sells the property to Herb Limited. The two-year rule is not relevant for Spice Limited's sale as there has not been an aggregate of 24 months' occupation since completion of development. The property is being sold by Spice Limited within five years of its completion, so Spice Limited is liable for 13.5% VAT on its sale to the new purchaser.

Imagine that Spice Limited had already occupied the property for, say, three years when it sells the property to Herb Limited (i.e. the sale is taking place within five years from the date of completion of the property). Provided that there has been no further development (or only minor development) of the property since its completion, the property would be regarded as old under the two-year rule when it is sold by Spice Limited. However, if development work has been carried by any party since completion and before the sale to Herb Limited, it would be necessary to see if this work is minor or significant. Where the work in the previous five years prior to sale comprises significant development, the property is regarded as new for VAT purposes and Spice Limited is liable for VAT on its sale to Herb Limited.

As can be seen from the above example, the application of the two- and five-year rules will require that there are adequate records regarding the VAT history of the property, including its date of completion and any subsequent works.

Exceptions to the Two- and Five-year Rules

There are notable exceptions to the two- and five-year rules, as follows:

Residential Property Developers (section 94(8) VATCA 10) Where property is residential, the supply by the person who developed it in the course of a property-development business or by a person connected with the property developer is always subject to VAT, provided the property developer had VAT-recovery entitlement. The two-year rule, five-year rule and twenty-year rule do not apply to such supplies of residential property.

Property Sold with a 'Connected' Building Agreement As we have seen regarding the system prior to 1 July 2008, the new VAT on property rules contain a 'connected building agreement' provision, whereby an undeveloped property or property that would normally be regarded as old (VAT-exempt property under section 94(2) VATCA 2010) is disposed of in connection with a building or development agreement, the disposal of the property is always subject to VAT in the hands of the vendor. This is an anti-avoidance measure, which was introduced to prevent the loss of VAT to the Exchequer in certain situations.

Option to Tax a Sale of Property (section 94(5) VATCA 2010)

Where a property is supplied when it is no longer considered new, the supply is exempt from VAT. This may have significant consequences for the vendor. For example, it will mean that no VAT can be reclaimed on costs associated with the transaction. It may also lead to a clawback of VAT previously recovered on acquiring or developing the property. The mechanism for calculating this clawback (the 'Capital Goods Scheme' (CGS) is outlined below).

To avoid these issues, the seller and the purchaser can jointly opt to tax the supply (i.e. apply 13.5% VAT on the sale) if they are both taxable persons carrying on businesses in the State. Where the option to tax is exercised, the seller does not charge VAT and instead the purchaser must account for the VAT on the supply on the reverse-charge basis, i.e. the purchaser accounts for the VAT as a sale in its own VAT return, taking a simultaneous deduction for the VAT to the extent that the property is going to be used by the purchaser for VATable purposes.

The joint option to tax is an optional election involving commercial agreement between the seller and purchaser. It does not require any application to Revenue. However, the joint option must be documented in writing by the 15th day of the month following the month during which the supply takes place. Consequently, it is common for the joint option to be included in the sales contract.

> **Tax Tip** The joint option to tax is only available if the purchaser is regarded for VAT purposes as being 'in business' in Ireland.

clawback that would otherwise arise for the vendor if a VAT-exempt sale is made. Also, if a joint option to tax is made and the purchaser subsequently uses the property for any VAT-exempt or non-business activities, the purchaser may trigger a VAT clawback.

> **Tax Tip** Instead of jointly opting to tax a sale, a possible alternative may be to proceed with a VAT-exempt sale and for the purchaser to compensate the vendor for the resulting VAT clawback (if any). The direct tax consequences of such a payment would, of course, have to be considered, e.g. whether an additional direct tax liability would arise in respect of the payment.

Letting of Property

As we have seen, in limited circumstances, if a landlord waived exemption prior to 1 July 2008, the waiver can potentially extend to leases granted after 1 July 2008. However, apart from these limited scenarios, new lettings granted in property since 1 July 2008 are exempt from VAT (paragraph 11, Schedule 1 VATCA 2010). There are exceptions for lettings of safes and certain machinery, car parking, hotel accommodation, etc., and these are subject to VAT in the normal manner.

Although lettings of property are VAT-exempt under the new VAT on property rules, the landlord may (with some exceptions) exercise an option to apply VAT to a letting in order to protect the landlord's entitlement to VAT recovery on the letting expenses (and avoid a clawback on previously reclaimed VAT). In this case, the landlord must charge VAT at the standard rate on the lease rentals. No distinction is made between leases for a period of 10 years or more and short-term lettings, as was the case before 1 July 2008. However, as outlined earlier in the chapter, certain very long leases (referred to as 'freehold equivalent interests') are treated for VAT purposes as a supply of the property, so it is important to consider each lease transaction on a case-by-case basis.

Option to Tax a Letting

A landlord who makes an exempt letting in a property is not entitled to deduct VAT incurred on the acquisition or development of the let area. However, where a landlord opts to tax a letting, that service (i.e. the rent) becomes subject to VAT at the standard rate. The landlord is entitled to deduct VAT incurred on the acquisition or development of a property that is to be used for the purposes of making taxable lettings.

The option to tax a letting should not be confused with the option to tax the sale of an old property discussed above as they are very different concepts. The legislation states that an option to tax a sale must be a joint option between the buyer and the seller. However, the option to tax a letting is a matter for the landlord and the legislation permits him or her either to simply issue a written notification to the tenant that the option is being exercised, or for the lease agreement to provide for this. Even so, it is still important for a landlord to protect his or her position legally and to confirm this with the tenant in writing in advance, as it may not be possible contractually to collect VAT from a tenant if they have not legally agreed that VAT will apply to the rents prior to agreeing the lease.

There are restrictions on the option to tax rents under section 97 VATCA 2010. These restrictions on the option to tax are mainly designed to prevent persons acquiring or developing properties for an exempt purpose and recovering VAT on the acquisition or development costs. The option to tax cannot apply (or will be terminated) in the following circumstances:
- where the property is occupied for residential purposes;
- where the letting is between connected persons (unless the tenant is entitled to deduct at least 90% of the tax chargeable on the rent);
- where the property is occupied by a person who is connected with the landlord, e.g. sub-tenant (unless that person has at least 90% VAT recovery).

As we have seen, the term 'connected' in this context is very widely defined in VAT legislation (section 97(3) VATCA 10) – see **Appendix 4.1**.

> **Tax Tip** Landlords should weigh up the likelihood that a tenant or
> occupant of the property is or will become connected to the landlord
> (e.g. by way of a share purchase or sale) and, if connected, the likeli-
> hood that their VAT recovery entitlement will fall below 90% at any
> time during the lease. Though the risk of this may well be regarded

taxable or by issuing a notice in writing to the tenant that the rents will
no longer be taxable, as provided for under section 97(1)(d) VATCA
2010. As already mentioned, an option to tax a letting will also be automatically terminated if any of the conditions referred to above apply.

Where an option to tax is terminated, or where a letting has been VAT
exempt and the landlord subsequently exercises an option to tax in
respect of the letting, the landlord may be deemed for VAT purposes
to have simultaneously sold and re-acquired the let property (under
sections 64(5) and (6) VATCA 2010). Where this rule applies, a CGS
adjustment (being either a clawback or an additional input credit) may
arise for the landlord.

THE 'TRANSITIONAL' VAT ON PROPERTY RULES

Different rules apply to transitional properties (as listed in section 95
VATCA 2010) and some key aspects of these are summarised in this
section.

Thus far we have considered some of the main aspects of the new and
old VAT on property rules. Transitional measures were introduced
from 1 July 2008 to bridge the gap between the new and the old rules.
These rules determine the VAT treatment of a disposal of a property
since 1 July 2008 that was held by a taxable person on 1 July 2008. It is
important to remember that under the old rules an interest in a property
included a leasehold interest (10 years or more) and, therefore, these
transitional rules apply to the assignment or surrender since 1 July 2008
of long leases, created prior to 1 July 2008.

Supplies of Freeholds – Transitional Measures

We will first look at the VAT treatment of freehold sales under the transitional VAT on property rules and then will outline the VAT treatment of other common property transactions.

Under the transitional VAT on property rules, where the party making the supply is entitled to deduct any of the VAT incurred on the acquisition or development of the property, the VAT rules we have outlined above (for properties completed on, or after, 1 July 2008) apply to the sale. Consequently, where the property is considered new (i.e. under the two- and five-year rules we have considered above), the supply of the property is taxable (at 13.5% at time of writing) in the hands of the vendor. The taxable amount is the full consideration for the supply, i.e. the vendor charges 13.5% VAT on the sales price and remits this to Revenue.

Under the transitional VAT on property rules, where the party making the supply was not entitled to deduct *any* of the VAT incurred on the acquisition or development of the property, the supply of the property on, or after, 1 July 2008 is exempt from VAT. The transitional rules also treat a property sale as VAT exempt if the party making the supply had no VAT recovery entitlement on the acquisition or development of the transitional property and any development work on the property since 1 July 2008 has only been minor development (section 95(3) VATCA 2010).

However, where the sale would normally be VAT-exempt under the transitional rules, the seller and the purchaser may jointly opt to tax the supply if they are both engaged in business (taxable persons) in Ireland. Where the option to tax is exercised (per section 94(5) VATCA 2010), the purchaser must account for the VAT on the supply on the reverse-charge basis (per section 94(6) VATCA 2010).

Sales of Reversionary Interests (No Second Supply Rule) – Transitional Measures

We have already seen that where a landlord created a pre-1 July 2008 long lease, the landlord was generally regarded as retaining a reversionary interest in the property (see below). Under the transitional rules, VAT is not charged on a sale of this reversionary interest (section 93(2) VATCA 2010), provided the property has not been developed by, on behalf of, or to the benefit of, the landlord since the time that the long lease was created. This is commonly known as the 'no second supply' rule.

Assignments or Surrenders of Long Leases –

acquisition of the lease or the development of the property, a subsequent assignment or surrender would be exempt from VAT. However, the tenant could agree with the assignee or landlord (depending on the circumstances) to jointly opt to tax the transfer of the leasehold interest. For such cases, a formula is set out in section 95(8) VATCA 2010 to determine the value of the transfer and also the relevant VAT amount. The formula is based on the amount of VAT reclaimed on the lease, reduced to reflect the number of 'intervals' in the 'Capital Goods Scheme' life of the lease that have expired at the time that the surrender or assignment takes place. (We look at the Capital Goods Scheme in more detail below.)

The assignee or landlord (as the case may be) then self-accounts for VAT on the reverse-charge basis, i.e. accounts for VAT on the assignment or surrender and, to the extent that the assignee or landlord has VAT-recovery entitlement on the transaction, also takes an input credit in the same VAT return.

Where the tenant was entitled to recover any VAT on the acquisition of their interest or development of the property, an assignment or surrender of the long lease after 1 July 2008 (during the Capital Goods Scheme life of the lease) will be subject to VAT. Generally, instead of the exiting tenant charging VAT, the assignee or landlord is again required to self-account for any VAT arising on a reverse-charge basis, e.g. where the assignee or landlord is VAT-registered (as per section 95(8) VATCA 2010).

The exiting tenant must provide a document to the assignee or landlord setting out the relevant VAT details in relation to the surrender or assignment. The assignee or landlord then uses this to comply with their obligations under the Capital Goods Scheme.

Waivers of Exemption – Transitional Measures

As already noted in discussing the new VAT on property rules, no new waivers of exemption can be granted after 1 July 2008 (subject to very limited exceptions). However, where a waiver of exemption was in place on that date, it remains in place until the landlord cancels it or until it is automatically cancelled (as per sections 7 and 7B VATA 1972 and section 96 VATCA 2010), e.g. certain lettings where the tenant or occupant is a connected party with less than 90% VAT recovery entitlement. An existing waiver of exemption does not extend to a property acquired or developed on, or after, 1 July 2008. However, development carried out from 1 July 2008 does not prevent the extension of that waiver to the property if the landlord had the waiver in place on 18 February 2008 and the development carried out from 1 July 2008 completes a development that was underway on 18 February 2008, by or on behalf of the landlord.

Connected Persons

A waiver of exemption, in so far as it applies to a letting between connected persons, was normally automatically cancelled with effect from 1 July 2008, unless the connected tenant (or connected occupant) had at least 90% VAT recovery on the letting. Where the connected tenant or occupant did not have 90% VAT recovery, the landlord was obliged to pay a cancellation adjustment in respect of the letting (as per section 7B VATA 1972 and section 96(8) VATCA 2010). The cancellation adjustment applied to that letting only. The amount due was the difference between the VAT deducted in connection with the acquisition and development of that property and the VAT accounted for, and paid, in respect of the rents of that property. The waiver would remain in place for other lettings or properties held by the landlord, subject to meeting the normal conditions. If, at any point after 1 July 2008 the VAT recovery rate of a connected tenant or occupant drops below 90%, the waiver in respect of that letting is automatically cancelled at that point.

However, as a transitional measure for landlords who had a waiver of exemption in place at 1 July 2008 for a letting with a connected party or occupant that has less than 90% recovery, Revenue will allow the waiver to remain in force if the VAT recovered by the landlord on acquisition of the property is effectively paid back to Revenue within 12 years of the date when the waiver was made, or if later, when the letting commenced (as per a formula set out in section 7B VATA 1972 and section 96(10) VATCA 2010).

THE CAPITAL GOODS SCHEME

We have seen that where a VAT-exempt supply of property is made, the vendor may suffer a VAT clawback under the Capital Goods Scheme (CGS) if VAT has previously been reclaimed on the property.

at any one time, an owner of a property may

multiple capital goods, and quite detailed VAT records ('capital goods records') are required to be kept for these by section 64(12) VATCA 2010 and regulation 27(1)(v) of the Value-added Tax Regulations 2010 (the 2010 VAT Regulations).[3]

'Intervals'

An 'interval' under the CGS is normally a period of 12 months. However, the second interval in the VAT life of a capital good often aligns with the owner's accounting year end, so it can be shorter than a year. Subsequent intervals then typically comprise 12-month periods, aligning with the successive accounting year ends. Consequently, the VAT life of a property and a refurbishment will generally be for a period of just under 20 years and 10 years respectively, with the intervals of each capital good aligning (after the initial interval) with the owner's year-end date.

EXAMPLE 4.2: INTERVALS (CAPITAL GOOD WITH A 20-INTERVAL 'VAT LIFE')

Let us assume that A Limited constructed a property for the purposes of its business (provision of IT services) and completed the development on 5 February 2012. A Limited has a year end

[3] S.I. No. 639 of 2010.

99

of 1 December and does not carry out any further development to the property from its completion date. The intervals in the CGS 'life' of the property would be as follows:

Interval	Starts	Ends
1	05/02/2012	04/02/2013
2	05/02/2013	31/12/2013
3	01/01/2013	31/12/2014
......	......	......
18	01/01/2020	31/12/2020
19	01/01/2021	31/12/2021
20	01/01/2022	31/12/2022

Operation of the Capital Goods Scheme

Under the CGS, where a business acquires a property or carries out a refurbishment of a completed property from 1 July 2008, the business is required to carry out an annual CGS review of its VAT-recovery entitlement on these capital goods until either the VAT life of the particular capital good ends or the business supplies the capital good to someone else, e.g. it sells the property. The business then needs to make VAT adjustment payments (or reclaims from Revenue) where the business's VAT recovery entitlement on the capital good (i.e. the property or refurbishment) varies during its VAT life. The VAT life of the capital good starts at the date of completion. However, if the property is supplied after completion, a new 20-interval VAT life then generally starts again from the date of the supply.

> **Tax Tip** If your client has carried out development works on a property, remember that a reverse charge applies to certain construction services that are subject to relevant contracts tax (see **Chapter 10**) since 1 September 2008, so your client may be treated as having reclaimed VAT on these works even if you cannot see any VAT being charged by the contractor.

The operation of the CGS can be seen broadly in the following example.

EXAMPLE 4.3: OPERATION OF THE CGS IN PRACTICE

work in line with its expected level of VAT recovery on those goods. Then, after the end of the first interval (i.e. after the first 12 months following the start of the VAT life for each capital good), Spice Limited is required to check whether it in fact had a different level of VAT recovery on those goods during the first 12-month period. If there is a difference, Spice Limited will either repay some of the previously reclaimed VAT to Revenue or make an additional claim of VAT from Revenue if its original estimate of VAT recovery was too low. This revised level of VAT recovery entitlement (identified at the end of the first 12 months) becomes the benchmark against which Spice Limited compares its VAT recovery for the capital good in subsequent intervals.

This means that for each subsequent interval, Spice Limited either makes no adjustment (if there has been no change in VAT recovery compared to the revised VAT recovery level), or makes repayments to Revenue or additional reclaims from Revenue (if its VAT recovery entitlement in any particular interval has changed from the revised level of VAT recovery that Spice Limited identified at the end of the first interval). Unless a property is sold or leased, the VAT adjustment due from Spice Limited for these subsequent intervals is normally capped at a maximum of either 5% (for the property) or 10% (for refurbishments) of the revised deductible VAT amount that Spice Limited identified at the end of the first interval. Spice Limited is required to continue this review for each interval and make adjustments as necessary, until either the VAT life of the relevant capital good ends, or, if earlier, Spice Limited sells the property (in our example, to Herb Limited). If the property is sold or leased, a CGS adjustment may arise that is not capped at the 5% or 10% maximum amounts and instead is based on the value of the remaining VAT life of the capital good in question, i.e. the adjustment can be expected to decrease as the VAT life of the capital good progresses, and no adjustment should arise for a capital good after the end of its VAT life.

Capital Goods Scheme Adjustments

As can be seen from **Example 4.3**, the implications of the CGS for a business can range widely from either having no real impact (e.g. where the business continues to have the same level of VAT-recovery entitlement on a capital good for the duration of its VAT life so no adjustment needs to be made) to scenarios where the business triggers a significant CGS adjustment. This could be because the business had perhaps taken VAT recovery on a property and subsequently makes a VAT-exempt sale or VAT-exempt lease in the property during its VAT life (thereby owing CGS liability to Revenue). Another scenario could be where the business has previously suffered irrecoverable VAT on a property, as a result of using it for VAT-exempt activities, and subsequently uses the property during its VAT life for VATable activities such as a VATable sale, thereby resulting in a potential CGS input credit claim for the business.

Significant CGS adjustments (i.e. adjustments that are not capped at a 5% level for the property or 10% for refurbishments) may also be triggered where the business's VAT recovery entitlement on the capital good in the interval differs by more than 50 percentage points from the revised VAT recovery level that was identified at the end of the first interval, e.g. if the VAT recovery rate was 80% at the end of the first interval but falls to 27% in a subsequent interval. This adjustment, which may be either a clawback or an additional input credit claim, is commonly referred to as a 'big-swing' adjustment and the relevant formula is set out in section 64(4) VATCA 2010.

Where a business owned a property or certain long leasehold interests prior to 1 July 2008, i.e. transitional ownership interests (as described above and set out in section 95(1) VATCA 2010), the application of the CGS rules is generally more limited (per section 95(11)). For example, a business that has a transitional ownership interest in a property is normally not required to carry out an annual CGS review on the property and is only subjected to the big-swing adjustment rules in certain circumstances (due to VAT provisions introduced with effect from 23 February 2010), but the normal CGS rules will apply to any refur-

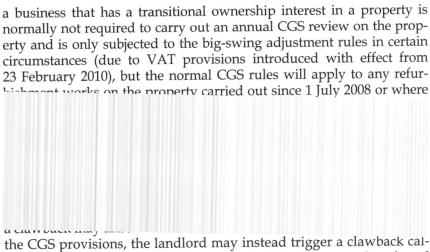

the CGS provisions, the landlord may instead trigger a clawback calculated under section 95(4) VATCA 2010. This is commonly referred to as a 'deductibility adjustment'.

COMMON VAT ISSUES TO WATCH FOR IN PROPERTY TRANSACTIONS

As can be seen from the above, there are a number of issues to be aware of when considering VAT on property rules. Examples of common issues and pitfalls in respect of the rules are outlined further below.

1. Determining an Accurate History of the Property

Determining the correct VAT treatment in relation to a property transaction depends entirely on having the correct information about the property itself. However, it is not always easy to get reliable information about the history of a property. For example, though under the Capital Goods Scheme, owners of property are generally required to keep records of capital goods, often these simply may not be available or may not be complete.

When a client or any property owner is asked when the property was last developed, they will have their own ideas as to what that means. In addition, a business may tell you that VAT did not arise when they acquired a property. This might suggest that there is no need for VAT to be considered for the next transaction; however, it is often the case that the reason the business believes VAT did not apply is because of any of the following.

(a) The property was acquired as part of a business and therefore the supply was outside the scope of VAT (as per section 20(2)(c) VATCA 2010).

(b) The client has a section 56B certificate from Revenue (see **Chapter 2,** formerly known as a VAT 13B certificate) and was able to acquire the property without paying VAT as a consequence.

(c) The client actually acquired a long leasehold interest and the VAT was dealt with by way of reverse charge, e.g. the VAT4A procedure may have been used if the client was acquiring a new lease before 1 July 2008, or the reverse-charge procedure may automatically have applied if the client was taking an assignment or surrender of a pre-1 July 2008 long lease (per section 4(8) VATA 1972).

It is vital to get to the bottom of the history fully in order to advise correctly on the next transaction. In this regard, it is important to try to gather as much documentation as possible in relation to the property. It is always a good idea to obtain a copy of the contract that governed the acquisition of the property and any associated maps, invoices, replies to requisitions by the purchaser (Pre-Contract VAT Enquiries (PCVE)) etc. It is also very useful to get photos of the property and, in some cases it may be helpful to visit the property to understand fully what level of development works may have been carried out.

Tax Tip Information concerning a property can potentially come from many sources, including the business itself, the bank that provided funding, the solicitor who acted for the business, Revenue, estate agents, etc.

---

2. Catering for Changes in Timing

Care is required when advising on VAT on property treatment if it is not certain when the transaction will take place. Take, for example, a client selling a commercial building, as illustrated below.

EXAMPLE 4.4: TIMING

Assuming that a business constructed a new building four and a half years ago and the building has been vacant since, the business would need to charge VAT and collect the VAT on completion/closing. However, in the event that the contract was signed and then for some unforeseen circumstance the closing was delayed for more than six months, then it is likely that the sale at that point ... ... from VAT and that the vendor would need to

3. Disregarded Transfers of Property

Certain transfers of property can be disregarded for VAT purposes under section 20(2)(a) and (b) VATCA 2010, e.g. transfers of property as security for a loan or debt, or the transfer back of the property held as security to the borrower when the loan or debt has been repaid. This means that there is no obligation to raise a VAT invoice or apply VAT on the transfer as there is no supply for VAT purposes. Another common category of disregarded transfers of property involves transfers of business (see further below).

4. Transfer of Business Relief

When a property is transferred as part of a business, VAT generally does not arise on the sale (section 20(2)(c) VATCA 2010). However, this throws up quite a few issues for the vendor and the purchaser. While the detailed rules for property transactions are beyond the scope of this book, it is worth specifically mentioning the following points in relation to transfers of business in the context of property transactions:

- The vendor needs to be able to demonstrate to Revenue that the transfer of business relief applies; otherwise, if the relief is not applicable, the vendor may be liable to Revenue for VAT it should have charged or even a clawback of VAT previously reclaimed, plus interest and penalties.
- The purchaser needs to be know and be assured it is not paying VAT in error where the parties believe that the relief does not apply; the purchaser may not then be entitled to a VAT refund if it tries

to reclaim VAT from Revenue that was not correctly chargeable in the first place.

- The relief only applies where the purchaser is an accountable person, so the vendor will normally want to obtain evidence of this from the purchaser before the sale, e.g. the purchaser's Irish VAT number.
- The question of whether let property can be regarded as a transfer of business has been the subject of evolving interpretation. Revenue guidance has confirmed[4] that the relief can apply to let properties or properties that have been let for a period of time before the transfer on a continuing basis. Normally, the relief cannot be extended to vacant property that has never been let, but the relief may be available for properties such as office blocks or shopping centres where some units are let (or have been let on a continuing basis) and some are vacant. Each case needs to be considered on its own facts. In cases of doubt, it may be appropriate to seek confirmation from Revenue whether the relief applies and it is also common practice for the sales contract to state the parties' view as to the VAT treatment applicable.
- Where the relief does apply, the purchaser should still establish what the VAT treatment of the property sale would have been if the relief had not been applicable. This is advisable for a number of reasons:
  - Even though the transfer is being disregarded for VAT purposes, if the purchaser subsequently uses the property for VAT-exempt or non-deductible activities, the purchaser may trigger a VAT clawback. This clawback is either based on the VAT that would normally have been chargeable on the sales price if the relief had not applied, or, as noted further below, on the VAT amounts inherited from the vendor.
  - The purchaser generally inherits the CGS position (VAT history) of the vendor in relation to the property under section 64(10) VATCA 2010 if the transfer of the property would normally have been VAT exempt or if the purchaser is taking an assignment or surrender of a pre-1 July 2008 long lease that would normally have been subject to VAT. In such a case, the purchaser would generally be treated as if he reclaimed any VAT that the vendor reclaimed on the acquisition or development of the property, etc. In the case of falling market prices, the sales price could be significantly lower than the costs incurred by the vendor. For example, the agreed sales price for a property could be €250,000 and if transfer of business relief applies, the purchaser would need to establish whether it is potentially stepping into or inheriting a larger VAT amount from the vendor

---

[4] See **Appendix B** for the relevant Revenue guidance (Revenue Information Leaflet of November 2015).

(e.g. where the cost of the property to the vendor was a multiple of the €250,000). Clearly, if the purchaser will be inheriting the VAT history of the property (and potentially multiple capital goods) from the vendor, it should ask for details of that VAT history as early as possible in the process as the VAT amounts involved may be significantly larger than the purchaser is expecting.

ery can only be taken by a vendor on costs relating to the transfer of goods qualifying for transfer of business relief where the transfer of the goods would normally have been subject to VAT. However, where the trade being transferred is a VATable business, it would be worth considering whether there is scope to reclaim VAT on sales-related costs.
- It is often the case that properties are held separate to the trading assets when a business is being disposed of; the parties need to consider if that will impact on the application of the relief.

5. Inheriting Capital Goods Scheme Liabilities from Tenant

There are specific rules dealing with works carried out by a tenant while they are in occupation of a property. Effectively, where a tenant carries out development works comprising a refurbishment (and reclaims the relevant VAT) and then surrenders or assigns the lease before the VAT life of the works has expired (i.e. 10 intervals), then the tenant will normally owe a clawback to Revenue unless the refurbishment works have been destroyed (section 64(7) VATCA 2010).

As an alternative, no clawback arises for the tenant in situations where the tenant had full VAT recovery on the works and the landlord (or assignee) agrees to take responsibility for the VAT history (i.e. effectively inheriting the CGS position on the refurbishment expenditure from the tenant). For this reason, many tenants seek to agree at the outset of a lease that a landlord will agree to this should the need arise. From the landlord's perspective, however, inserting such a clause is unlikely to be attractive as it would involve agreeing at the outset to take responsibility for an amount that has not yet been quantified.

This is a matter that is increasingly forming part of commercial discussions when leases are being negotiated.

6. Tenant Works Making Building 'New'

It is important to remember that any works carried out by a tenant can impact on the VAT treatment of a sale of the property (with or without the tenant being in place). Under the old VAT on property rules, works carried out by a tenant could often be ignored by a landlord if the works were not deemed to be for the benefit of the landlord. However, under the new rules, development of the property carried out by any party can impact on the status of the property. For that reason, landlords will often insist on approving any works that a tenant proposes to carry out and will also seek full details (description and cost) so that it has all necessary information in the event of a sale of the property.

7. Connected Parties

It is very important to know if you are dealing with a transaction involving connected parties as this can impact hugely on the VAT treatment. It is important to be aware of the definition of the term 'connected parties' in the context of property transactions (section 97 VATCA 2010) and it is worth noting that it includes "bodies of persons acting in pursuit of a common purpose".

Where the parties are connected, the following are some of the consequences of which to be wary:
- A landlord cannot opt to tax a letting to a connected party (or a letting where there is a connected occupant) unless the connected tenant/occupant has at least 90% VAT recovery on an ongoing basis.
- A receiver (or liquidator or mortgagee-in-possession) cannot jointly opt to tax a sale to a party connected with it or the borrower, even if the purchaser has full VAT recovery (section 94(7)(d) VATCA 2010). (There is more commentary on sales by receivers, liquidators and mortgagees in possession in **Chapter 8**.)
- Where certain construction work services are provided in Ireland between connected parties, instead of the services provider charging VAT, a reverse-charge VAT mechanism applies, i.e. the recipient is obliged to self-account for VAT arising on the services (section 16(5) VATCA 2010). We will see in **Chapter 10** that a reverse-charge VAT procedure may also apply to certain construction services that are subject to relevant contracts tax.

- Market value can be imposed by Revenue for VAT purposes on a transaction where the parties are connected and where the purchaser does not have full VAT recovery. In this context, it should be noted that the definition of connection differs somewhat and is set out in section 38 VATCA 2010, e.g. it refers to parties who are connected by ~~financial and legal ties~~

Laura runs a PR business and bought a newly built commercial property in 2009 for €2 million plus VAT of €270,000. She reclaimed the VAT and used the property for fully VATable consultancy purposes for six years. Laura then sold the property to her daughter for the market value price of €1 million. The assumption in this example is that as six years have passed since Laura's purchase, there are 14 intervals remaining in the 20-interval VAT life of the property at the time of sale (i.e. including the interval during which the sale by Laura takes place). For the purposes of CGS, the remaining VAT life is attributed a value based on the VAT previously reclaimed by Laura, being €270,000 × 14/20 = €189,000.

As the sale would normally be VAT-exempt and Laura does not want to suffer a VAT clawback, she agrees with her daughter to exercise a joint option to tax (her daughter is VAT registered and intends to use the property for fully VATable purposes). The amount of VAT arising on the jointly opted sale would be €135,000 (being the €1 million sales price × 13.5%) and this VAT is self-accounted for by Laura's daughter on a reverse-charge basis in her VAT return.

However, as this €135,000 VAT amount is less than the €189,000 CGS value attributed to the property, unless Laura's daughter agrees to take over the VAT history of the property, Laura will have a VAT liability on the sale of €54,000 (i.e. €189,000 − €135,000). This agreement must be made in writing and Laura must provide her daughter with a copy of the capital goods record for the property. Laura's daughter is then treated as reclaiming €189,000 of VAT on the purchase of the property, regardless of the actual sales price.

8. Option to Tax not Possible

There are many situations where the sale of a property will not automatically be subject to VAT, e.g. due to the two- and five-year rules, as discussed above. However, the vendor will often wish to jointly opt to tax the sale in order to avoid a VAT clawback and will seek agreement from the purchaser in this regard.

In certain cases, if a vendor is faced with the prospect of a VAT clawback where a VAT-exempt sale is made but the purchaser does not have full VAT recovery entitlement, the vendor may seek a price increase in order to proceed with a VAT-exempt sale, or the purchaser may seek a price reduction in order to agree to the joint option. At the same time, it is important to be aware that it is not always possible to opt to tax the sale. As we have seen, the joint option to tax can only be put in place where the transaction involves parties who are carrying on businesses in the State (taxable persons); however, this will not always apply, which can be a problem. This is again best explained by way of example.

EXAMPLE 4.6: RESTRICTIONS ON THE JOINT OPTION TO TAX A SALE

A hotel operator bought a property and large gardens in a remote area from an unconnected third party and reclaimed the VAT arising, with the intention of redeveloping it into a 'hideaway' hotel. Due to financial difficulties, the redevelopment did not occur and the operator did not trade from the property; instead, it eventually put the property up for sale after lying vacant for a number of years. As the property will be considered old at the time of sale, the operator is concerned that it will suffer a CGS clawback if it makes a VAT-exempt sale. Therefore, its preference would be to obtain the purchaser's agreement to exercise a joint option to tax. However, the only expression of interest is from a prospective purchaser who is a private individual and who wants to use the property for private purposes. Unfortunately for the operator, the joint option to tax is not available where the purchaser is not a 'taxable person' (i.e. in business) so the operator would need to weigh up whether it is willing to proceed with the sale, despite any VAT clawback arising for it under the CGS.

9. Waiver of Exemption Cancellation

We have looked above at the waiver of exemption on lettings and it is very important to be aware when a waiver of exemption has been cancelled. When a waiver is cancelled, an adjustment amount may be ~~due to Revenue (section 7B VATA 1972 and section 96 VATCA 2010).~~

~~applies to Revenue in~~ of the last property covered by the waiver. In that respect, it will be necessary to consider if the landlord continues to hold any other properties covered by the waiver after making a sale. In addition, it may be necessary to consider if the landlord previously had properties covered by the waiver which were sold, as these figures may need to be taken into account in the calculation of the cancellation liability.

As already outlined, a waiver of exemption can also be automatically cancelled where the landlord and tenant are connected and the tenant does not have at least 90% VAT recovery. VAT legislation effectively imposes a minimum VAT amount that must be remitted in these cases and failing to meet this amount will lead to a cancellation of the waiver (for the relevant property) and potentially a VAT liability to Revenue.

10. Dealing with VAT Clauses

The Law Society of Ireland issues standard VAT clauses that can be used in sales contracts.[5] These clauses are updated to cater for changes in legislation and to try to deal with the commercial issues that can arise. If you are advising on VAT clauses, it is obviously important to select the correct clauses appropriate to the transaction in question and to be satisfied that the wording reflects what the client wants to achieve.

[5] Law Society of Ireland, Special Condition 3.

The party that issues the contract (sales contract or lease agreement) will often insert clauses that are favourable to their own client so these need to be reviewed by both parties.

As we have seen above, replies to VAT requisitions on title from the purchaser (commonly called Pre-Contract VAT Enquiries (PCVEs)) may also need to be completed and these also need to be reviewed carefully before they are submitted.

11. Leases versus Licences

We have examined the VAT treatment of lettings and transactions in leases under the old, new and transitional VAT on property rules. Of course, a key assumption when applying these rules is that the transaction in question involves a letting. By contrast, where a licence is granted over land or immovable property in Ireland, the rules for leases are not relevant and instead the licence is in principle subject to VAT at the standard VAT rate.

Indicators that a letting is being granted include the occupant's right to exclusive occupation over a defined area for a defined period and fee. Often the position will be clear, but each case needs to be reviewed on its own facts and care should be taken, especially in grey areas, as the VAT implications can vary significantly.

12. Holiday Homes

Specific VAT rules apply to holiday accommodation where the landlord has 'elected' to VAT register and charge VAT on the rentals (i.e. in order to reclaim VAT on the acquisition and development of the holiday home). For example, depending on the facts of the case, the CGS may apply or, where the landlord cancels the election, the landlord may trigger a cancellation liability based on the amount of VAT deducted on the property, reduced by a formula (in section 8(2) VATCA 2010) to reflect the length of time since the holiday home was first let.

13. Tenant Dilapidations

'Dilapidations' in the context of property transactions typically refer to the property's condition while it is occupied or when a lease on the property ends. The tenant may have an obligation to repair and maintain the leased property. Where a tenant makes a payment to a landlord in full and final settlement of its dilapidation liabilities under a lease, no VAT generally applies, as the payment is not consideration for a supply. However, in practice it is advisable to check whether the payment is being made for any other liabilities or as consideration for any other supplies being made, in case other VAT implications may arise.

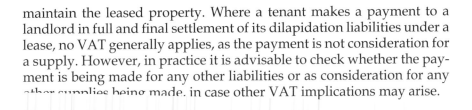

or developed since 1 january 2011 and are set out -
(1A) VATCA 2010 and the CGS provisions. However, the key issue to be aware of is that a VAT cost can generally be expected if a property is not being used for VATable business activities.

15. Premiums Paid by Landlords or Tenants

Where a landlord makes a payment (commonly referred to as a 'premium') to a tenant or a tenant pays a premium to its landlord in relation to a lease (not a freehold equivalent), the VAT treatment of the premium broadly depends on the type of letting involved.

A premium payable in respect of the surrender or assignment of a pre-1 July 2008 long lease is generally not subject to VAT. For example, a landlord could pay a tenant a premium to surrender a lease early, in which case VAT should not apply to the premium (but remember that VAT may apply to the surrender itself under section 95 VATCA 2010).

For other leases, VAT generally arises at the standard rate on payments by a tenant to the landlord if the underlying lease rentals are subject to VAT (e.g. due to a waiver of exemption or an option to tax) or on payments between an exiting tenant and assignee in relation to the assignment of the lease.

Where a landlord makes a payment to induce a tenant to enter into a lease (e.g. a contribution to fit out), the payment will generally not attract VAT unless, for example, the tenant is providing a service to the landlord in return for the payment. A tenant would normally not be viewed as providing a service simply as a result of agreeing to take the lease, but an example given by Revenue of a potential service

provided by the tenant is where a well-known brand proprietor provides an advertising-type service to the landlord by agreeing to be a
tenant in a shopping centre in return for a premium payment.

Conclusion

When advising on the VAT treatment arising from property transactions,
the approach will largely depend on which party you are representing.
If you are acting for the vendor or landlord, you will want to ensure that
VAT is charged and collected where it is due and any potential claw-
backs are avoided. If you are acting for a purchaser or tenant, you will
only want your client to pay VAT where it is necessary and to minimise
any risks for your client accordingly.

Under the VAT and property regime that applied pre-1 July 2008, sales
were either subject to VAT or they were not. Under the new rules, the
introduction of the system whereby parties can agree to jointly opt to tax
an otherwise VAT-exempt sale has meant that parties need to engage
early in order to determine what the consequences are for a particular
course of action and what the VAT status for each party is. It is vital
to get a full picture (including understanding the VAT history of the
property) as early as possible so that you can correctly advise your
client and negotiate the best solution by taking all the circumstances
into consideration.

This chapter has focused on VAT on property rules and we have seen
that where VAT recovery has previously been taken on a property,
adjustments may need to be made during the 'VAT life' of the property,
e.g. under the Capital Goods Scheme as a result of selling or leasing
the property in question. In the next chapter we will look at the general rules governing VAT recovery and the circumstances where VAT
incurred may not be reclaimable by a business.

Appendix 4.1: Connected Parties

Definitions of 'Connected' – section 97(3) VATCA 2010

"(a) In this subsection—
'control', in the case of a body corporate or in the case of a partnership,
has the meaning assigned to it by section 4(2) [VATCA 2010];
'relative' means a brother, sister, ancestor or lineal descendant.

(b) For the purposes of this section, any question of whether a person is connected with another person shall be determined in accordance with the following:

    (i) a person is connected with an individual if that person is the individual's spouse or civil partner, or is a relative, or the spouse or civil partner of a relative, of the individual or of

another person or persons;

    (iv) a body of persons is connected with another person if that person, or persons connected with him or her, have control of that body of persons, or the person and persons connected with him or her together have control of it;

    (v) a body of persons is connected with another body of persons—

        (I) if the same person has control of both or a person has control of one and persons connected with that person or that person and persons connected with that person have control of the other,

        (II) if a group of 2 or more persons has control of each body of persons and the groups either consist of the same persons or could be regarded as consisting of the same persons by treating (in one or more cases) a member of either group as replaced by a person with whom he or she is connected,

        (III) if both bodies of persons act in pursuit of a common purpose,

        (IV) if any person or any group of persons or groups of persons having a reasonable commonality of identity have or had the means or power, either directly or indirectly, to determine the activities carried on or to be carried on by both bodies of persons, or

        (V) if both bodies of persons are under the control of any person or group of persons or groups of persons having a reasonable commonality of identity;

    (vi) a person in the capacity as trustee of a settlement is connected with—

        (I) any person who in relation to the settlement is a settlor, or
        (II) any person who is a beneficiary under the settlement."

Definition of 'Control' (as referred to in section 97(3) VATCA 2010) – section 4(2) VATCA 2010

"(2) In this Part 'control'—

(a) in relation to a body corporate, means the power of a person to secure, by means of the holding of shares or the possession of voting power in or in relation to that or any other body corporate, or by virtue of any powers conferred by the articles of association or other document regulating that or any other body corporate, that the affairs of the first-mentioned body corporate are conducted in accordance with the wishes of that person,

(b) in relation to a partnership, means the right to a share of more than one-half of the assets, or of more than one half of the income, of the partnership."

Definition of 'Body of Persons' (as referred to in section 97(3) VATCA 2010) – section 2(1) VATCA 2010

"2(1) 'Body of persons' means any body politic, corporate or collegiate, any company, partnership, fraternity, fellowship and society of persons, whether corporate or not corporate."

- Introduction
- VAT Recovery – General
- How VAT is Reclaimed
- Non-deductible VAT
- Partial VAT Recovery
- Timing of the VAT-Recovery Rate Calculation
- VAT Exemption
- VAT-exempt Traders
- Conclusion

Introduction

Ensuring that the correct amount of VAT is recovered is just as important as ensuring that the correct amount of sales VAT is paid to Revenue.

For the final consumer of goods and services (e.g. private individuals),

* VAT-recovery principles for traders involved in making VAT-exempt
  supplies.

VAT Recovery – General

Any business incurring VAT (input tax) on purchases will want to know:
* how VAT can be recovered;
* how much VAT can be reclaimed; and
* how soon VAT recovery can occur.

VAT is incurred (and therefore the question of VAT recovery is
relevant) in a range of ways, including: VAT paid on 'domestic' purchases of goods and services from Irish suppliers; 'reverse-charge'
VAT for which a business self-assesses (e.g. on purchases from foreign
suppliers); and import VAT incurred on goods brought into Ireland
from non-EU countries.

VAT law contains detailed rules dealing with VAT-recovery entitlement (key provisions of which are contained in sections 59 to 62A
of the Value-Added Tax Consolidation Act 2010 (VATCA 2010)). As
a starting point, it should be noted that interest and penalties can be
applied for incorrect VAT reclaims (see **Chapter 7** for further details)
and that the general rule for taking VAT recovery is that the following
four conditions must all be met:
1. The claimant must be an 'accountable person', i.e. VAT-registered or
   required to be VAT-registered. (We will consider further below how
   businesses that are not Irish VAT-registered but incur Irish VAT on
   expenditure may reclaim this VAT.)

2. The VAT being reclaimed must have been correctly charged and documented, e.g. by way of a valid VAT invoice (see **Chapter 1**) or, in the case of an import of goods from outside the EU, a valid single administrative document ('SAD'). Indeed, in the area of VAT recovery it cannot be over-emphasised how important it is as a general rule for the claimant to ensure that it obtains and keeps appropriate VAT documentation to support any VAT recovery taken. The expenditure on which VAT is being reclaimed must also not fall within a list of specifically disallowed items (outlined later in the chapter under Non-deductible VAT).

Tax Tip In principle, the right to VAT recovery arises at the time the VAT is chargeable, i.e. when the claimant obtains a valid VAT invoice for the supply in question. However, bear in mind that a subsequent adjustment to VAT recovery may be triggered in certain circumstances, e.g. where a discount is given by the supplier and a credit note is issued to the customer against a previously issued invoice. With respect to land and buildings, adjustments to VAT recovery may arise under Ireland's detailed VAT on property rules and the Capital Goods Scheme (CGS) (see **Chapter 4**).

---

3. The costs must not fall within a list of expenditure items that are specifically disallowed (non-deductible) in VAT law. The list of non-deductible items is contained in section 60 VATCA 2010 and is described further below.

4. The claimant must be able to demonstrate that the expenditure in question was incurred for the purposes of the claimant's business activities that are either subject to Irish VAT (at any VAT rate) or are 'qualifying activities', i.e. activities that are not liable to Irish VAT but are nevertheless specifically permitted under VAT law to qualify for VAT recovery on related costs. Examples of '**qualifying activities**' are as follows:

   • Transport of passengers and their accompanying baggage outside the Republic of Ireland. For example, if an airline is flying passengers from Dublin to Paris, this activity qualifies the airline for VAT recovery on related costs, such as advertising and marketing (although passenger transport in Ireland is normally VAT exempt).
   • Distance sales of goods that are treated (under the place of supply rules) as being supplied in another EU Member State, provided the supplier is VAT registered in that other EU country. The place of supply rules and the VAT treatment of distance sales of goods (e.g. certain mail-order sales and sales of tangible books, CDs etc., over the internet) are examined in **Chapter 2**.

- Certain financial services (e.g. insurance, loans, share sales, granting of credit guarantees) supplied outside the EU or directly in connection with the export of goods outside the EU.
- The issue of new stocks, new shares, new debentures or other new securities by a VAT-registered person. This is commonly referred to as the 'Kretztechnik' principle, after the Court of Justice of the

consultancy services and the p—
ness to a foreign (non-Irish established) business customer in another country. In these cases, the Irish supplier does not charge Irish VAT on the supplies (as a reverse charge instead applies) yet VAT recovery is permitted for the supplier on its related costs.

For ease of reference in this chapter, activities (both qualifying activities and activities where Irish VAT is charged) that allow for VAT recovery to be taken on related costs are collectively called 'deductible activities'. If a business incurs VAT on expenses that relate solely to non-deductible activities, no VAT recovery can be taken. Consequently, a business incurring such expenses would generally book these in its accounts as the gross or VAT-inclusive amount, given that the VAT is an absolute cost to the business and not reclaimable from Revenue. Examples of non-deductible activities that generally do not allow for VAT recovery on related costs are private (non-business) activities or certain VAT-exempt activities (Schedule 1 VATCA 2010 contains a list of VAT-exempt activities; examples include the provision of medical care as well as the provision of school/university education).

VAT Recovery and Transfer of Business Relief

Transfer of business relief was discussed in **Chapters 2, 3** and **4**. In cases where VAT transfer of business relief (under section 20(2)(c) VATCA 2010) applies to asset transfers, a special VAT-recovery rule (section 59(2A) VATCA 2010) applies whereby VAT recovery is permitted on related services (e.g. professional fees) to the extent that the sale of the underlying assets would have been liable to VAT in the absence of the relief.

[1] C-465/03.

> **Tax Tip** If a business has paid VAT on general overheads (i.e. expenditure) that relates partly to deductible activities that permit VAT recovery and partly to non-deductible activities (e.g. non-business activities or certain VAT-exempt supplies), the claimant would need to carry out an apportionment of the expenses in question in order to take the appropriate level of input credit. (Examples of apportionment methods are examined further below under 'VAT Apportionment Methods'.)

How VAT is Reclaimed

Irish VAT-registered traders generally claim input credits from Revenue by recording a deduction in Box T2 of the relevant VAT 3 return form (see **Chapter 1**). VAT reclaims can also be made under regulation 36 of the Value-Added Tax Regulations 2010[2] (the '2010 VAT Regulations') by making a written claim to the Revenue that sets out the grounds for a refund as well as a computation of the refund, and also by providing back-up documentation if requested (see below).

In the VAT 3 return form, the VAT credit being taken is recorded in Box T2 and may either offset/reduce a VAT liability (shown in Box T1) in the same return (thereby resulting in a net VAT payable position in Box T3) or result in a net VAT repayable position, reflected in Box T4 of the return.

> **Tax Tip** VAT-registered traders that are in a continual VAT repayment position may consider seeking approval from Revenue to file VAT returns on a monthly basis in order to expedite reclaims.

VAT reclaims are processed by the Office of the Collector-General and can take a number of weeks. It is common, particularly in cases of large VAT reclaims, new VAT registrations or start-up businesses that have not yet made any sales, for Revenue to require back-up evidence to support the reclaim made. This information can include copies of the relevant invoices making up the claim, a description of the activities carried out by the business and confirmation whether the business expects to move into a VAT-payable position in its returns (and if so, the expected timing of this).

> **Tax Tip** If VAT is reclaimed on receipt of an invoice but the invoice remains unpaid six months following the end of the bi-monthly period during which recovery was taken, the business will then be

---

[2] S.I. No. 639 of 2010.

> required to make a VAT-recovery adjustment whereby it effectively repays Revenue the VAT relating to the unpaid amount. If the person subsequently makes an additional or full payment, a proportional re-adjustment is permitted under section 62A VATCA 2010.

expenditure (e.g. construction of particular farm buildings and certain specified fishing equipment) by filing a Form VAT 58 or VAT 58A reclaim. In addition, certain VAT Refund Orders are in place to permit VAT reclaims from the Revenue by certain other unregistered claimants, e.g. reclaims of VAT on certain aids and appliances by people with a disability, etc.[3]

Reclaiming Foreign European Union VAT

Different procedures apply in respect of reclaiming foreign VAT from other EU tax authorities. An Irish VAT-registered business that incurs VAT on purchases in another EU Member State (that would normally be reclaimable by local VAT registered businesses) but who is not established or VAT registered in that country may file an electronic reclaim (electronic VAT refund (EVR) claim) on the Revenue On-Line Service (ROS), which Revenue then forwards to the relevant tax authority for review and processing. Claims are subject to specified minimum thresholds and a strict filing deadline of 30 September following the calendar year during which the VAT in question was incurred (although it is worth noting that the Netherlands permits claims going back five years). In a similar manner, non-Irish EU traders that incur Irish VAT may seek to reclaim this by filing EVR claims using their State's own electronic portal and their local tax authority then forwards these to the Irish Revenue.

It may be possible for an Irish business to reclaim VAT (or its equivalent) incurred in non-EU countries. However, this can be difficult in practice, and will depend on the country in question and the nature of the expense incurred.

---

[3] The relevant forms are available on the Revenue website at www.revenue.ie/en/tax/vat/forms/ (accessed August 2016).

Non-European Union Traders

With respect to non-EU traders that have incurred Irish VAT but are not established or VAT-registered in Ireland, they may seek to reclaim the VAT by making a direct reclaim to Revenue (again, subject to certain specified minimum thresholds, etc.) via Form 60OEC. This procedure is also commonly referred to as a 'Thirteenth Directive reclaim', after the EU Council Directive that permitted the reclaim procedure. The filing deadline for claims by non-EU traders is somewhat tighter than that in EVR claims, i.e. 30 June following the calendar year during which the VAT was incurred. The claim should be accompanied by original invoices as well as a recent certificate issued by the competent authority of the relevant non-EU country providing specified particulars in relation to the claimant.

Tax Tip VAT recovery should only be taken by the party that has received the good or service in question. This will usually be apparent from the circumstances and contractual arrangements, but should always be considered on a case-by-case basis. VAT law also deems certain supplies to be made. For example, if a person is indemnified under an insurance policy for legal services by a barrister/solicitor, the legal services are deemed to be supplied to the insured person and are therefore deductible by that person subject to satisfying normal VAT recovery rules.

Non-deductible VAT

As already outlined, in the normal course, VAT incurred on non-business (e.g. private) activities and VAT-exempt business activities cannot be reclaimed (see Schedule 1 VATCA 2010, which outlines VAT-exempt activities). In addition, irrespective of whether certain costs are being incurred for business purposes or deductible activities, VAT law specifically prohibits taking VAT recovery on certain expenses, which include:

- Food, drink, accommodation (except for certain conference-related accommodation, see below) or other personal services for the VAT-registered person, its agents or employees, except to the extent, if any, that the expenditure is incurred in relation to a supply of services in respect of which the VAT-registered person is accountable for VAT.
- Conference-related accommodation that qualifies for VAT recovery comprises hotel/guesthouse accommodation for a conference delegate for a maximum period starting from the night before the start of the conference and ending on the date that the conference concludes. The conference itself must have been organised to cater for

50 or more delegates at a conference venue and written confirmation must be obtained from the conference organiser setting out certain particulars of the conference.

- Entertainment expenses (such as a Christmas party) incurred by the VAT-registered person, its agents or employees.

(including the intra-Community acquisition and importa-

(s 60 VATCA 2010)

the first time since 1 January 2009 and that less than 156g/km. A partial clawback of the reclaimed VAT may arise if the business usage of the vehicle falls below 60% or if the vehicle is sold.
- Petrol (this prohibition does not apply to petrol that is purchased for stock-in-trade).

Tax Tip Most commercial vehicles (e.g. vans, lorries, etc.) and diesel fuel are not included in the express prohibition on VAT recovery and instead are subject to general VAT-recovery rules.

- Procurement of contract work involving the handing over of any goods that normally are disallowed for VAT recovery purposes. For example, if a person paid a chef to prepare a meal from ingredients provided to the chef, and paid a fee to the chef, then any VAT charged by the chef on the fee would not be recoverable if VAT would not have been recoverable had the person simply purchased the food.

Tax Tip Practitioners should keep in mind that the VAT-recovery rules differ in a number of respects from deduction principles under other tax heads, e.g. income tax or corporation tax deductions. These mismatches commonly create pitfalls for many businesses that may inadvertently reclaim VAT on disallowable items.

Partial VAT Recovery

We have seen that, as a general rule, VAT is deductible to the extent that it is incurred for business activities that are subject to VAT or are qualifying activities. VAT incurred solely for 'deductible activities' is recoverable in full (subject to meeting any relevant conditions, such as obtaining a valid VAT invoice). Conversely, VAT incurred solely for the purposes of carrying out 'non-deductible activities' must be disallowed in full. This is commonly referred to as 'direct attribution' of the costs to either deductible or non-deductible activities.

This leaves a third category of costs that do not relate either wholly to deductible activities or wholly to non-deductible activities, for example, general overheads. These costs are commonly referred to for VAT purposes as **'dual-use inputs'** and may include costs such as audit fees, general operational/infrastructure costs, rent, light, heat, etc.

VAT legislation permits recovery in relation to dual-use inputs to the extent that they relate to a business's deductible activities. Consequently, although this issue is not relevant for certain traders, an apportionment may need to be carried out by businesses that are engaged in both deductible and non-deductible activities, and the level of VAT recovery taken (i.e. the business's VAT recovery rate) must be reviewed on an annual basis. (**Example 5.1** below illustrates the point.)

The review period for these purposes either consists of a calendar year, or more commonly, where the business makes up accounts for 12-month periods ending on an accounting year-end date, the review period comprises all the bi-monthly VAT periods that end during the accounting year. For example:

EXAMPLE 5.1: IDENTIFYING THE **VAT** REVIEW PERIOD

If a VAT registered person's accounting year end date is 31 May, the review period for the purposes of VAT apportionment and the annual review comprises the period from 1 May to the following 30 April (i.e. the six bi-monthly periods from the May/June VAT period to the following March/April VAT period, inclusive).

VAT Apportionment Methods

Relevant VAT legislation dealing with VAT apportionment methods (which themselves are commonly referred to as 'partial exemption' or 'VAT-recovery-rate' methods) can be found in section 61 VATCA 2010 and regulation 17 of the 2010 VAT Regulations.

Commonly, a 'turnover method' is used when VAT recovery is taken on general overheads in line with the ratio of the business's deductible turnover to total turnover. VAT legislation dictates that the 'turnover method' should be used but only if the following conditions are satisfied:

- the method used must correctly reflect the extent to which the dual-use inputs (general overheads) are used for the purposes of deductible supplies; and
- the method must have due regard to the range of total supplies and

As can be imagined, where two traders in the same industry levels of VAT on general-overhead expenditure but apply different VAT recovery-rate methods, the level of their respective VAT reclaims could potentially differ significantly. Also, if a trader applies different VAT-recovery-rate methods within its own business (e.g. for different business units or income streams within the business) this may lead to the business having a blended or overall VAT-recovery rate on general overheads that, when broken down, represents potentially very different levels of VAT recovery being taken by each individual business unit or cost centre on their costs. Both of these are illustrated in **Examples 5.2** and **5.3** below.

EXAMPLE 5.2: VAT RECOVERY METHODOLOGY

A Limited and B Limited are both Irish VAT-registered companies operating from rented premises in Galway and each operating the same two business lines: the sale of bedroom furniture and the separate sale of VAT-exempt insurance. They are charged VAT on rents by their respective landlords. Both companies have an Irish customer base.

As the companies carry out a mix of VATable and VAT-exempt activities, they are required to restrict VAT recovery on costs that wholly relate to their VAT-exempt insurance activities and to carry out an apportionment of their general overheads.

A Limited identifies that its furniture sales account for 70% of its turnover, so it applies a 70% VAT recovery rate to all its overheads. B Limited identifies that although its furniture sales account for

70% of its turnover, it actually uses 90% of its rented premises for these activities. B Limited decides that the most appropriate method for its VAT recovery is to reclaim 90% of the VAT it incurs on rents, light, heat and property maintenance costs (i.e. applying a floor-based or square-footage method to this category of expenditure) and to reclaim 70% of general overheads that do not relate specifically to the premises, e.g. audit fees.

It can be seen from this example that even where two taxpayers appear identical, the apportionment methods they apply can result in significant differences in their VAT reclaims on dual-use costs. As such, taxpayers need to be able to demonstrate that the method they are using is appropriate for their activities and in their particular circumstances, particularly where they are not using the 'turnover method'.

EXAMPLE 5.3: DIFFERING VAT RECOVERY METHODOLOGIES

Quick and Easy is an Irish VAT-registered subsidiary of a foreign-based bank. It employs 40 people, 32 of whom are engaged solely in VAT-exempt lending activities, with the remaining eight working exclusively in VATable leasing activities. As the company carries out a mix of VATable and VAT-exempt activities, it is required to restrict VAT recovery on costs that wholly relate to its VAT-exempt lending activities and to carry out an apportionment of its general overheads. Although 90% of its turnover is derived from its VAT-exempt lending activities, the company decides against applying a turnover method to its general overheads (which would normally indicate a 10% VAT recovery entitlement). Instead, as its VAT-exempt activities are carried out by 80% of its employees, the company decides to apply a method based on head count and consequently reclaims 20% of VAT on its general overheads. It can be seen that this approach results in a higher level of VAT reclaims. As already outlined in the last example, the company would need to be able to demonstrate the appropriateness of this method to Revenue.

Finance Act 2016 contains amendments to the provisions in relation to the apportionment of VAT on general overhead costs for partially VAT-exempt entities. These provide that the proportion of recoverable VAT on general overhead costs should be calculated using a turnover method unless same method does not correctly reflect the use of the overhead costs, in which case an alternative method of apportionment must be used.

...method may vary for

Certain businesses prefer to calculate their VAT ... real-time basis (e.g. for each bi-monthly period), whereas others provisionally use the VAT-recovery rate that was calculated in the preceding review period and then make a 'true-up' adjustment (i.e. a reclaim from Revenue or payment to Revenue) at the end of the current review period as a means of reflecting the correct VAT recovery rate.

> **Tax Tip** Revenue allow businesses to make their VAT-recovery-rate adjustment (if relevant) in any one of the three bi-monthly VAT periods immediately following the end of the review period in question.

It is possible for VAT-registered persons to use an estimated VAT-recovery rate when reclaiming VAT on dual-use inputs, on the condition that details of the method are provided to Revenue at the same time as the first VAT return in which the estimated VAT recovery rate is used. This could be relevant, for example, where a business has just commenced trading or has introduced a new income stream and does not have reliable historic information on its VAT-recovery rate in a preceding period. In this situation, Revenue may then challenge the method used.

> **Tax Tip** It should be remembered that there are specific VAT on property rules dealing with VAT recovery and VAT recovery adjustments with respect to immovable goods (land and buildings). These are outlined in **Chapter 4**.

VAT Exemption

As already noted, from a supplier perspective, VAT is generally not reclaimable on costs incurred for the purposes of VAT-exempt activities (except for certain qualifying activities). Also, from a customer perspective, VAT is generally not reclaimable unless it has been correctly charged. As such, it is important for practitioners to be able to identify if a transaction is VAT exempt or correctly chargeable to VAT. Subject to meeting the relevant specific conditions set out in Schedule 1 VATCA 2010, examples of VAT-exempt activities in Ireland include:

- public postal services;
- medical services, dental services, optical services;
- supplies by certain non-profit organisations;
- certain sporting facilities and admission to sporting events;
- child fostering services and crèche childcare services;
- certain educational services;
- national broadcasting and television services (excluding advertising);
- various financial services (e.g. loans, mortgages, share sales, insurance and reinsurance, the management of certain qualifying funds) and related agency services;
- certain transactions in investment gold;
- certain betting and gambling activities;
- certain disposals of immovable goods (land and buildings) and also the letting of immovable goods (exceptions to this include the provision of car parking, use of toll roads and the hire of safes);
- funeral undertaking;
- the supply of water by local authorities and Irish Water;
- transporting passengers and their accompanying baggage; and
- supplies of most movable goods, provided the claimant incurred VAT on acquisition and used them for business purposes but had no VAT recovery entitlement on purchase. For example, if an insurance broker pays VAT on buying a computer and has no VAT recovery entitlement as the computer is being used solely for the provision of VAT-exempt insurance services in Ireland, VAT exemption would apply if the insurance broker subsequently sells the computer.

Tax Tip A general principle of the VAT system is that business transactions should be subject to tax. VAT exemption is an exception to this, and therefore the listing of VAT-exempt activities in the legislation should be interpreted narrowly.

The scope and parameters of VAT exemption in respect of specific transactions can be contentious and the principles underpinning exemption are also subject to evolving interpretation at EU level, in particular when questions are referred on specific VAT exemption matters to the CJEU by Member States.

When considering whether VAT exemption applies, practitioners should ensure that they refer to Schedule 1 VATCA 2010 and check whether the specific criteria for VAT exemption are met. Strictly, VAT-exempt activities should also be distinguished from activities that are ~~... of VAT (e.g. deemed non-supplies, such as transfers ... 20(2)(c) VATCA 2010) and ... certain~~

related expenditure ... e.g. obtaining a valid VAT invoice.

VAT-exempt Traders

In practice the expression 'VAT-exempt traders' can be somewhat misleading. This is because traders carrying out VAT-exempt supplies are not relieved in principle from being charged VAT by other traders, i.e. they are not somehow exempted from incurring any VAT on their expenditure. It should also be remembered that although a supplier of VAT-exempt goods or services is not accountable for VAT on them, the trader may nevertheless be an accountable person (and therefore be required to VAT register). This could be due to, for example, carrying out other supplies that are subject to VAT (subject to relevant VAT-registration thresholds), or as a result of making intra-Community acquisitions of goods from other EU countries or receiving reverse-charge goods or services. As a result, although being VAT registered would not impact on the VAT treatment of any VAT-exempt supplies themselves, ostensibly 'VAT-exempt traders' may nevertheless be required to file ongoing VAT returns and pay VAT liabilities for other activities, in the normal manner.

EXAMPLE 5.4: MIXED ACTIVITIES

Peter is a dentist and is not registered for VAT. He decides to construct and sell a new office block near where he lives. As a result, Peter will be obliged to register for VAT in respect of the sale of the newly built property. This should not impact on Peter's VAT recovery in respect of his dental practice (i.e. this activity will still be exempt with no VAT recovery for Peter on associated costs).

Peter's friend, Paul, is also a dentist who lives in Dundalk. Paul takes out an advertisement in a Belfast newspaper hoping to attract customers from Northern Ireland. Paul will be obliged to register for VAT in Ireland and to self-account for VAT in respect of the advertising service received from the Belfast-based advertiser. This should not impact on Paul's VAT recovery in respect of his dental practice (i.e. this activity will still be exempt with no VAT recovery for Paul on associated costs).

It can be seen from the above that VAT exemption can be a tricky area to navigate. In this context, the EU Commission has been undertaking a review of how VAT exemption does and should operate in the financial services industry. This is commonly referred to as the 'Financial Services Review'. Among other issues, there is a question as to whether the current VAT-exemption principles (established in the 1970s) are outdated compared to the reality of financial services products and therefore need to be redefined. Conversely, it is being considered whether extended VAT-exemption principles might result in an inappropriate tax advantage for the financial sector in comparison with other industry sectors. Practitioners should be aware of the Financial Services Review and its future effect on significant changes in the overall EU VAT-exemption system, although at the time of writing a timeline has not been specified.

Conclusion

Although it is something that sounds quite straightforward, in practice it can be difficult to ensure the correct amount of VAT is recovered. While VAT can generally be reclaimed by Irish VAT-registered traders, provided the necessary procedures are met, it is always worth bearing in mind that VAT incurred in relation to the following cannot be reclaimed in an Irish VAT return:
• costs relating to specific disallowable items (e.g. entertainment, etc.);
• costs relating to VAT-exempt activities (that are not "qualifying" activities);

- costs relating to non-business activities;
- costs incurred where foreign VAT has been correctly charged (as foreign VAT cannot be reclaimed in an Irish return).

Incorrectly reclaiming VAT is a very common issue for Irish traders to watch out for and is something that frequently arises during a Revenue ʼll deal with a variety of other common

- Introduction
- Ensuring the Correct VAT Rate is Used
- Value of Transactions for VAT Purposes
- Cash Receipts Basis
- Common Invoicing Issues
- Expressing Doubt on the VAT Treatment of a Transaction
- Asset Finance and Financial Services
- Requirement to Retain Records
- VAT Cash-flow Issues
- Conclusion

Introduction

In the previous chapter, we examined the issue of VAT recovery. Although it is something that, in theory at least, appears to be straight-forward, it is a concept with which businesses sometimes struggle in .... Consequently, it is not unusual for issues relating to VAT

dealing with ......

VAT accounting;
- common invoicing and record-keeping issues; and
- making an adjustment where the price agreed between the parties is subsequently amended.

Ensuring the Correct VAT Rate is Used

As most readers will be aware, the default or standard VAT rate in Ireland is currently 23%. However, there are also other rates at 13.5% and 9% (commonly referred to as the 'reduced rates'), 4.8% (for sales of livestock) and 0%. These rates are set out in section 46 of the Value-Added Tax Consolidation Act 2010 (VATCA 2010). The activities in Ireland that attract the reduced rates and the 0% rate are listed in Schedules 2 and 3 VATCA 2010 respectively. Although in this book we focus on Irish VAT, for illustrative purposes we also include some information on the VAT rates applied in other EU Member States (as at 1 January 2016) in **Appendix A**.

> **Tax Tip** It should be noted that the 4.8% VAT rate (applicable to sales of livestock by VAT-registered traders) differs from the flat-rate addition collected by farmers on certain agricultural supplies. The latter is currently 5.2% and forms part of a special VAT regime for non-VAT registered farmers. Details of the VAT system for flat-rate farmers can be found in section 86 and Schedule 4 VATCA 2010.

0% VAT Rate Examples of activities attracting 0% VAT in Ireland include certain transactions involving exports of goods, services relating to vessels and aircraft, food and drink, printed matter, children's clothing and footwear, medicines and fertilisers. Conditions specified in Schedule 2 VATCA 2010 need to be met in order for these activities to qualify for zero-rating.

13.5% VAT Rate Examples of supplies attracting the 13.5% rate, subject to meeting the specified conditions in Schedule 3 VATCA 2010, include certain fuels, construction services, repair work, cleaning and maintenance services, works of art, photographic supplies and beauty treatments.

9% VAT Rate Examples of activities attracting the 9% rate, subject to meeting the specified conditions in Schedule 3 VATCA 2010, include:
- the supply of food and drink (excluding alcohol, soft drinks and bottled water) in the course of catering;
- the supply, by means of a vending machine, of food and drink that would otherwise be zero-rated;
- hot take-away food and hot drinks;
- hotel lettings, including guesthouses, caravan parks, camping sites, etc.;
- admissions to cinemas, theatres, certain musical performances, museums, art gallery exhibitions;
- amusement services of the kind normally supplied in fairgrounds or amusement parks;
- the provision (excluding non-profit making organisations) of facilities for taking part in sport;
- printed matter, e.g. newspapers, magazines, brochures, leaflets, programmes, maps, catalogues, printed music (excluding certain printed books, which are zero-rated); and
- hairdressing services (whereas certain other beauty treatments, such as facials, nail treatments, tanning, sunbed services etc., qualify for the 13.5% rate).

Correct VAT-rate Treatment

It can be difficult in practice to pinpoint whether a specific transaction qualifies for one of the lower VAT rates, VAT exemption or defaults back to the standard rate, particularly in the context of, say, a new product line being introduced by a supplier or a new service offering in an industry. If there is doubt as to the correct VAT rate treatment, or whether VAT exemption may apply, VAT-registered traders can ask Revenue for a formal determination. Revenue must communicate their determination to the applicant, unless they feel the matter is already sufficiently free from doubt or Revenue have already issued a previous determination on the subject. Alternatively, Revenue can choose to publish a determination where this has not been asked for. The procedure for seeking or appealing a determination is set out in section 51 VATCA 2010.

> **Tax Tip** Any requests to Revenue for VAT rate determinations must be made in writing. Applicants should also expect Revenue to request full details of the nature of the transaction(s) in question and, for example, Revenue may consult with experts in order to understand the context or industry more fully.

The key question here from a VAT rate perspective is whether the supplier is making multiple supplies (in which case the sales price will need to be apportioned, with differing VAT rates or VAT exemption, as the case may be, being applied to each element) or else making a 'composite supply'.

Composite Supply A composite supply occurs where a principal good or service is being supplied, with some ancillary supplies being provided for the better enjoyment of that main/principal supply. In the case of a composite supply, the entire sales price attracts the VAT rate applicable to the principal element. For example, where a new mobile phone is sold with an instruction manual, although certain printed matter can qualify for the 0% rate, the booklet would typically be viewed as being ancillary to the sale of the phone so that the standard rate (23%) would apply to the entire sales price.

Multiple Supply By contrast, an example of a 'multiple supply' is the sale of a hamper of goods. Unlike a composite supply, a multiple supply involves the sale of a number of individual goods or services that could be supplied independently and that are physically and economically dissociable from each other. In the case of a multiple supply, although a single price is paid by the customer, for VAT purposes the price (consideration) is apportioned between the different rates. Therefore, in the case of a hamper, the portion of the price attributable to items such as alcohol and chocolate would attract the standard rate, whereas portions of the sales price allocable to zero-rated food items would be taxed accordingly.

This detailed apportionment approach can be somewhat cumbersome for low-value transactions, so in carrying out an apportionment traders are permitted effectively to disregard certain very low value items. This simplification generally does not apply to beverages and it is necessary that the total VAT-exclusive cost to the supplier of any disregarded items must not exceed the lower of €1 or 50% of the VAT-exclusive price for the multiple supply. The specific simplification provisions can be found in regulation 12 of the Value-Added Tax Regulations 2010 (the '2010 VAT Regulations').[1]

Identifying composite and multiple supplies is not always straightforward and care should be taken in this area to consider transactions on a case-by-case basis. Some helpful principles can be found in the Irish Supreme Court case of *Inspector of Taxes v. Cablelink Ltd. & Ors* (2003)[2] and the Court of Justice of the European Union (CJEU) case of *Card Protection Plan (CPP) v. Comissioners of Customs & Excise.*[3]

The 'Two-thirds Rule'

A VAT-rating provision that can cause confusion in practice (particularly for agreements involving physical labour) is the 'two-thirds rule' (contained in section 41 and paragraph 15 of Schedule 3 VATCA 2010). This sets out that where the cost to the supplier of movable goods supplied under a services agreement exceeds two-thirds of the contract price, the VAT rate applicable to the goods applies to the entire contract. In practice, where this rule applies, it can result in an increased VAT rate of 23%, i.e. from the 13.5% VAT rate that might otherwise be expected for agreements to carry out physical work, repair, etc. The following example illustrates the point:

EXAMPLE 6.1: THE TWO-THIRDS RULE

Joe is a painter and has the following house-decorating job:

Price quoted to customer	€3,000 plus VAT
Made up as follows:	
Cost of materials at 23% (excluding VAT)	€2,200
Labour, overheads, profit	€800
Total	€3,000

As the cost of materials (€2,200 excluding VAT) exceeds 2/3rds of the full price of the job (excluding VAT), the 23% VAT rate applies to the entire job price.

[1] S.I. No. 639 of 2010.
[2] [2003] IEHC 625.
[3] Case C–349/96.

However, this rule does not apply if the goods that are being provided are zero-rated food and drink (e.g. where they are being provided as part of an agreement to provide catering services) and also does not apply to the provision of certain reverse-charge construction services, e.g. services comprising 'construction operations' that are subject to ~~relevant contracts tax (RCT).~~

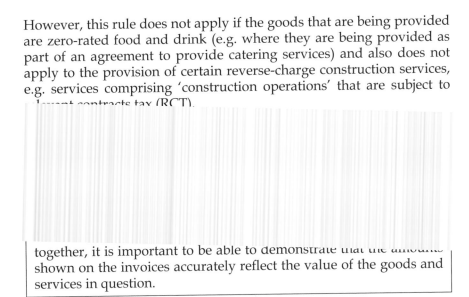

together, it is important to be able to demonstrate that the amounts shown on the invoices accurately reflect the value of the goods and services in question.

Value of Transactions for VAT Purposes

As VAT is a tax on transactions (and consequently may be due even where a business is in a loss-making position) it is critical to be able to identify the value of a transaction for VAT purposes. This is commonly referred to as the 'taxable amount' in relation to the transaction. Often it will be clear from the circumstances what the taxable amount is for the transaction, but mistakes in this area can prove costly and VAT law also contains deeming provisions that specify how the taxable amount will be identified in particular scenarios.

The general rule for identifying the value of a transaction for VAT purposes is that **VAT is charged on the total consideration received by the supplier** (section 37 VATCA 2010). This includes all amounts that the supplier is entitled to receive in return for the supply of the goods or services in question, including any amounts receivable by the supplier in respect of taxes, commissions, costs and charges whatsoever (but excluding the VAT amount itself).

It is important to note that VAT is therefore generally due on the full amount charged to a customer as illustrated in **Example 6.2**.

Example 6.2: Taxable Amount

An accountant agrees to assist a client with the preparation and submission of the client's tax return, in return for a fixed fee of €1,000 plus expenses. If the expenses work out as €100 (e.g. travel expenses) then VAT should be charged on the entire amount of €1,100.

It is of course possible for a supplier to incur costs while acting as agent of a client, which do not actually comprise a payment in return for the supplier's goods or services. For example, an accountant might pay a Companies Registration Office (CRO) fee on behalf of a client, or a solicitor might pay a stamp duty liability or a court fine for a client. In such cases, it is possible for the accountant or solicitor to recoup these amounts from the client without VAT applying (on the basis that they are simply amounts being reclaimed which were paid on the client's behalf). In the case of solicitors, Revenue have published guidelines on how their billing operates and these can be found on Revenue's website.[4] However, where any payment is received from another party and VAT is not accounted for on that element, it is very important to be satisfied that it is correct to do so.

> **Tax Tip** In error, many practitioners issue fees for their services treating any expenses or extras as non-VATable payments, incorrectly believing that these amounts cannot be subject to VAT. It is important that any expenses are reviewed to see if their VAT treatment should instead follow the VAT treatment of the fees for the services.

Tipping

There can sometimes be a fine line between 'tips' and 'consideration'. VAT law deems that if the consideration received by a supplier in relation to goods or services supplied exceeds the amount that the supplier was entitled to receive, the taxable amount includes the excess amount (section 39 VATCA 2010). However, Revenue accepts that in the services sector, although charges (e.g. service charges) presented on the bill form part of the VATable consideration for the service in question, voluntary payments (tips) made by customers and not appearing on the bill are outside the scope of VAT.

---

[4] See www.revenue.ie/en/tax/vat/leaflets/solicitors.html for more information.

'Buy One, Get One Free' Promotions

In the case of 'buy one, get one free' marketing promotions, it is commonly accepted that the second item is not actually being given away for 'free', although at face value it might appear that a gift or a self-supply is taking place and that consequently its taxable amount is nil. Instead,

Value of 'Self-supplies' and Purchases from Abroad

In cases where a 'self-supply' (as discussed in **Chapter 3**) is taking place (e.g. where a VAT credit has been taken on a movable business asset and the asset is then appropriated for personal use or is used for VAT-exempt activities), we have seen that a VAT charge arises in order to claw back the VAT recovered. Consequently, the taxable amount is based on the cost to the person when the goods were acquired. VAT arising on intra-Community acquisitions of goods from other EU countries or the receipt of services from outside Ireland (e.g. reverse-charge VAT that is self-assessed by the recipient) will also be based on the cost to the recipient.

Of course, Irish VAT liabilities are paid to Revenue in euro; therefore, if an invoice is received in a foreign (non-euro) currency, it will be necessary to translate the taxable amount of the invoice into euro in order to calculate the correct value of the transaction and the accompanying VAT charge. The business should normally use Central Bank of Ireland exchange rates, or else the business may agree specific foreign exchange (FX) procedures with Revenue. Care should be taken to identify the correct time of supply for the transaction so as to apply the appropriate FX rate and record the transaction in the appropriate VAT period.

Price Adjustments, Discounts and Bad Debts

Where there is an upwards price adjustment (e.g. if a supplier were to increase the consideration for a supply after invoicing the customer), there will also be an increase in the taxable amount of the transaction. It follows that the supplier's VAT liability also increases accordingly and that the supplier may be required to issue an additional invoice. Conversely, where a supplier charges VAT on an invoice and then gives a discount to the customer (e.g. a volume-based discount or a discount to reflect that payment has been made within an agreed period), the supplier will want to make a VAT adjustment to reflect the price reduction that has been given. Certain procedural requirements may apply, such as the obligation to provide a valid VAT credit note. We have seen in **Chapter 1** that VAT legislation sets out specific details that must be shown on valid VAT invoices and credit notes, and the timing within which they must be raised.

It is not uncommon for suppliers and business customers in longstanding trading relationships, or businesses engaged in a high volume of transactions with their customers, to agree certain discounts and rebates. Rather than VAT administration requirements forming a barrier or block to these genuine commercial arrangements, VAT law permits the parties to agree that standard VAT credit-noting procedures will not be followed between them with respect to the discounts. In this scenario, if a VAT invoice is raised but the price is subsequently reduced or discounted, there is no requirement to raise a standard VAT credit note and the amount of VAT on the invoice is not altered, so the supplier remains liable to VAT on the original invoiced amount and the customer does not make any VAT adjustment for the discount that is given. Where the parties are agree to this procedure, this simplification can ease the administrative burden of tracking multiple discounts for VAT purposes.

Tax Tip Although VAT legislation does not specify that the agreement between the parties must be in writing, this is highly recommended in order to avoid confusion or uncertainty on the agreed position.

Bad Debts

Of course, not all customers pay the agreed price for a supply and suppliers are frequently faced with bad debts. If a supplier that accounts for VAT on the invoice basis, and who has identified a bad debt, has already remitted VAT to Revenue on the supply in question and has taken all reasonable steps to obtain payment, VAT relief can be claimed on the bad-debt amount by the supplier, provided certain conditions are met. These include being able to demonstrate that the defaulting customer is not a connected party and that the debt in question has been written off in the supplier's accounts and is eligible, if relevant, for an income tax/corporation tax deduction.

Appendix C to this book reproduces the text of the Revenue VAT leaflet *Bad debts (excluding hire-purchase)*, which deals with bad debt relief.

Tax Tip While, strictly, there is no requirement in VAT law to obtain prior Revenue authorisation to make a VAT bad debt adjustment, it is not uncommon for businesses to notify Revenue, especially regarding large adjustments that may alter the typical profile of the business's VAT returns.

ately and any subsequent invoice for the balance should make reference to the advance payment.

Where a supplier has accounted for VAT on a deposit but the customer cancels the transaction (e.g. cancels a hotel reservation) before the transaction takes place and if the supplier retains the deposit payment, the supplier can make an adjustment for the VAT that has previously been accounted for on this. (The conditions for claiming relief are set out in section 74 VATCA 2010.) Where the supplier has previously issued a VAT invoice for the supply and then claims relief for the cancelled deposit, the supplier must issue a document to the customer, which is effectively treated as a VAT credit note.

Unjust Enrichment

If a VAT overpayment is made to Revenue by mistake (e.g. due to the application of a too-high VAT rate on sales), in order to obtain a refund from Revenue it may be necessary for the supplier to demonstrate that the repayment will not lead to the supplier's 'unjust enrichment'. In considering whether there would be unjust enrichment, Revenue will normally look at a range of factors, including whether the overpaid amount was effectively passed on by the supplier to its customers (and therefore the supplier would essentially have a windfall if the VAT repayment is made). (Further details on unjust enrichment can be found in section 100 VATCA 2010.)

Tax Tip Where Revenue believe an overpaid VAT amount was already passed on to customers and therefore that there would be unjust enrichment if a VAT repayment is made, the claimant can nevertheless obtain the repayment to the extent that it undertakes to (and actually does) repay the VAT amounts to its customers within a specified period.

Margin Schemes

Whereas we have seen that VAT is generally applied to the full consideration for a supply, VAT law also provides for a range of 'margin schemes'. These typically result in VAT only being accounted for on the *margin* earned, with a restriction on VAT recovery. Examples of these include the optional margin schemes for certain means of transport, agricultural machinery, second-hand goods and antiques as well as the mandatory margin schemes for certain sales by auctioneers and travel agents (the last being commonly referred to as the Travel Agents' Margin Scheme (TAMS)). VAT law also contains a special scheme for the taxation of certain transactions in investment gold. Further details of these schemes are contained in sections 87 to 90 VATCA 2010.

Special Schemes

There are special VAT schemes for certain businesses. Examples include the special scheme for auctioneers (more can be found in respect of this in section 89 VATCA 2010 and on Revenue's website[5]) and also the special scheme for retailers (which we have outlined further below).

VAT issues in the retail sector can be complex, especially given the large volume of transactions and the wide range of VAT rates that may apply to the different sales made. For retailers, the consideration for a sale is generally accepted to be the amount that is actually received by the retailer, after the customer has used discount vouchers and coupons, etc. This approach has been endorsed in CJEU cases such as *Boots Company Plc v. Commissioners of Customs and Excise*[6] and *Argos Distributors Ltd v. Commissioners of Custom & Excise*[7]. Similarly, in *Elida Gibbs Ltd v. Commissioners of Customs and Excise*[8], a supplier manufacturing toiletry products offered cash refunds to customers in order to encourage repeat purchases and was found to be ultimately liable to account for VAT only on the net amount received.

Where a retailer sells a voucher, VAT typically does not apply until the voucher is redeemed and then at that stage, VAT is charged by the supplier for the goods that are purchased with the voucher. However, practitioners should be aware that there are particular VAT provisions for the sale of phone cards, vouchers, coupons, tokens, etc., through

---

[5] See www.revenue.ie/en/tax/vat/leaflets/auctioneering.html.
[6] Case C-126/88.
[7] Case C-288/94.
[8] Case C-317/94.

intermediaries and agents. These are contained within section 43 VATCA 2010. Also, it should be noted that the overall VAT regime for vouchers is currently under review at EU level and further changes are expected in this area.

Revenue permit a special scheme for retailers that sell goods attracting

Non-monetary consideration

We have seen that the taxable amount for a supply is the full amount that the supplier is entitled to receive in return for that supply. It is possible that the consideration may not be wholly in money's worth, such as a barter transaction whereby the parties may be exchanging goods or services instead of one party paying cash, as illustrated in **Example 6.3** below.

Example 6.3: Barter Transactions

> Mary owned a development site in Dublin. Linda (a property developer) wanted to buy the site. Instead of paying cash to Mary for the site, Linda agreed to construct a new extension on Mary's house in return for Mary transferring the site to Linda. As no cash changed hands, both parties incorrectly assumed that they did not need to worry about VAT.

If the consideration received is not wholly in monetary form, then it is necessary under section 37 VATCA 2010 to impute a value for the purposes of calculating the taxable value of the transaction and the relevant amounts of VAT. Where cash is not changing hands, this area can often be overlooked, so it is important in practice to ensure that all elements of consideration in a deal or transaction are identified, whether in monetary form or otherwise.

---

[9] See www.revenue.ie/en/tax/vat/leaflets/retailers-special-schemes.html for more details.

Market Value

It is also important to note that Revenue may make a determination to impose market value on a transaction for VAT purposes in certain circumstances, particularly where the parties to the transaction are connected and one of the parties is not entitled to full VAT recovery. These rules are set out in section 38 VATCA 2010 and it should be noted that 'connection' in this context is defined broadly.

Cash Receipts Basis

VAT-registered traders who account for output VAT (VAT on sales) on the invoice basis must remit VAT to Revenue based on invoices raised (or invoices that should have been raised) and are generally only permitted to take VAT recovery where valid invoices have been obtained. However, it is also possible for certain traders to account for output VAT on the cash receipts basis (also known as the 'receipts' or 'moneys received basis'). This is provided for in section 80 VATCA 2010 and is broadly available to traders whose turnover does not exceed €2 million annually, or traders who derive at least 90% of their turnover from taxable supplies to unregistered customers.

A trader applies to Revenue in writing in order to be authorised to account for VAT in this manner, or selects the appropriate box on its tax registration form (e.g. TR1 or TR2).

Where an applicant has been authorised to apply the cash receipts basis, its output VAT position in a VAT period will largely be dependent on the payments that have actually been received. The cash receipts procedure cannot be applied to transactions with connected parties.

With respect to input credits, the authorised trader can still reclaim VAT on foot of valid VAT invoices received where these have not yet been paid (i.e. there is no requirement for the trader to wait until they have paid purchase invoices to reclaim the VAT from Revenue). However, this is subject to the requirement on all traders in section 62A VATCA 2010 to make VAT adjustments if their purchases are not fully paid within six months following the bi-monthly period in which the claim was made.

Common Invoicing Issues

As already outlined in **Chapter 1**, VAT law specifies the circumstances in which a valid VAT invoice or credit note must be issued and the particulars that must be shown in order for the invoice or credit note to be regarded as valid for VAT purposes, as well as the strict time limits for raising these.

Instead of the supplier issuing a VAT invoice to a VAT-registered customer, the parties may agree to implement self-billing (section 71 VATCA 2010). This can work well in practice where the customer has the appropriate systems in place. However, a practical risk to note is

an equal footing

systems criteria and specifications are met. These are outlined in regulation 21 of the 2010 VAT Regulations.

Expressing Doubt on the VAT Treatment of a Transaction

As outlined above, it may be unclear what the taxable amount or the VAT rate applicable to a transaction is, or perhaps the place of supply of a transaction is not straightforward. In cases where a VAT-registered trader is doubtful on any aspect of the VAT treatment of a transaction, the trader can notify Revenue of this (in a letter to the relevant district that deals with the trader's VAT affairs) when filing the relevant VAT return.

Section 81 VATCA 2010 sets out a number of conditions that need to be met in order to be regarded as making a valid expression of doubt. It is therefore necessary that the expression of doubt sets out full details of the fact pattern and the applicant's view of the technical analysis applicable, why there is indeed doubt on this, etc. Consequently, this can involve the applicant having to carry out detailed research on relevant legislation and case law.

We will see in **Chapter 7** that interest is normally due (at a rate of 0.0274% per day or part of a day) on unpaid VAT or VAT that is paid late. The potential benefit of making an expression of doubt is that where the treatment that has been applied by the trader was incorrect but Revenue accept that the doubt in question (and the intention behind the trader's application) was genuine and the trader pays any VAT shortfall in the VAT return for the period in which Revenue's decision is notified, no interest is applied to the VAT shortfall.

> **Tax Tip** While the expression of doubt mechanism is a welcome one, practitioners should note that strict time limits and procedural requirements apply. For example, the alignment of the application with the bi-monthly VAT return filing deadline is tighter than the filing deadline for income tax returns.

> **Tax Tip** Practitioners should also be aware that in addition to any penalties pursued from the taxpayer, penalties may be applied to persons who knowingly assist in the preparation, or submission, of incorrect VAT returns (e.g. a €4,000 penalty under section 117 VATCA 2010).

Asset Finance and Financial Services

VAT issues arising in asset finance and financial services transactions (e.g. share transactions, insurance, transfer of receivables, factoring) can be very complex, as it is often necessary to consider the place of supply of the transactions, the scope for VAT exemption to apply to all or some of the transactions, as well as the impact of the arrangements on VAT recovery entitlement. Conversely, we have also seen in **Chapter 2** that certain transactions, while legally being effective and fully enforceable, are disregarded for VAT purposes, e.g. the transfer of ownership of goods as security for a loan or debt or the transfer back of those goods when the loan in question has been repaid.

Factors that may be relevant in the VAT analysis include determining the exact nature of any services being performed, if and how ownership over assets is being transferred, the location of any such assets at the time of the transaction and the location of the counterparties to the transaction themselves. The contractual terms should of course be reviewed closely, including identifying allocation of risk between the parties (especially where any warranties or indemnities are being provided). With respect to transactions involving other jurisdictions, it may be necessary to obtain specific foreign VAT or local sales tax advice.

Requirement to Retain Records

Unless otherwise expressly agreed with Revenue, a trader must keep all records which affect or may affect its VAT affairs for a period of six years from the date of the latest transaction to which they relate.

Records relating to property transactions (e.g. copies of leases) must be kept for the duration of the interest that the trader holds in the property plus a further six years.

Examples of records to be retained include the business's books, records, linking documents, invoices, credit notes, receipts, accounts vouchers,

recorded and stored and where the system has controls and meets certain specifications.

VAT Cash-flow Issues

Given that VAT is a tax on most business transactions and also that the standard VAT rate in Ireland is at the time of writing 23%, this means that even if a trader is operating successfully and has full VAT-recovery entitlement on its deductible expenditure, significant VAT cash-flow issues can arise and need to be managed.

We have already seen that a trader's VAT cash-flow position with respect to sales is likely to be impacted by whether the trader operates VAT on the invoice basis or on the cash receipts basis. In addition, a trader seeking to minimise its VAT cash-flow issues may be eligible for various other relieving measures and should ensure that it follows appropriate procedures in order to expedite VAT refunds and reduce VAT costs. Examples of steps that a trader may be able to take to manage VAT cash-flow costs include the following:

- Timely VAT registration by start-up businesses in order to reclaim VAT on expenditure appropriately.
- Obtaining authorisation from Revenue for VAT grouping (see **Chapter 1**).
- Obtaining Section 56 zero-rating authorisations for exporters.
- If in a continual VAT repayment position, obtaining authorisation from Revenue to file monthly VAT returns in order to expedite VAT refunds.

[10] See http://www.irisoifigiuil.ie/archive/2012/january/Ir270112.pdf (accessed December 2016).

- Responding fully to Revenue verification queries with respect to reclaims and filing annual VAT returns of trading details on a timely basis (otherwise, in practice, Revenue may withhold refunds).
- Submitting timely electronic VAT refund (EVR) claims on ROS in order to reclaim foreign EU VAT.
- Providing the trader's Irish VAT number to foreign EU suppliers in order to avoid foreign VAT being incorrectly applied to certain reverse-charge transactions.

Conclusion

VAT is a self-assessment tax, so businesses need to ensure that VAT is being applied appropriately on sales and that VAT is being deducted appropriately on purchases. In **Chapter 5**, we examined common issues that arise in relation to VAT on purchases. This chapter covered common issues that arise in relation to sales VAT, such as accounting for VAT at the correct VAT rate and ensuring that it is based on the correct amount. In addition, we outlined some other VAT issues that are often encountered, including the requirement to keep full records.

Chapter 7 will deal with Revenue audits and interventions and will outline some procedures for dealing with VAT issues arising in such circumstances.

- Introduction
- Types of Revenue Intervention
- What to do on Receiving Notification of a Revenue Audit
- The Revenue Audit Process
- E-audits
- Qualifying Disclosures
- Preparing for the Revenue Audit
- The Opening Meeting of the Audit
- The Audit Settlement
- 'No Loss of Revenue'
- Self-correction
- Innocent Error
- Technical Adjustments
- Statutory Penalties
- Inability to Pay
- Revenue Powers
- Tax Tips Relating to the Revenue Audit Process
- Conclusion
- Appendix 7.1 – Sample Notification of a Revenue Audit

Introduction

Revenue audits are an essential component of any self-assessment tax system. Although it is not possible for the Revenue Commissioners to review every return under every tax head for every taxpayer, they must ~~..~ ~..~~~ ~.~~~~.~~ ~~.~ ~~.~~~~~~~ where there is the greatest chance that

interact with taxpayers in order to assess compliance and will also describe the procedure whereby a taxpayer who wishes to regularise its position may make a disclosure to Revenue regarding an error (or errors).

To put matters more in context, as a starting point we have set out below some statistics on Revenue audits, taken from Revenue's 2015 Annual Report.

AUDIT YIELDS (REVENUE ANNUAL REPORT 2015)

Total audits;	6,612
Total yield:	€327.9 million
Average yield per audit:	€44,592

Types of Revenue Intervention

There are several ways in which Revenue can correspond with a taxpayer. For example, it is quite common for Revenue to query certain figures contained within a VAT return, particularly when the taxpayer is in a start-up or refund position. In other cases, Revenue may initiate what is commonly called an 'aspect query'. Examples of aspect queries would include a request for information about a particular transaction in which the taxpayer is involved, or perhaps a request for information about third parties with which the taxpayer has dealings.

Finally, Revenue may seek to conduct what is commonly called a 'profile interview' with a taxpayer in order to better understand the nature of the taxpayer's activities.

None of the above interventions necessarily mean the taxpayer is being (or will be) subject to a formal Revenue audit. They are often queries arising from the submission of a return or from information required as part of Revenue's risk-profiling system. Quite often, these situations can be dealt with by simply providing the relevant information and no further issues arise. However, interventions can also lead to formal audits and the taxpayer should therefore consider if any further action is required in this regard.

At the other end of the scale, Revenue may commence an investigation. An inquiry (or investigation) letter from Revenue is generally a signal that a Revenue official has good reason to believe that a serious tax offence has been committed and that he or she is investigating with a view to criminal prosecution. It is strongly recommended that legal advice is obtained in relation to all such matters (the procedure for dealing with such investigations is outside the scope of this publication).

Between the intervention (aspect query or profile interview) and the investigation is the formal audit. A taxpayer will know that an audit is to commence as Revenue will generally write to the taxpayer (and usually their tax agent) to confirm this. The letter[1] will contain the wording 'Revenue Audit' and will contain the relevant details including:
1. what period will be reviewed;
2. what tax heads will be reviewed; and
3. where and when the audit is to take place.

It is important to note that the interventions referred to above (e.g. aspect queries and profile interviews) are not the commencement of formal audits, though they may *lead* to an audit. Accordingly, the taxpayer may still be able to benefit from making an 'unprompted qualifying disclosure' (see below) even if one of these interventions has taken place.

Tax Tip Make sure to understand if the communication from Revenue is an investigation, an audit or a non-audit intervention. This will dictate how best to deal with the query. If there is any doubt, this should be clarified with Revenue as soon as possible.

---

[1] For an example of such a letter, see **Appendix 7.1** at the end of this chapter.

> **Tax Tip** If the taxpayer is subject to a non-audit intervention, consider if an unprompted qualifying disclosure may be appropriate.

What to Do on Receiving Notification of a Revenue Audit

amount of work to do in order to prepare for the audit, or where the taxpayer or relevant staff are on leave, etc. It is typically availed of by larger clients, especially where the client believes that it be may necessary to make a disclosure.

It is also advisable to consult the most recent *Code of Practice for Revenue Audit and Other Compliance Interventions*[2] (the 'Code of Practice'). This is a guidance (non-statutory) document, which outlines how Revenue deal with audits and what a taxpayer can expect from a Revenue officer. The Code of Practice was substantially updated and published in 2010 and has been revised several times since then. It is therefore important to ensure that the most recent version is being consulted as it is expected that the Code of Practice will continue to be amended. The last update (at the time of writing) was in November 2015 and therefore this chapter addresses the November 2015 version.

> **Tax Tip** On receipt of a formal audit notification, consider if additional time is required to prepare for the audit. The taxpayer must request the additional 60-day period within 14 days of the issue of the Revenue audit notification.

The Revenue Audit Process

Let us imagine that you have received notification from Revenue of an audit. In this section, we summarise what the audit process involves and what you can typically expect.

[2] See www.revenue.ie/en/practitioner/codes-practice.html

Audit Selection

A Revenue audit is the examination of compliance with tax legislation. Audits are rarely random and are generally based on informed selection from knowledge banks (e.g. existing knowledge gathered from other audits in the same sector, etc.) or computer-based profiling on Revenue's REAP (Risk Evaluation, Analysis and Profiling) software. Revenue have also increased their focus on targeting particular business sectors and conducting 'streetscapes' (i.e. auditing businesses in specific locations).

Notification

Notice is received in the form of a letter containing the phrase 'Notification of a Revenue Audit' (see **Appendix 7.1** to this chapter). Generally, 21 days' notice is given and the letter is copied to the taxpayer's tax agent (if Revenue have these details). From the date of issue of the letter, there is no longer the opportunity to make an 'unprompted qualifying disclosure' in respect of the particular tax head/period and in respect of related liabilities in other tax heads/periods.

Unannounced Visits

Unannounced visits from Revenue officers may occur if the officer is in the area. Upon arrival, the officer should normally offer to rearrange the visit for a more convenient time. However, this option is not available for spot-checks carried out relating to record-keeping or the correct operation of cash points. Such checks often take place on all businesses in the same geographical area (e.g. street) during the same visit. *Note:* An unannounced visit is not the commencement of a formal audit, although clearly it could lead to one.

Location

An audit is generally carried out at the taxpayer's place of business. This is usually the principal place of business rather than the registered office (if the taxpayer is a company). Should the taxpayer have no premises, the audit can take place at the private residence of an individual, but generally only with the prior consent of the individual. It is possible for the audit to take place at the relevant Revenue office or at the tax agent's place of business, although the latter is the least preferred location for Revenue. Irrespective of where the audit is carried out, the Revenue officer usually visits the business premises at some stage during the process.

Conduct

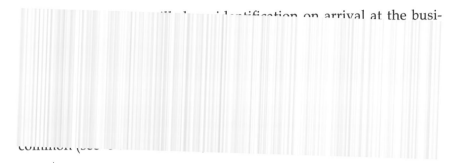

...ification on arrival at the busi-

Period of Review

The Revenue officer will focus on the period indicated in the audit notice (e.g. the notice may have specified that the audit relates to six consecutive bi-monthly VAT periods). However, if issues arise and the Revenue officer believes that tax defaults have taken place in previous or later periods, these periods can also be reviewed following approval from the relevant Revenue manager.

Data Protection

The purpose of the collection of data by Revenue is to ensure the correct operation of the taxation system. Any information provided to Revenue is strictly confidential and subject to the rules of the Data Protection Act 2003.

E-audits

The term 'e-audit' is used to describe audits consisting, exclusively or non-exclusively, of an examination of records held electronically. When it comes to examination, there is no distinction between records kept manually and those kept on computer systems; Revenue's Code of Practice is still in operation with regard to the conduct of the audit and the procedures involved. Some small-scale electronic checks may take place as part of an audit, but generally if an extensive e-audit is required the taxpayer will be notified of this in writing.

Traditionally, e-audits took place for businesses with high volumes of transactions such as large retailers, as the e-audit procedure allowed for quick analysis of large numbers of transactions. This method, however, is expanding and its use is increasing across all business areas. The adoption by Revenue of data analysis software means that data can be analysed and inconsistencies easily identified due to the tailored nature of the search program.

Electronic Files

Files of a specific nature and format may be requested by Revenue. This information will then be handed over electronically by the taxpayer to the Revenue officer for storage on encrypted Revenue systems. Revenue have a data security policy in place for the storage of data to ensure the safeguarding of sensitive information.

Need for Information Technology Involvement

Concerns have been voiced by taxpayers and advisors regarding the scope of the information being examined by Revenue. It is important to note that the information should be provided to Revenue on an electronic medium populated by the taxpayer. Therefore, for many businesses, a person from their IT department is likely to be involved in the process. In practical terms, their involvement should be managed by the taxpayer and their discussions with Revenue limited to IT-related matters.

E-audit Testing

The testing software used by Revenue is extremely powerful and can process huge amounts of data. It can be programmed to search for data such as inconsistent numeric patterns, large transactions, weekend postings, gap detection and more detailed inconsistencies.

The following are some examples of what Revenue typically examine:
- Invoicing errors – gaps or duplicates in sequential invoice numbers can be detected.
- Non-deductible items – the software can search for references on purchase invoices to items such as food, entertainment, hotel, and so on; in other words, items where input credit is typically not allowable.

- VAT-rate errors on supplies of goods/services – product files and sales data can be analysed to determine which items have been sold at reduced or zero VAT rates and how much is involved.
- Irregular postings – the software can easily identify the dates and times when postings were made (e.g. unusual late-night or weekend postings may indicate that a transaction is worth further examination).

Tax Tip Where members [...] payer will usually want to ensure that IT staff do not engage in discussing aspects of the business with Revenue, other than the supply of the relevant files requested.

Qualifying Disclosures

Revenue's Code of Practice describes a 'qualifying disclosure' as follows:

> "a disclosure of complete information in relation to, and full particulars of, all matters occasioning a liability to tax that give rise to a penalty, is made in writing, is signed by or on behalf of the taxpayer that is accompanied by:
> a) a declaration, to the best of that person's knowledge, information and belief, that all matters contained in the disclosure are correct and complete; and
> b) a payment of the tax or duty and interest on late payment of that tax or duty."[3]

A qualifying disclosure is a disclosure made to Revenue before the commencement of a Revenue audit. It is typically made at the opening meeting with Revenue. However, in certain cases, it may be beneficial to forward a draft copy of the disclosure to Revenue prior to the opening meeting as this might enable the agent or the taxpayer to discuss certain matters with the Revenue inspector prior to the commencement of the audit, possibly enabling the taxpayer to amend the disclosure if necessary.

[3] *Code of Practice for Revenue Audit and Other Compliance Interventions* (November 2015), Paragraph 3.7. Available at www.revenue.ie/en/practitioner/codes-practice.html.

A qualifying disclosure must contain certain information. It should be in writing and signed by the taxpayer, together with a taxpayer statement that the disclosure is correct and complete to the best of the taxpayer's knowledge, information and belief. It should include details of tax owing as well as the interest due to Revenue. It should also be accompanied by a cheque for the tax, plus interest. There is no requirement to calculate the level of penalty as this can usually be agreed at the end of the audit. A disclosure will still be accepted by Revenue as 'qualifying' where all of the criteria are satisfied with the exception of payment, as long as the taxpayer enters into an acceptable payment plan with Revenue (and assuming the obligations under the payment plan are met).

A taxpayer may wish to make a qualifying disclosure for the following reasons:
- the level of penalty applied will generally be much lower;
- the taxpayer name and settlement will not be published by Revenue; and
- Revenue will generally not initiate an investigation with a view to prosecution (however, it should be noted that decisions around prosecution are not made by Revenue).

Types of Qualifying Disclosure

There are two types of qualifying disclosure:
- a prompted qualifying disclosure; and
- an unprompted qualifying disclosure.

Prompted Qualifying Disclosure This is effectively a disclosure made after receiving notice from Revenue that an audit is about to commence (but before the audit itself has commenced).

A prompted qualifying disclosure is defined in Revenue's Code of Practice as:

> "a qualifying disclosure that has been made to the Revenue in the period between—
> a) the date on which the person is notified by Revenue of the date on which the audit will start, and
> b) the date the audit starts."[4]

Unprompted Qualifying Disclosure This is effectively a disclosure made to Revenue before notification of an audit is received. An unprompted qualifying disclosure will result in lower 'tax-geared' penalties than a prompted qualifying disclosure.

[4] *Ibid.*, Paragraph 3.8.

162

An unprompted qualifying disclosure is defined in the Code of Practice as:

> "a qualifying disclosure that the Revenue are satisfied has been voluntarily furnished to them;
>
> a) before any audit or investigation had been started by
>
> ~~into any~~ matter occasioning a liability to tax, and
>
> ~~of the date on which~~

Tax Tip When preparing a qualifying disclosure, ~~ensure~~ of the conditions have been satisfied and consider whether there is merit in sharing a draft with Revenue prior to the day on which the audit is due to commence.

Tax Tip It is possible to inform Revenue that a taxpayer intends to make an unprompted, voluntary disclosure (where there has been no audit notification) and to request a 60-day period in order to prepare and submit the disclosure.

Preparing for the Revenue Audit

The amount of time needed to prepare for a Revenue audit will depend to a large extent on the size and complexity of the business, the period of time covered by the audit and whether there are any particular matters of concern to the taxpayer. Clearly, if the taxpayer intends to make a qualifying disclosure with respect to VAT, then some work will be required in order to identify and quantify any VAT liabilities. At the very least, a taxpayer should review the following matters in advance of the audit:

- The VAT returns submitted for the period that is subject to audit to identify if any obvious errors were made.
- The accounts for the same period to identify if there are any items included that may attract further scrutiny. For example, if there is a large VAT debit or credit amount at the period end, is there a

[5] *Ibid.*, Paragraph 3.9.

simple explanation? If any tax provisions have been included in the accounts, then these may need to be considered. It is very important to consider if any items in the accounts suggest that the taxpayer was aware of a VAT issue but did not act on it. This could lead Revenue to conclude that an underpayment was 'deliberate' – such a scenario would need to be handled carefully.

- If there are any unusual transactions, such as one-off or capital transactions, was the VAT treatment considered in respect of these transactions?
- Consider if there were any material transactions in the period that could have significant consequences if the VAT treatment was incorrect or if there were any particular transactions where the VAT treatment was not clear cut.

The Opening Meeting of the Audit

Most Revenue inspectors will want to discuss the nature of the business with the taxpayer at the outset of the audit. Where the taxpayer is a corporate entity, Revenue will expect that someone senior (e.g. a director of the company) will be in attendance. Depending on the nature of the business, in most cases, the questions will typically relate to:
- nature of the goods/services supplied;
- level of turnover;
- number of staff;
- who the largest suppliers and customer are;
- locations of the business and whether properties are rented/owned, etc.;
- transactions involving the principal of the business (e.g. if premises are rented from a shareholder or director).

The Audit Settlement

It is possible that no additional liabilities will be due to Revenue at the conclusion of the audit. In fact, it sometimes happens that a taxpayer discovers they are due a refund. Unfortunately, however, these situations are quite rare and in the vast majority of cases, some amount of tax is due to Revenue, mainly because of innocent error.

In addition to the tax, Revenue will generally insist on collecting interest. Interest is charged at a rate of 10% per annum (calculated on a daily basis) for VAT underpayments (generally considered to be quite a penal rate).

Finally, Revenue will seek to collect a penalty, which is based on the amount of the tax underpaid and known as a 'tax-geared penalty'. Allowance is made for a number of factors, including:

- Was the error disclosed by the taxpayer?
- Was the error material and was it deliberate?
- ~~operate~~ with the Revenue officer?

	Default		
All defaults where there is a qualifying disclosure	Penalty table for defaults that occurred on or after 24/12/2008	Prompted qualifying disclosure and co-operation	Unprompted qualifying disclosure and co-operation
All qualifying disclosures in this category	*Careless behaviour without significant consequences*	10%	3%
First qualifying disclosure in these categories	*Careless behaviour with significant consequences*	20%	5%
	Deliberate behaviour	50%	10%
Second qualifying disclosure in these categories	*Careless behaviour with significant consequences*	30%	20%
	Deliberate behaviour	75%	55%
Third or subsequent qualifying disclosure in these categories	*Careless behaviour with significant consequences*	40%	40%
	Deliberate behaviour	100%	100%

[6] *Ibid.*, Paragraph 5.6.2.

No Qualifying Disclosure	Category of Default	No Co-Operation	Co-Operation Only
All defaults where there is no qualifying disclosure	*Careless behaviour without significant consequences*	20%	15%
	Careless behaviour with significant consequences	40%	30%
	Deliberate behaviour	100%	75%
Liability to a tax-geared percentage penalty generally arises on the difference between (a) the amount of tax (if any) paid or claimed by the person concerned for the relevant period on the basis of the incorrect return, claim or declaration as furnished/made, and (b) the amount properly payable by, or refundable to, that person for that period.			

As you can see from **Table 7.1** above, the level of tax-geared penalty is much greater where a disclosure has not been made.

Note: the terms 'deliberate behaviour', 'careless behaviour with significant consequences' and 'careless behaviour without significant consequences' are explained in the Code of Practice. These are important and should be considered carefully. In particular, the amount of the penalty increases significantly where Revenue form the view that VAT has been underpaid as a result of deliberate behaviour, so it is essential to understand these concepts. In addition, a taxpayer is much more likely to be referred for prosecution where Revenue believe that the taxpayer has underpaid deliberately.

Table 7.1 above shows how the tax-geared penalty amount can range from 3% to 100%. In the vast majority of Revenue audits, the penalty will be in the lower range. Where a qualifying disclosure is made, then the penalty amount will mostly be in the 3–20% range, on the basis that most errors are not made 'deliberately'. While all taxpayers will want to minimise the penalty amount, many will primarily be concerned with ensuring that the penalty is capped at 15%, as this should ensure that the settlement will not be published (see the section below dealing with publication).

It is possible that the taxpayer will not agree with the level of tax-geared penalty that the Revenue officer is seeking to apply. Unfortunately, in such cases the Revenue officer has the power to have the matter dealt with in a public court, which effectively results in the publication of the settlement by another means. However, the vast majority of audits are concluded without recourse to this

Exchequer being in a tax-neutral position. 'no loss of revenue' ('NLOR') situations, an example of which is set out below.

EXAMPLE 7.1: NO LOSS OF REVENUE

Assume Company A sold goods to Company B but forgot to charge VAT, in error. Assuming Company B is fully tax compliant and is involved in fully VATable activities and would have been able to reclaim all of the VAT charged to it (had Company A charged the VAT), then it could be argued that there is no loss to Revenue in these circumstances. Where the taxpayer can demonstrate that this applies, Revenue will generally not seek to collect the tax. However, Revenue are still likely to seek a penalty and possibly some amount of interest if the Exchequer was out of funds at any stage as a result of the error (even if only for a short period).

Table 7.2 below outlines the relevant tax-geared penalties that will be sought in NLOR situations, i.e. where 'no loss of revenue' can be demonstrated to Revenue's satisfaction.

TABLE 7.2: NO LOSS OF REVENUE – TAX-GEARED PENALTIES[7]

No Loss of Tax Revenue Default	Category of Default	No Loss of Revenue Qualifying Disclosure	
All *'careless behaviour'* no loss of revenue tax defaults where there is a 'qualifying disclosure'		Prompted qualifying disclosure and co-operation	Unprompted qualifying disclosure and co-operation
First qualifying disclosure in this category	*Careless behaviour*	Lesser of 6% or €15,000	Lesser of 3% or €5,000
Second qualifying disclosure in this category	*Careless behaviour*	Lesser of 6% or €30,000	Lesser of 3% or €20,000
Third or subsequent qualifying disclosure in these categories	*Careless behaviour*	Lesser of 6% or €60,000	Lesser of 3% or €40,000
No Loss of Revenue (NLOR) Tax Default	**Category of Default**	**Co-Operation Only**	
All 'careless behaviour' no loss of revenue tax defaults where there is no 'qualifying disclosure'	*Careless behaviour*	Lesser of 9% or €100,000	

'No loss of revenue' claims will not be accepted when:
- deliberate default exists;
- there is a general failure to operate the tax system;
- 'no loss of revenue' is not proven to the satisfaction of Revenue;
- there is no co-operation from the taxpayer; and
- careless behaviour exists and there is neither a qualifying disclosure nor taxpayer co-operation.

Self-correction

A taxpayer can 'self-correct' a return without paying a penalty if the error is identified and rectified within certain timeframes. For VAT

---

[7] *Ibid.*, Paragraph 3.5.7.

purposes, the correction must usually be made before the due date for filing the corporation tax or income tax return for the taxpayer for the chargeable period within which the relevant erroneous VAT period ended. This generally involves writing to Revenue to explain the error and including payment for the underpaid tax along with interest. Where the amounts involved are less than €6,000 for the relevant VAT

Innocent Error

A penalty will generally not be sought by Revenue where an underpayment of tax has resulted from an 'innocent error'. A Revenue officer will consider several factors when deciding if an error should fall into this category. A taxpayer would typically need to have a good compliance record and the error should not have arisen from failure to keep proper books and records, etc. In addition, the amount of tax underpaid would also be a factor. Interest will still be applied.

Technical Adjustments

No penalty will be applied where an officer accepts that a liability has arisen as a result of a technical adjustment. Technical adjustments arise from differences in interpretation of tax law. For a Revenue officer to accept such a position, they would need to be satisfied that due care has been taken by the taxpayer and that the interpretation taken by the taxpayer was reasonable. This will all be influenced by the amount of published material on the topic (e.g. case law or Appeal Commissioner decisions) and in particular if there has been Revenue guidance issued. Interest will still be applied.

It is important to note that Revenue will not accept that a tax liability has arisen merely from a technical adjustment in cases of tax avoidance involving complex transactions.

---

[8] *Ibid.*, Paragraph 3.2.

Statutory Penalties

There are a range of statutory penalties contained within VAT legislation. These are fixed amounts (usually €4,000 per offence) for a large number of different offences, including:

* failing to keep proper records;
* failing to issue correct VAT invoices;
* failing to complete VIES returns (nil threshold);
* submitting a VAT return after the due date; and
* failing to notify Revenue that a 'Section 56B authorisation' no longer applies (this penalty applies for each bi-monthly VAT period involved). (This authorisation was described in further detail in **Chapter 2,** Supplies of Goods.)

These penalties are in addition to the tax-geared penalties (max 100%) that have been described above and apply to underpayments of tax. In most audit situations, Revenue will typically only seek the tax-geared penalties. However, it is important to remember that Revenue have the ability to seek substantial penalties even in cases where there have been no underpayments.

Inability to Pay

It is not always possible for a taxpayer to fund an immediate settlement with Revenue. In cases where there is a genuine inability to pay (and Revenue accepts that the business is a viable one), it may be possible to enter into a phased-payment arrangement with the Collector-General. To avail of this process, a significant amount of information must be provided to Revenue and the agreed period will generally be limited to two or three years maximum. Once agreed, it is very important that the taxpayer meets the payment requirements.

Revenue Powers

It is important to note that Revenue have extensive powers which enable them to gather information necessary to establish if tax has been underpaid. These powers include:

* the power to enter and search a business premises at reasonable hours;
* the power to examine books, records and certain 'linking documents' (e.g. working papers drawn up in the making of accounts or returns

that show details of the calculations linking the records to the accounts or returns) and take copies;
- the power to question staff working on premises;
- the power to compel persons (such as financial institutions as well as professional advisors in certain cases) to provide certain information relevant to another party;

is incorrect.

Assessments issued under these sections are often referred to as 'Section 22' and 'Section 23' assessments respectively as these were the sections that included the relevant provisions prior to the VAT Act being consolidated in 2010.

Publication

If a taxpayer is discovered to have underpaid tax and the settlement (including tax, interest and penalties) totals €33,000 or more, the taxpayer will face having the result of the audit published in:
- *Iris Oifigiúil* (the Irish State Gazette);
- national newspapers; and
- the website of the Revenue Commissioners.

Publication will not proceed where:
- a qualifying disclosure is accepted before the audit has commenced; or
- the penalty does not exceed 15% of the tax ultimately due; or
- the total of tax, interest and penalty is less than €33,000.

It is important to note that the settlement should not be published where any of the conditions above are satisfied. However, as also mentioned above, if the Revenue inspector and the taxpayer cannot agree on the penalty amount and the inspector seeks to have the matter decided in open court, then the settlement could *effectively* be published even though it may satisfy all of the conditions referred to above.

Prosecution

Prosecutions are not within the scope of Revenue's Code of Practice. Should a taxpayer become aware that an investigation into their affairs has commenced or is about to commence, it is important to seek legal advice.

Tax offences that are most likely to be prosecuted include:
- deliberate omissions from tax returns;
- false claims of repayment;
- use of forged or falsified documents;
- facilitating fraudulent evasion of tax;
- systematic schemes to evade tax;
- use of offshore bank accounts to evade tax; and
- failure in remitting fiduciary taxes.

Tax Tips Relating to the Revenue Audit Process

Based on our experience, the following points are worth considering if you have been selected for a Revenue audit:
- Carefully examine the period and tax heads under review as this will impact on the approach you will take to the audit.
- It may be advisable to seek additional time before the audit commences (in the event that you believe it will take time to prepare the relevant calculations or carry out a thorough review).
- Consider if a comprehensive review needs to be carried out or if any particular transactions need to be examined in more detail.
- Ensure any disclosure meets the requirements as outlined by Revenue.
- Be sure to know the appropriate level of penalty relating to any tax underpayments and in particular consider if there is scope to argue that a penalty should not be applied or that a lower penalty is applicable. Revenue's Code of Practice should be consulted as this can be very helpful in understanding Revenue's likely approach to the audit and how best to deal with any potential issues that arise.
- While preparing for the audit, you may discover errors that resulted in tax being overpaid. Consider whether it is appropriate to include these amounts in the disclosure or whether they should be addressed during or after the audit has been concluded.
- Consider if any issue impacts on more than one tax head. For example, if it is discovered that VAT was incorrectly reclaimed on

entertainment expenses, it should be established if the corporation tax treatment for that expenditure was also incorrect.
- If additional VAT is due to Revenue, consider if it is possible that the corporation tax or income tax due for the period in question may be overstated (which would reduce the net payment due to Revenue).
- In our experience, there is almost always something to dis-

- Before getting into the detail, take a big picture of the VAT treatment applied to the sales and purchases of the business. Consider if the amounts of VAT that are being recorded in the VAT returns are consistent with the sales and purchases in the financial statements for the same period. It is always worth carrying out a high-level reconciliation to ascertain if there are likely to be any significant variations.

The following is a short list of items that frequently arise during Revenue VAT audits and it is worth considering if any may apply to the business:
- Reclaiming VAT in error on 'non-deductibles' such as client/staff entertainment, food/drink, petrol, etc.
- Failing to self-account for VAT on receipt of services or acquisition of goods from abroad.
- Failing to account for VAT at the correct rate (this is most common in retail environments or other scenarios where a large range of different goods/services are supplied).
- Failing to account for VAT on all sales where systems errors occur within accounting software.
- Failing to account for VAT on miscellaneous transactions such as sales of capital assets which are not recorded in the accounting software in the usual manner.
- Incorrectly dealing with property-related transactions such as sales or sublets of property.
- Failing to review previously reclaimed VAT where the relevant supplier has not been paid within the six-month period.
- Reclaiming VAT without receiving valid VAT invoices from suppliers.

Conclusion

As noted at the start of this chapter, Revenue audits go hand-in-hand with the self-assessment tax system. However, there is a range of other ways that Revenue may choose to interact with a taxpayer which do not constitute a formal audit. Taxpayers and practitioners should ensure they are clear on the type of Revenue intervention that is being proposed.

Interest and penalties (which can prove costly) may apply to tax errors and publication of defaulters may also occur. Consequently, familiarity with Revenue's Code of Practice is essential and if a tax error is identified it is important to consider whether a disclosure to Revenue should be made.

As VAT is a self-assessed tax, the question arises as to how VAT is operated in practice in insolvency scenarios. Therefore, in the next chapter, we consider the key VAT implications where forced sales take place.

Appendix 7.1 – Sample Notification of a Revenue Audit

 **Revenue**

www.revenue.ie

Oifig na gCoimlsiniirf Ionuim

Office of the Revenue Commission
[Region]

I wisn to inform you that has been

Scope of Audit	VAT
Period for Audit	
Date and Time of Audit	

A Revenue auditor will call to your place of business and will show his/her identity card on arrival. Please arrange to have available all records including all linking documents for the period specified.

Issues may arise during the course of the audit, which will require the auditor to extend the audit to include a review of other tax returns for other periods.

The audit may include an examination, using e-audit techniques, of the records held on and processed by computer systems, as well as the system processes and controls in place. Data downloads may be required to ensure the accuracy of the returns submitted. A pre-audit meeting to discuss the e-audit aspects may be required and, if so, I will contact you.

Revenue recognises that this audit may cause a degree of inconvenience for you. If for good and sufficient reason the date and time of the audit is not suitable please contact me without delay so that an alternative date can be arranged.

Finally, if you have any outstanding returns and remittances please have them ready for presentation to the auditor on his/her arrival.

Yours faithfully,

_____

[Name]
District Manager

_____   _____

This matter is being dealt with by,
Phone Number: eMail MyEnquires FAO

- Introduction

- VAT Review on Appointment of an Insolvency Practitioner or Mortgagee in Possession

- VAT Obligations for Liquidators

- VAT Obligations for Receivers

- VAT Obligations for Mortgagees in Possession

- VAT Obligations or Issues Particular to Insolvency and Property Transactions

- Entitlement of Insolvency Practitioners and Mortgagees in Possession to Input Credit

- Other VAT Issues Arising in Insolvency Situations

- Relevant Contracts Tax

- Conclusion

Introduction

Irish VAT legislation imposes certain obligations on insolvency practitioners (receivers and liquidators) and mortgagees in possession, i.e. scenarios in which a lender (mortgagee) is selling a property under the terms of a mortgage deed when there has been an act of default by

have VAT obligations on disposing of goods or providing services using the property of a borrower. It also extended the obligations that could arise under the Capital Goods Scheme (CGS). This chapter addresses the obligations arising under current VAT legislation.

The VAT obligations that can arise for receivers, liquidators and mortgagees in possession (MIPs) arise mainly under sections 22(3), 28(4) and (5), 64(12A), 65(4) and 76(2) of the Value-Added Tax Consolidation Act 2010 (VATCA 2010). Certain transactions involving National Asset Management Agency (NAMA) entities are also dealt with under section 16(1) VATCA 2010. (Further information can be found in Part 04.00.01 of the Revenue Operational Manual, *Guidelines on Tax Consequences of Receivership and Mortgagee in Possession (MIP)*,[1] which deals with all tax heads. This Revenue guidance was updated with respect to receivers and MIPs by *eBrief* 102/2015 and *eBrief* 110/2015.

VAT Review on Appointment of an Insolvency Practitioner or Mortgagee in Possession

It is important for an insolvency practitioner or MIP (as the case may be) to carry out a review and establish as much information about the VAT status of the borrower and the VAT history of the assets as early as possible after appointment.

Particular difficulties can arise with property disposals, as the VAT on property legislation is complex and therefore it is important for

[1] Revenue Commissioners, Operational Manual, Part 04.00.01 (October 2015).

insolvency practitioners and MIPs to be aware of these rules (discussed in more detail in **Chapter 4**).

Determining the correct VAT treatment in relation to property transactions relies heavily on knowing the full VAT history of the property. In a regular (non-insolvency) situation, a client (or the client's professional advisor, such as a solicitor or accountant) can generally provide full information in relation to the history of the property, such as:

(a) When was the property acquired?
(b) Was VAT charged on its acquisition?
(c) Was that VAT reclaimed?
(d) Why was the property acquired?
(e) What has it been used for since acquired?
(f) Has it been developed since it was acquired? When, and to what extent, etc.?

In an insolvency situation, the answers to the above questions are not always easy to find.

Take, for example, a 'fixed-charge' receiver appointed over a large residential development where the borrower was the developer of the property. It may seem likely that the borrower had constructed the units to sell on the open market and that therefore the borrower had recovered all of the VAT on expenses incurred in relation to the project. However, it is possible that the borrower had intended to rent the units once complete and perhaps did not register for VAT in the first place. This could have significant consequences for the obligations of the receiver (on rental or sale).

It is therefore vital that as much information as possible is obtained early in the process as it can become more difficult as time passes to establish the facts.

> **Tax Tip** It may be possible to source information from the borrower, the lender and Revenue. In addition, examining the physical appearance of the property (e.g. through photos), as well as information available concerning planning permission, may provide helpful information in relation to the VAT history.

Examples of Relevant Information

The following is a sample of the range of information that may be required in order to advise fully on what the VAT treatment may be on a future sale or letting of a property:
• name and full address of the property;
• name and details of the borrower (person/partnership/company);

- the borrower's VAT number (provide all relevant names and VAT numbers where there is more than one party involved);
- the date the property was acquired (or leasehold interest was assigned, if applicable);
- type of property (industrial/commercial/residential);
- type of interest held (e.g. freehold, leasehold);
- ... acquired (includ-

either by the current or previous ...
- how much VAT (if any) was reclaimed on development; and
- copies of VAT invoices or other documents received.

In addition, if the property is subject to a letting, the following information may be helpful:

- name of the current tenant;
- when the current lease commenced;
- terms of the lease (years and rent amount);
- confirmation if VAT is charged on the rents or if VAT was charged upfront when the lease was created;
- details of any development works the tenant has undertaken;
- confirmation if a 'waiver of exemption' applied in relation to short-term lettings whereby VAT was remitted to Revenue on lease rentals; and
- confirmation if any VAT clawback applied as a result of the letting (e.g. for certain property developers).

VAT Obligations of Liquidators

A 'liquidator' is a person appointed to conduct a winding-up (dissolution) of a company. Companies may be wound up voluntarily or by order of the court. As a liquidator has the power to secure and dispose of assets, on appointment the liquidator should consider if he or she is required to register for VAT (with a separate VAT registration for each particular case) and account for VAT to Revenue (either on sales or lettings). Often, the position is straightforward; for example, a liquidator disposing of equipment previously used in a VAT-registered manufacturing business will typically be obliged to account for VAT on the sale, and therefore the liquidator must register for VAT.

> **Tax Tip** In the normal course, an Irish-established trader may not be obliged to VAT register until its turnover exceeds a certain threshold. However, assuming the underlying borrower is an accountable person, it should be noted that the VAT-registration thresholds do not apply to liquidators and receivers, and they must register irrespective of the value of their taxable disposals.

In other situations, the disposals may not be subject to VAT, and therefore the liquidator will not be obliged or entitled to register for VAT. For example, the sale of the computers of an insurance broker would not typically be subject to VAT in normal circumstances as the insurance broker would not have been entitled to reclaim the VAT incurred when the goods were purchased. Typically, the activities of an insurance broker are VAT exempt.

Due to the complexities of VAT on property law, where the only asset to sell is an immoveable good (such as a building), it may require some investigation and professional advice to determine if a particular disposal is liable to VAT. It is important to note that a disposal of property may not be subject to VAT, but the liquidator could be obliged to make a payment to Revenue under the CGS in order to repay Revenue a portion of the VAT that was previously recovered by the borrower on the property. It may be possible for the liquidator to avoid this CGS clawback by making a joint election with the purchaser to apply VAT on the sale (i.e. 'opting to tax' the sale), but this is not possible in every circumstance and needs to be investigated thoroughly before a decision is made.

Finally, it is worth noting that a disposal of a property includes a distribution of the asset to the shareholders of the company. This will usually involve disposing of the property to a connected party, so specific VAT market-value rules (see **Chapter 6**, Other Common VAT Issues) and connected-party rules (see **Chapter 4**, VAT on Property) will need to be considered in relation to such transactions.

VAT Obligations of Receivers

Where a borrower has mortgaged or charged its assets and is in default, the lender may appoint a receiver to take control of and sell the assets towards the satisfaction of the debt owing by the borrower. A receiver may be appointed under a fixed charge or a floating charge. A receiver appointed under a fixed charge is generally only entitled to sell or rent the specific assets that are subject to the charge, whereas a receiver appointed under a floating charge is generally entitled to sell any of the company's available assets in order to discharge the debt owed to the lender. In both cases, the receiver's duty is generally to take charge of the assets, to sell them and to use the proceeds to discharge the debt owed to the lender.

The receiver must ascertain if the sale or rent of the asset will be subject to VAT and if it is, must register for VAT, charge VAT on the sale and

receivership, the company/

ers. If a sale is made by the MIP and the sale is subject to VAT, VAT should be accounted for by the MIP using its own VAT number, i.e. unlike the position for receivers and liquidators, in practice there is no requirement for the MIP to effect separate VAT registrations for each particular case. If a clawback of VAT arises under the CGS as a result of the sale of an asset, then the MIP will be obliged to make the payment.

VAT Obligations or Issues particular to Insolvency and Property Transactions

Insolvency practitioners and MIPs should keep the following VAT on property points in mind:

1. The insolvency practitioner/MIP may be obliged to account for VAT on sale of the assets.
2. The insolvency practitioner/MIP may be obliged to account for VAT on services provided using the assets of the borrower (e.g. rental income).
3. If a property is sold or rented and no VAT is charged, the insolvency practitioner/MIP may be liable for a clawback of VAT arising under the CGS.
4. The insolvency practitioner/MIP may be obliged to make adjustments (positive and negative) which arise under the CGS during the period in which they have control of the asset.
5. The insolvency practitioner/MIP may be obliged to provide information under the CGS (e.g. to a purchaser) relating to the property when their appointment has ended or the asset has been disposed of.
6. The insolvency practitioner/MIP cannot exercise a 'joint option to tax' in respect of the sale of a property to a purchaser connected with the borrower or the insolvency practitioner/MIP, even if the

purchaser has full VAT recovery and the property is being disposed of for market value. This is an anti-avoidance mechanism, although it potentially catches a very wide range of transactions.

7. Purchasers of property will generally look for replies to the Law Society of Ireland's Pre-Contract VAT Enquiries (PCVE). The purpose of the PCVE document is to outline the VAT history for the property and the basis for the proposed VAT treatment of the sale. Insolvency practitioners and MIPs need to exercise care in completing this as it generally forms part of the contract. It is often not possible to confirm the VAT history for the property conclusively and it may be necessary to ensure the purchaser is aware of this. (A copy of the PCVE can be found at www.lawsociety.ie.)

Entitlement of Insolvency Practitioners and Mortgagees in Possession to Input Credit

Insolvency practitioners and MIPs will generally incur costs in the course of their activities and so it is necessary to consider their VAT-recovery entitlement on these.

Typically, the receiver, liquidator or MIP will register for VAT on appointment if it is clear that disposals will be made at some point in the future which will be subject to VAT. This should allow VAT recovery on costs incurred that relate to the taxable sales, e.g. professional fees.

If a liquidator, receiver or MIP sells a number of assets, only some of which are subject to VAT on disposal (e.g. a mixture of VATable sales of property and VAT-exempt sales of property or shares), an apportionment of deductible VAT will be required. VAT registration also allows for the recovery of the VAT charged on the provision by a professional services firm of the services of a receiver or liquidator and their staff. However, it is important to consider the position prior to making the VAT registration application. In particular, care should be given when answering questions about the intention of a receiver, as this may have implications or trigger queries further along the process, especially where Revenue expect a VATable sale to be made and, instead, a VAT-exempt sale is made and no VAT is remitted.

Where the sale of an asset is made by an MIP, and the sale is one which would entitle the vendor to VAT recovery on costs associated with the sale, it may be desirable for the invoices in respect of those costs incurred to be made out to the MIP. The costs involved are typically those of lawyers, estate agents, other professionals, and so on. There will generally be no issue where an MIP has taken control of an asset without any other party being involved and makes a VATable sale. However, it is not unusual for a receiver to be appointed to take control of an asset and to prepare the asset for sale. During that period a receiver will typically incur costs on which VAT can be recovered, but those invoices are usually made out to the receiver. Where the sale is ultimately made by an MIP, the entitlement to recover VAT on these costs can come into

uidator/receiver/MIP who has disposed of a business, consider if recovery can be taken on the basis that a VATable business was being carried on by the liquidator/receiver/MIP (rather than simply considering if the assets being sold are subject to VAT).

Other VAT Issues arising in Insolvency Situations

Transfer of Business Relief

When a person decides to sell a business (either in the normal course of selling a business or in an insolvency scenario), it can generally be done in one of two ways:
1. If the person is a sole trader, he or she can only choose to dispose of the assets of the business.
2. However, if the person operates through a company, then he or she may be more likely to dispose of their shareholding in the company, rather than just selling off the assets of the company.

The VAT issues that arise under both scenarios are very different. The transfer of business relief provisions impact on insolvency practitioners as they are often disposing of assets that may well be viewed as the sale of a business.

Where businesses are transferred, VAT law contains relieving provisions (described in more detail in **Chapters 2** and **3**, for sales of tangible and intangible assets respectively) whereby no VAT is charged on the sale, provided certain conditions are met. Care needs to be taken when deciding whether or not VAT transfer of business relief applies. If a vendor incorrectly charges VAT on the transfer of a business and the purchaser pays the VAT, Revenue are entitled to refuse to give an input credit in respect of such incorrectly charged VAT. Accordingly, it is vital that the purchaser of an asset (where a business or part of a business is being taken over) resists any attempt by the vendor to charge VAT on the transaction. If doubt exists, the purchaser should request the vendor to seek clarification of the VAT position from the Revenue District dealing with the vendor's VAT affairs. Equally, if a vendor does not charge VAT when it should have been charged, then it will remain liable for the VAT. Consequently, prior to completing the transaction, it is often in both parties' interest to seek clarification from Revenue on whether the transfer of business provisions do, in fact, apply.

Revenue have clarified their view that the sale of a rented property to a VAT-registered person may be subject to transfer of business provisions, although, at the time of writing, the application of the relief to the sale of rented property is still an issue that generates debate. Care is therefore needed in determining whether the relief applies to a particular transaction.

Tax Tip It will be necessary to consider the impact on VAT recovery for the insolvency practitioner/MIP where transfer of business relief applies to a sale of property. The entitlement to recover VAT is not clear in all cases and may depend on the underlying VAT status of the property, what the property was used for prior to sale, etc.

VAT Groups

As we have seen in **Chapter 1**, Registration and Administration, two or more persons can apply to Revenue to be included in a VAT group. It is important to note that granting such an application is at the discretion of Revenue.

The principal advantage of forming a VAT group is that VAT is not chargeable on transactions between VAT group members on most transactions. The exception to this is that sales of property are not covered by the VAT-grouping provisions and VAT must be charged on taxable sales of freehold property between VAT-group members. As the sale and purchase of the property will be reflected on the VAT-group return, some cash-flow benefits still arise as the VAT on the purchase will be automatically offset partly or wholly against the VAT due on the sale, depending on the purchaser's VAT-recovery entitlement.

If a receiver or liquidator is obliged to register for VAT, it is possible for the liquidator or receiver to join an existing VAT group or form a new VAT group to benefit from the advantages of VAT group membership, subject to the usual VAT-grouping rules. It should be noted, however, that members of a VAT group are jointly and severally liable for the VAT liability of the VAT group as a whole, and this potential exposure for a liquidator or receiver may make membership of a VAT group unattractive.

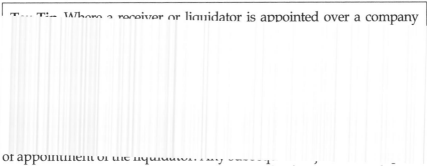

to the company's VAT returns (e.g. as a result of receiving credit notes from suppliers or writing off bad debts) will be made by submitting supplementary VAT returns for the last taxable period for which the company was registered.

Receivers appointed under a fixed charge only have the power to dispose of a specific asset. If the company continues to trade, its VAT registration number will remain in place so that it can remit VAT to Revenue as normal.

The VAT registration of a liquidator or receiver should be cancelled as soon as it has carried out all of its functions that give rise to a VAT charge. A liquidator or receiver should obviously ensure that it has reclaimed all VAT to which it is entitled (including VAT on its own fees) prior to the cancellation of its VAT registration.

Liquidators and receivers may register for VAT in error in the belief that they will have taxable disposals to make, only to discover that none of their disposals are subject to VAT. The VAT registrations of a liquidator or receiver should be cancelled when it is realised that it is not required and any VAT input tax previously reclaimed from Revenue may need to be refunded to Revenue.

VAT and Bad Debt Relief

In general, bad debt relief arises when a customer fails to pay in full or part and where that supplier has accounted for VAT to Revenue in respect of the supply. Bad debt relief is available only to traders who account for VAT on the invoice basis; it is not available to those operating VAT on the cash receipts basis or for certain connected-party transactions. (The relief is considered in greater detail in **Chapter 6**.)

Bad debt relief can apply in insolvency situations. It should be noted that it may be difficult to secure a refund from Revenue where the borrower has other outstanding tax liabilities. A review would need to be carried out of the relevant debts to determine the potential quantity and the history surrounding each of the debts. A decision can only then be taken as to whether or not a claim should be made.

Examiners

As already noted, this chapter focuses on the VAT position for receivers, liquidators and MIPs.

However, we have also set out below some brief comments with respect to examiners and examinership.

An examiner is a person appointed by the courts to assess whether the company can viably continue to trade and, if so, to prepare a plan for this. During the period of 'examinership', debts cannot be executed against the company and Revenue enforcement activity is suspended. In circumstances where an examiner is appointed, the company will typically continue to account to Revenue for VAT due on its supplies of taxable goods and services.

Relevant Contracts Tax

Although relevant contracts tax (RCT) is dealt with in more detail in **Chapter 10**, it is very easy to overlook the potential application of RCT in the context of insolvency assignments.

RCT arises most frequently for insolvency practitioners when dealing with clients in the construction industry. Liquidators, receivers and MIPs often dispose of assets and do not get involved in carrying out construction operations. In these cases, RCT should not be of too much concern. However, in order to sell (or rent) an asset, the insolvency practitioner or MIP (as the case may be) may need to carry out some works to the property. This could range from minor finishing works to a property (e.g. painting) to more substantial construction works where a receiver or liquidator takes control of a partly completed development. RCT may be relevant in respect of payments for nearly all such work. The insolvency practitioner/MIP therefore needs to determine the RCT status early in order to ensure tax compliance. In a typical situation, the receiver or liquidator and/or the lender will be eager to make progress with the assets to generate income. Additionally, it is often the case that third-party contractors are due monies for work carried out to date and will demand payment for previous services as well as advance payment before carrying out further work.

> **Tax Tip** Before making payments to any contractors, it is important that the RCT position is clarified as it is the person making the pay-

As outlined in Chapter 10, ... applies to a construction service. The VAT treatment applying to certain services that are subject to RCT was amended from 1 September 2008. From that date, when a contractor issues an invoice for certain construction services provided, the VAT element is dealt with by way of reverse charge, whereby the customer (principal contractor) self-accounts for VAT on the services in its VAT return. The contractor issues an invoice to the principal, instructing the principal to self-account for the VAT. This is another reason why it is important to determine the RCT treatment before payments are made.

Revenue's Position on the Application of RCT

Given the interaction between VAT and RCT, it is important to be aware of the main aspects of the RCT regime. Consequently we have set out below two extracts from Revenue guidance, which deal with the tax obligations arising in insolvency scenarios.

REVENUE OPERATIONAL MANUAL 04.00.01 – GUIDELINES ON TAX CONSEQUENCES OF RECEIVERSHIP AND MORTGAGEE IN POSSESSION (MIP)

3.5 RCT

Tax legislation provides no exemption from the operation of Relevant Contracts Tax (RCT) in the case of receivership or where there is a MIP. Revenue considers that all aspects of the RCT legislation, including deduction by the principal contractor and the offset by Revenue of RCT against outstanding taxes, must be applied as normal, notwithstanding the fact that a receiver has been appointed to a business or the mortgagee is in possession.

Where the receiver acts as a Principal

A receiver who is appointed to a business in the construction, meat processing or forestry sectors, who engages a subcontractor to carry out relevant operations, is a principal contractor for RCT purposes. A MIP who engages a subcontractor may also be a principal contractor depending on the circumstances. A receiver/MIP (who is a principal under the legislation) is, therefore, obliged to operate the RCT system on relevant payments made to the subcontractor in the same way as any other principal contractor. This includes registering with Revenue as a principal contractor and obtaining a 'deduction authorisation' in relation to all relevant payments made. If there is any doubt as to whether a particular contract is a relevant operation for RCT purposes, the receiver/MIP should contact the local Revenue office dealing with the borrower's tax affairs.

Appointments over separate borrowers will be examined separately, i.e. the appointment of Mr X as receiver over a construction company will not automatically deem all Mr X appointments to be within the RCT regime – each appointment will be examined separately.

In cases where a receiver/MIP is carrying out construction work to meet health and safety or planning guidelines, each case would have to be examined and judged on its own facts and merits. Factors to be considered would include the type and range of works being carried out, whether this work was being carried out in conjunction with other work or as part of wider construction work and what was the ultimate intention with regard to the property. Where there is doubt as to the position regarding cases which involve health and safety or planning guidelines requirements, details should be submitted to the relevant local Revenue office.

Where the receiver acts as a Subcontractor

Any RCT deducted from a subcontracting business in receivership and remitted to Revenue will be offset against outstanding taxes of the business in the order statutorily provided for, with any balance being repaid to the receiver provided all of the business' tax obligations are met. Section 530V(4) distinguishes between RCT deducted on foot of a contract entered into by a business prior to ~~~~~~~~~~~ and new contracts entered into by the receiver (in his

entered into after his/her appointment and the receiver obtains a new RCT reference number in respect of the receivership, the RCT system automatically grants a deduction rate of 20%, as a three year compliance history does not exist for the new receivership RCT registration. However, the requirement to have a three year compliance history can be disregarded, and the rate changed to 0%, if the receiver has met all the other conditions for the 0% rate and the risk to Revenue is minimal.

REVENUE EBRIEF NO. 03/11 – 21 JANUARY 2011:
RELEVANT CONTRACTS TAX (RCT) IN LIQUIDATION, RECEIVERSHIP OR EXAMINERSHIP

Tax law provides no exemption from the operation of RCT in the case of liquidation, receivership or examinership. Revenue takes the view that all aspects of RCT law – including deduction by the principal contractor and offset by Revenue of RCT against outstanding taxes – must be applied as normal, notwithstanding the fact that a liquidator, receiver or examiner has been appointed to the subcontracting company.

As such, any RCT deducted from a company in liquidation, receivership or examinership and remitted to Revenue will be offset against outstanding taxes in the order statutorily provided for, with any balance being repaid to the liquidator, receiver or examiner.

Revenue does, however, distinguish between RCT deducted on foot of a contract entered into by a company prior to receivership or liquidation and new contracts entered into by the receiver/liquidator (in his capacity as receiver/liquidator of the company) should the receiver/liquidator continue to trade the business. In such cases, if the contract which gave rise to the RCT deduction was entered into by the liquidator/receiver following their appointment, the RCT deducted should be offset only against liabilities of the post-appointment period, with any balance being repaid to the liquidator/receiver. If it is not clear whether the relevant contract was entered pre- or post- appointment, the receiver/liquidator should be asked to clarify the position. The tax number of the subcontractor shown on the RCT Deduction Card might be informative in this situation.

It should be noted that where a company successfully exits examinership and tax has been written off in line with the Court-approved scheme of arrangement, these taxes cannot be subsequently written back in for the purposes of offset.

Conclusion

Insolvency practitioners and MIPs need to be equipped to deal with VAT in respect of their activities and any forced sales. Most VAT difficulties arise when dealing with property transactions as the VAT rules surrounding such assets are complicated. Property transactions are the most common type of transactions that insolvency practitioners/MIPs encounter and there can be a lack of information available regarding the VAT history of the borrower and assets. Therefore, it is important for practitioners and lenders to be aware of the relevant VAT rules to ensure tax compliance and help avoid costly errors. In addition, if any works will be carried out to the property, it is important to be aware of how the VAT rules interact with RCT.

We will look at the RCT regime in more detail in **Chapter 10**. However, first we will look at how Ireland's VAT regime operates within the wider EU framework of VAT and consider how EU VAT law impacts on the Irish VAT system.

9
Anti-avoidance

- Introduction
- The Impact of European Union VAT Legislation on Irish VAT
- The Role of the Court of Justice of the European Union in relation to VAT
- General Principles of European Union Law
- Ireland's General Anti-avoidance Rules
- Mandatory Disclosure
- Base Erosion and Profit Shifting (BEPS) Project – (VAT Implications)
- Conclusion

Introduction

At this point, it is worthwhile taking a step back to consider the European Union sources of Irish VAT law, how Irish legislation fits into the wider EU framework of VAT and why it is important to be aware of this backdrop of EU law when advising on VAT matters. Certain

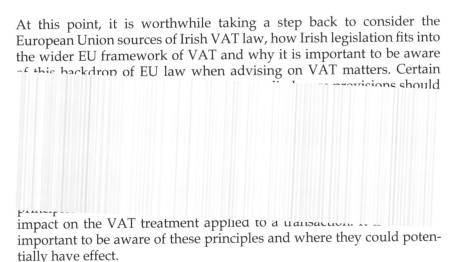

provisions should

impact on the VAT treatment applied to a transaction. It is important to be aware of these principles and where they could potentially have effect.

In addition, most readers will be aware that there has been an increased focus on tax planning and avoidance in recent years. While it is outside the scope of this book to describe these in detail, this chapter outlines some of the main aspects of relevant EU and Irish 'anti-avoidance' provisions that need to be considered.

The Impact of European Union VAT Legislation on Irish VAT

When considering how VAT legislation should be applied to a particular transaction or scenario, it is important to bear in mind that the overall Irish VAT system (including the Value-Added Tax Consolidation Act 2010 (VATCA 2010) and the Value-Added Tax Regulations 2010 (the '2010 VAT Regulations')[1]) is based on EU law.

Each Member State of the European Union is required to have a VAT system modelled on EU Directives and EU Regulations (these sources of EU law are discussed in more detail below) and when a new Member State accedes to the EU, it is required either to introduce a conforming VAT system, or, if it already has a VAT-type system in place, to align this with the EU code. A percentage of the VAT that is collected by the Member States is used to fund the various EU governing bodies and the EU Commission actively monitors if each Member State is implementing the system correctly.

---

[1] S.I. No. 639 of 2010.

EU Directives

The EU law governing the Irish VAT system takes a number of forms. The cornerstone of EU VAT law is the EU Directive[2] commonly referred to as the 'Recast Sixth Directive', as it updated and 'recast' the previous cornerstone EU VAT legislation, which was the EU's Sixth Directive on VAT. [3]

EU Directives require Member States to achieve a particular result but do not prescribe the specific way that the Member State must achieve that result. So, for example, the Recast Sixth Directive sets out the framework of the VAT system but generally does not dictate the ways in which Member States must implement the rules. Instead, each Member State implements national legislation to specify this and Ireland has chosen to implement the Directive by way of the VATCA 2010 and the VAT Regulations 2010.

To give an example of how the Recast Sixth Directive and the Irish legislation interact, the EU Directive (Article 132) sets out a mandatory rule that Member States shall VAT-exempt the provision of medical care by certain professionals, but it is left to the Member States to define the professionals covered. Irish legislation then sets out the parameters of the Irish VAT exemption in paragraph 2 of Schedule 1 VATCA 2010.

Derogations As a general rule, unless Ireland has obtained agreement from the EU Commission that it can derogate from a mandatory provision in an EU Directive, the EU law takes supremacy over Irish legislation. An example of a derogation was Ireland's authorisation to derogate from EU VAT law with respect to aspects of the old Irish VAT on property system (see **Chapter 4**).

Consequently, if an EU Directive is aimed at providing taxpayers with certain rights and it is precise, clear and unconditional (i.e. it does not give the Member State discretion as to its implementation) but the Member State has implemented conflicting rules (or has not implemented the EU rules at all) without having a relevant derogation on the matter, then the taxpayer can generally seek to rely on the EU rule to claim the rights when it is dealing with the Member State. This is commonly referred to the Directive as having 'direct effect'.

---

[2] Council Directive 2006/112/EC of 28 November 2006 on the common system of value-added tax.

[3] Council Directive 77/388/EEC of 17 May 1977 on the harmonisation of the laws of the Member States relating to turnover taxes – Common system of value-added tax: uniform basis of assessment.

EU Regulations

EU Regulations are another source of EU law and, importantly, they have direct applicability. There is no need for Ireland to implement the EU Regulations into national legislation because the EU Regulations are already part of Irish law without any further action required. Therefore,

At first glance, the interaction between the VATCA 2010 and the 2011 Implementing Regulation can be confusing. However, this can be broadly presented as follows.

As discussed below, the Recast Sixth Directive sets out 'place of supply' rules that Member States are required to apply in determining the location (country) of supplies of services. These place of supply provisions for services have been implemented into Irish national law (by way of sections 33–35 VATCA 2010) including provisions regarding the place of supply of catering services. However, it is the 2011 Implementing Regulation that defines 'catering services' for the purposes of the rules and this definition has direct and binding effect, i.e. it forms part of Irish law. Similarly, the 2011 Implementing Regulation specifies how a supplier of cross-border services can identify the location and status of its customer for VAT purposes in certain circumstances, as well as identify scenarios where the supplier will be obliged to charge VAT instead of the customer applying the reverse-charge mechanism. (The reverse-charge procedure for cross-border services is examined in **Chapter 3**.)

> **Tax Tip** In order to advise on VAT matters, make sure you have access to the suite of relevant VAT legislation, the key components of which are the (Irish) Value-Added Tax Consolidation Act 2010, the (Irish) VAT Regulations 2010, the (EU) Recast Sixth Directive and the (EU) 2011 Council Implementing Regulation.

---

[4] Council Implementing Regulation (EU) No 282/2011 of 15 March 2011 laying down implementing measures for Directive 2006/112/EC on the common system of value-added tax.

The Role of the Court of Justice of the European Union in relation to VAT

So far we have considered the relevance of EU Directives and Regulations for the Irish VAT system. Another important source of EU VAT law for anyone advising on VAT matters is the extensive body of case law from the Court of Justice of the European Union (CJEU), previously and still commonly referred to as the European Court of Justice (ECJ).

The CJEU plays a crucial role in the interpretation of EU law. As a general rule, if a provision in EU law is binding on a Member State, then the CJEU's judgment on how the provision should be interpreted is similarly binding. National courts in the EU can refer questions of EU law to the CJEU.

The importance of the CJEU for the development of the Irish VAT system cannot be understated. For example, CJEU case law has clarified key concepts such as how 'intending traders' should be treated for VAT purposes[5] (see **Example 1.2** in **Chapter 1**) as well as setting out anti-avoidance guiding principles in respect of VAT (which are outlined further below).

> **Tax Tip** You can search for CJEU judgments (as well as finding the non-binding opinions of the Advocate Generals of the CJEU) at http://curia.europa.eu/juris/. The search function allows you to search by reference to the citation of the case, the names of the parties and subject matter.

The CJEU not only hears referrals of questions from EU Member States. If the European Commission considers that a Member State has failed to implement EU VAT law appropriately or is in breach of EU VAT law, the Commission can take infringement proceedings against that Member State. Infringement proceedings broadly involve three stages:

- a formal notice from the European Commission asking the Member State to present its views;
- a reasoned opinion giving the Member State a reasonable period of time to remedy the matter (usually in the region of two months); then
- a referral to the CJEU for a decision on the matter.

---

[5] Case C-268/83, *D.A. & E.A. Rompelman v. Minister van Financiën* and Case C-110/94, *Intercommunale voor zeewaterontzilting (INZO) v. Belgian State*.

A recent example of proceedings involving Ireland included the European Commission's (successful) argument that Ireland's VAT rules for public bodies (in particular, the scenarios in which a public body should be regarded as a taxable person, i.e. acting in business for VAT purposes) should be amended. These rules were then updated in July 2010 – see section 14 VATCA 2010).

In judgments of the CJEU (or the non-binding opinions of the Advocate-Generals of the CJEU) on VAT matters, there will frequently be references to general principles of the EU legal system, which guide how EU VAT law should be interpreted and applied. Examples of some of the more commonly mentioned concepts are:
- fiscal neutrality (stemming from the principle of equal treatment);
- narrow interpretation of exceptions;
- proportionality;
- legitimate expectation (stemming from the principle of legal certainty); and
- abuse of rights.

The general principles can be said to 'overlap' to an extent and are often mentioned together. It is beyond the scope of this book to consider any of the general principles of EU law in great detail and clearly their application in any particular scenario will depend on the specific context. However, a brief summary of some of the main principles is provided below, and how, instead of being entirely academic in nature, they can play an important role in the field of VAT.

Fiscal Neutrality and Equal Treatment

The Recast Sixth Directive states at the outset in its preamble that in order to achieve a free internal market in the EU, it is necessary that any VAT system does not distort competition or hinder the free movement of goods and services. Consequently, the principle of 'fiscal neutrality' is a key concept for the EU VAT system. Very broadly, this means that (within the parameters of the Recast Sixth Directive) VAT should impact in the same way on any party carrying on the same activity or supplying the same product or service. This is illustrated in the following examples:

EXAMPLE 9.1: *HMRC v. THE RANK GROUP PLC*

An example of the practical CJEU's application of the fiscal neutrality principle is the *HMRC v. The Rank Group plc*[6] case in which the Court ruled that, in the particular circumstances, UK VAT rules should not apply different VAT rates for certain types of games that were extremely similar from the consumer's point of view.

EXAMPLE 9.2: *HMRC v. BRIDPORT AND WEST DORSET GOLF CLUB*[7]

Another example is where the CJEU concluded in the more recent case of *HMRC v. Bridport and West Dorset Golf Club* regarding non-profit-making golf clubs that the Recast Sixth Directive envisages that VAT exemption should apply equally to green fee income received from members and non-members. The VAT-exemption provisions in Irish VAT law were specifically amended (in Finance Act 2014) to reflect the outcome of this case.

Narrow Interpretations of Exceptions

Another general principle of the EU VAT system is that there should be a narrow or restrictive interpretation of any exceptions to the main objectives of EU VAT law, the scope of any VAT exemptions or any derogation from EU law.

Therefore, although the principle of fiscal neutrality is a crucial aspect of the EU VAT system, this does not mean that Member States can, for example, simply choose to extend an existing low VAT-rate treatment of particular activities or types of goods or services to all other activities that, at least at face value, appear similar in nature. Instead, it is always necessary to consider the particular provision of the Recast

[6] Case C-259/10.
[7] Case C-495/12.

Sixth Directive, i.e. whether the EU rule has *deliberately* been framed in a narrow way, in which case although a Member State might like to, for example, extend the parameters of a 'low' VAT rate or even introduce a new low VAT rate, it may not have flexibility to do so as it needs to act within the ambit of EU law.

VAT law should not be excessive or disproportionate to what is necessary in order to achieve that objective.

An example of the CJEU considering the general principle of proportionality is the *EMS-Bulgaria Transport OOD* case[8] in which the Court was asked to consider time limits in Bulgarian VAT law for making reclaims. The CJEU concluded that a Member State can have a time limit for reclaims, provided that the time limit does not render the right of VAT recovery excessively difficult or impossible in practice. (As provided for in section 99 VATCA 2010, Irish VAT law generally applies a four-year time limit for Irish VAT-registered businesses to reclaim VAT.)

Legitimate Expectation and Legal Certainty

The principle of legitimate expectation is commonly mentioned together with the principle of legal certainty, i.e. legal rules should be sufficiently precise and clear so that a taxpayer can identify its rights and obligations.

Taxpayers do not have any absolute guarantee that VAT law will not change and indeed, VAT rules are constantly evolving. However, the CJEU has held that the principle of legitimate expectation forms part of the EU VAT system and therefore should be appropriately observed by the Member States when they exercise the powers conferred on them by EU VAT law. An example of this principle in action is the *Marks & Spencer plc v. Commissioners of Customs & Excise*[9] case.

---

[8] Case C-284/11.
[9] Case C-62/00.

EXAMPLE 9.3: *MARKS & SPENCER PLC V. COMMISSIONERS OF CUSTOMS & EXCISE*

In the *Marks & Spencer plc v. Commissioners of Customs & Excise* case, a retailer made a claim for repayment of UK VAT it had previously remitted on its sales. Before the reclaim application was processed, however, the relevant UK VAT law was amended to introduce a three-year time limit (instead of a six-year limit) for VAT reclaims. This curtailment had immediate effect and also applied retrospectively to any as yet unsettled VAT reclaims, so a significant amount of VAT that the retailer had originally claimed (within a six-year time frame) was now time-barred.

When the matter came before the CJEU, the Court agreed with the retailer that the immediate and retroactive provisions (e.g. without adequate transitional period or due warning, etc.) breached the principle of legitimate expectation.

As a result of this judgment, the UK subsequently permitted a three-month transitional period during which certain retrospective claims could be made if particular conditions were met.

Abuse of Rights

So far, we have looked at a number of general EU VAT principles that can potentially favour the taxpayer. However, the CJEU has also developed an 'abuse of rights' principle, which involves a purposive (rather than literal) reading of EU VAT law and this principle needs to be remembered and respected when advising on the VAT implications of any arrangements or structures.

VAT is not intended to be a barrier to genuine commercial transactions and the CJEU has indicated that where a business is considering two types of transactions, the business should not automatically be required to proceed with the transaction that involves paying the higher amount of VAT. However, this flexibility is tempered by the 'abuse of rights' principle under which a taxpayer cannot rely on or use EU law for 'abusive' or any fraudulent ends.

Leaving the matter of fraud to one side, broadly, an 'abuse of rights' scenario involves a transaction (or transactions) that is technically within the strict letter of the relevant VAT law but results in a tax advantage that is contrary to the *purpose* of the particular EU VAT provision. In order to be regarded as abusive, the extent to which the transaction(s) in question must have been aimed, when viewed objectively, at obtaining the tax

facilities but would have suffered a significant level of 'upfront' irrecoverable VAT if it bought or built the facilities directly as it was engaged in VAT-exempt financial services. The taxpayer arranged for associated companies to purchase land, engage builders to construct the premises and then lease these back to the taxpayer. The associated companies claimed VAT recovery on the expenditure, but the UK tax authorities viewed the particular arrangements as lacking commercial reality and disallowed the VAT recovery claims.

EXAMPLE 9.5: *BUPA HOSPITALS LTD AND GOLDSBOROUGH DEVELOPMENTS LTD V. COMMISSIONERS OF CUSTOMS & EXCISE*

In *BUPA Hospitals Ltd and Goldsborough Developments Ltd v. Commissioners of Customs & Excise*,[11] following the announcement of new legislation in the UK that would result in irrecoverable VAT on the purchase of certain pharmaceutical items, the taxpayer arranged for connected companies to act as its suppliers and agreed large lump-sum prepayments with them (approximately £100 million)

[10] Case C-255/02.
[11] Case C-419/02.

prior to the legislation change taking effect, covering future supplies of unspecified pharmaceutical products and prostheses. When the taxpayer claimed an input-VAT credit on the prepayments, the UK tax authorities considered the arrangements were a tax avoidance scheme and disallowed recovery of the VAT.

EXAMPLE 9.6: THE *PART SERVICE* CASE

Another example is the *Part Service* case (*Ministero dell'Economia e delle Finanze v. Part Service Srl*)[12] in which the Italian tax authorities challenged leasing transactions that involved the end customer entering into two separate contracts with two companies in the taxpayer's group. The tax authorities viewed these separate contracts as representing in substance a single supply to the customer that had been artificially split for 'value shifting' type purposes, i.e. to reduce the amount of the charges that were ultimately being subjected to VAT. The court issued guidance on abusive practice and referred the matter back to the national court to decide in the context of the fact pattern.

What is the Impact on the Taxpayer if there is an Abuse of Rights? Where an abuse of rights scenario exists, effectively the transaction(s) can be redefined by the tax authorities of the particular Member State so as to enforce the outcome that would have applied if the abusive transaction(s) had not taken place.

This means that the tax authority can potentially 'look through' to the substance of the abusive arrangements (or disregard the abusive arrangements that were put in place) and the taxpayer may consequently lose the right to VAT deduction or may trigger a VAT liability. Additionally, the taxpayer may incur interest. (In Ireland, Revenue can raise estimates and assessments where they believe VAT is due or VAT has been incorrectly claimed, for example in sections 110 and 111 VATCA 2010).

---

[12] Case C-425/06.

Ireland's General Anti-avoidance Rules

Aside from the general EU principle regarding 'abuse of rights', taxpayers and advisors also need to carefully consider specific Irish legislation dealing with anti-avoidance.

sonable to consider, based on a number of specified factors, that an action is a tax-avoidance transaction, Revenue may deny the particular tax advantage and, additionally, a 30% surcharge (previously 20% for pre-24 October 2014 transactions) can be applied on the quantum of the tax advantage. In order to protect itself from the surcharge, in certain circumstances a taxpayer may file a 'protective notification' (or 'qualifying avoidance disclosure') to Revenue in relation to the transaction in question, which makes Revenue aware of the transaction at an earlier stage than they may otherwise have become aware. The benefit to the taxpayer in filing such a notification is that the lower surcharge will not apply in the event that the particular transaction is ultimately deemed (e.g. by the courts) to be a tax-avoidance transaction.

As VAT is an EU tax (and, as we have seen, EU law takes precedence over national law) the question has arisen of how these 'national' anti-avoidance rules interact with the 'abuse of rights' principle of EU law. In this regard, the Irish High Court has concluded in *Cussens & Ors v. Brosnan*[13] that it was not strictly necessary for Ireland to have introduced any national anti-avoidance provisions with respect to VAT because Revenue could re-characterise anti-avoidance transactions (or 'sham' transactions lacking commercial reality) in light of the EU abuse of rights principles. At the time of writing, the *Cussens* judgment is currently under appeal.

As can be seen from the above, this evolving area of VAT law is nuanced and is not straightforward. A key point to remember, however, is that while a business can generally arrange its normal and genuine commercial affairs as tax efficiently as possible, tax authorities may challenge

[13] [2008] IEHC 169.

artificial arrangements that are implemented to give rise to a tax advantage, e.g. any non-commercially driven tax planning.

> **Tax Tip** When considering how arrangements should be put in place, make sure to consider the applicability, if any, of the relevant anti-avoidance and abuse of rights provisions, including considering what is the commercial rationale for the arrangements being structured in that way and their commercial substance.

Mandatory Disclosures

In the context of anti-avoidance rules and the 'abuse of right' principle, you may wonder how a tax authority becomes aware of and keeps up to speed on potentially abusive structures or aggressive VAT planning ideas. Ireland has a mandatory disclosure tax regime, which covers, among other taxes, VAT. This regime places an obligation on promoters, marketers and users of 'disclosable transactions' (see below) to notify Revenue about certain aspects of those transactions. Penalties (including penalties for each day that there is a failure to disclose) can be applied where a mandatory disclosure was required but not made. Promoters and marketers could include accounting firms, law firms and other advisors. Users would typically refer to the client or the person involved in the transaction(s) in question.

Disclosable Transactions

Broadly, a 'disclosable transaction' is a transaction, or any proposal for a transaction, that enables (or might be expected to enable) a person to obtain a tax advantage, where the tax advantage is (or might be expected to be) the main benefit or one of the main benefits of the transaction. The terms 'transaction' and 'proposal for a transaction' are broadly framed.

In order to be disclosable, the transaction (or proposal for a transaction) generally needs to fall within a specified 'hallmark' list (and certain transactions are specifically excluded from mandatory disclosure by the relevant regulations and Revenue guidelines). The primary duty to disclose falls on the promoter of a scheme (a disclosable transaction or series of transactions), but the user of a scheme may be required to disclose in certain circumstances. Taxpayers who have used a disclosable scheme (regardless of whether the disclosure was made by that taxpayer or by someone else) may not utilise the 'protective notification' regime mentioned above in relation to Irish national anti-avoidance rules.

Aims of the Mandatory Disclosure Regime

Aims of the mandatory disclosure regime include helping Revenue to obtain early information about tax schemes and assisting Revenue with identifying loophole areas of the tax code that in their view could encourage aggressive tax planning. However, as the regime can result

In their *Guidance Notes on the Mandatory Disclosure Regime*, Revenue state that the mandatory disclosure rules "do not impact on ordinary day-to-day tax advice between a tax advisor and a client that involves, for example, the use of schemes that rely on ordinary tax planning using standard statutory exemptions and reliefs in a routine fashion for bona fide purposes, as intended by the legislature."[14]

Revenue have also indicated that it is reasonable to assume that the tax advice given by most tax advisors to clients would be of an ordinary, routine nature.

Tax Tip You can find some illustrative examples of what Revenue would generally regard as ordinary day-to-day tax advice in their *Guidance Notes on the Mandatory Disclosure Regime*. With respect to VAT, these include advice:
- in relation to the operation of 'transfer of business' relief (see sections 20(2)(c) and 26 VATCA 2010);
- on the VAT implications of property transactions including the option to tax and the Capital Goods Scheme (see **Chapter 4**);
- on the application for VAT grouping (see **Chapter 1**);
- on the portion of VAT that can be deducted on expenditure (see **Chapter 5**);
- on preparation for a Revenue audit and ongoing advice in the course of the conduct of the audit (see **Chapter 7**).

---

[14] Revenue Commissioners, *Guidance Notes on the Mandatory Disclosure Regime* (January 2015), para 1.1. See www.revenue.ie/en/practitioner/law/notes-for-guidance/mandatory-disclosure/guidance-notes-mandatory-disclosure-regime.pdf (accessed January 2016).

Where a scheme is disclosed under the mandatory disclosure regime, Revenue will either assign a unique number to the scheme and notify the discloser of that transaction number, or notify the discloser that the scheme was not disclosable under the regime. A promoter is required to give the transaction number to anyone who markets the scheme on the promoter's behalf and also to persons to whom a scheme is sold. Parties entering a scheme may also need to include the transaction number on the relevant return of income.

The rules surrounding the regime are complicated and in this chapter we provide only a high-level overview of certain aspects. For the detailed provisions on the mandatory disclosure regime, relevant legislation in this area includes:

- Chapter 3 of Part 33 of TCA 1997 (as amended by Finance Act 2014);
- the Mandatory Disclosure of Certain Transactions Regulations 2011 (S.I. No. 7 of 2011); and
- the Mandatory Disclosure of Certain Transactions (Amendment) Regulations 2015 (S.I. No. 28 of 2015).

Tax Tip In addition to considering the impact of abuse of rights and anti-avoidance principles when advising on VAT matters, you should also take into account Ireland's mandatory disclosure tax regime for 'disclosable transactions'.

Base Erosion and Profit Shifting (BEPS) Project – (VAT Implications)

Tax practitioners should be aware of recent important international developments in the form of the Organisation for Economic Co-Operation and Development's (OECD) Base Erosion and Profit Shifting (BEPS) Project,[15] the Action Plan which was published in a final report in October 2015.

The BEPS Action Plan is essentially aimed at tackling corporate tax planning strategies that exploit 'loopholes' in current tax regimes or utilise 'treaty shopping' in order to artificially reduce the quantum of taxable profits and/or artificially shift profits to jurisdictions where they can avail of more favourable tax treatment. As well as representing one of the most significant changes to the international corporate tax regime in recent years (including the call for significant increases in transparency

---

[15] Final report available at http://www.oecd.org/ctp/beps-2015-final-reports.htm

via country-by-country reporting so that tax authorities can obtain a global picture of the operations of multinational enterprises), the BEPS Action Plan also addresses indirect tax, including a recommendation that VAT is collected in the country of consumption (see **Chapters 2** and **3**, which detail a number of 'reverse-charge' measures that are already in force for cross-border transactions).

Now that the BEPS Action Plan and ....

presented, the next phase is implementation. Thus, a number of significant changes can be expected in the international tax (including VAT) landscape in coming years.

Conclusion

There are a number of key principles of EU law that can impact on the VAT treatment applied to transactions. One of the most important principles is the concept of 'abuse of rights', which may impact on certain transactions. Where a transaction is deemed to be 'abusive', then a taxpayer could incur a significant VAT liability.

In addition, taxpayers also need to be familiar with specific Irish legislation dealing with anti-avoidance and mandatory disclosure.

In the next and final chapter we will discuss relevant contracts tax (RCT). While RCT is not part of VAT legislation, there is an overlap between RCT and VAT as the VAT treatment applied to certain transactions is dependent on whether or not RCT also applies. Many advisors deal with VAT and RCT on a regular basis as both taxes need to be considered in relation to construction projects and property development businesses, etc.

[16] See https://ec.europa.eu/taxation_customs/sites/taxation/files/com_2016_148_en.pdf

- Introduction

- What is Relevant Contracts Tax?

- Why it is Important from a VAT Perspective to get RCT Right

- When Does Relevant Contracts Tax Apply?

- What Happens when Relevant Contracts Tax Applies?

- The Impact of RCT on the VAT Treatment of Certain Construction Operations

- The 'Two-thirds Rule' and Relevant Contracts Tax

- Relevant Contracts Tax in the Context of Insolvency

- Conclusion

- Appendix 10.1: Extract from Revenue Guidance Note for School Boards of Management on dealing with RCT/VAT

Introduction

As we have seen in **Chapter 8**, the VAT implications of certain construction services can be impacted by their treatment for the purposes of relevant contracts tax (RCT). For example, where services comprising 'construction operations' for RCT purposes are provided in Ireland

construction services and also how RCT is typ

What is Relevant Contracts Tax?

RCT is a withholding tax, i.e. the payer is required in certain circumstances to withhold or deduct tax from the payment due to a contractor and pay that tax to Revenue. It applies where a person (such as an individual, partnership or corporate) known as a 'principal' makes a payment to another person, known as a 'contractor' or a 'subcontractor', for services (known as 'relevant operations') in the industries of:
- construction;
- forestry; and
- meat processing.

This chapter focuses on 'relevant operations' in the construction industry as the RCT analysis of those activities impact on their VAT treatment (whereas the VAT treatment of forestry and meat processing activities is not determined by their RCT treatment).

(**Note**: although the terms contractor/subcontractor are used in the legislation, many people use the term 'subbie'.)

RCT does not apply to employer/employee relationships. In such cases, Pay As You Earn (PAYE) would obviously need to be considered.

Why it is Important from a VAT Perspective to get RCT Right

The legislation governing RCT is dealt with in Chapter 2 of Part 18 (sections 530–531) of the Taxes Consolidation Act 1997 (TCA 1997) and associated regulations. Although the relevant legislation is quite short, it is a very tricky area. Many people do not operate RCT correctly and are often very surprised to find out how expensive it is when they fail to get it right, as demonstrated by the following example.

EXAMPLE 10.1: OPERATION OF RELEVANT CONTRACTS TAX

Donal engaged Michael to carry out some works to a property for him. They agreed a price of €100,000 and Michael carried out the work. Michael invoiced Donal (€100,000 plus VAT of €13,500) and Donal paid him the full amount of €113,500. About a year later, Donal was the subject of a Revenue audit. The Revenue inspector notified Donal that in the particular circumstances, he should have operated RCT on the payment to Michael. In addition, it turned out that Michael had not been certified by Revenue as either a zero-rate or standard-rate contractor (we look at the rates of RCT further below). As a result of the failure to operate RCT correctly, Donal was liable to a penalty of €35,000 (35% of the payment made to the subcontractor).

Furthermore, the inspector noted that Donal may not be entitled to the VAT refund that he claimed on the construction services as he should not have paid the VAT to Michael (this was on the basis that the VAT amount should have been dealt with by way of reverse charge as per section 16(3) VATCA 2010).

When Does Relevant Contracts Tax Apply?

For RCT to apply, the following components are necessary:
1. There must be a principal.
2. There must be a contractor.
3. The contractor must be engaged under a 'relevant contract'.
4. There must be a 'relevant payment'.

Who or What is a 'Principal' for the Purposes of RCT?

According to section 530A TCA 1997, RCT can only apply where the principal is:

"(a) in respect of the whole or any part of a relevant contract, the contractor under another relevant contract,

(b) a person—
  (i) carrying on a business that includes the erection of buildings or the development of land (within the meaning of *section 639(1)*) or the manufacture, treatment or extraction of materials for use, whether used or not, in construction operations,

thinned or felled trees in sawmills or other like premises or the supply of thinned or felled trees for such processing,
(c) a person connected with a company carrying on a business mentioned in *paragraph (b)*,
(d) a local authority, a public utility society (within the meaning of section 2 of the Housing Act 1966) or a body referred to in subparagraph (i) or (ii) of section 12(2)(a) of that Act or *section 19* or *45* of that Act,
(e) a Minister of the Government,
(f) any board or body established by or under statute or any board or body established by or under royal charter and funded wholly or mainly out of moneys provided by the Oireachtas,
(g) a person who carries on any gas, water, electricity, hydraulic power, dock, canal or railway undertaking, or
(h) a person who carries out the installation, alteration or repair in or on any building or structure of systems of telecommunications."

The most common example in the context of construction is where a developer or builder contracts out various 'relevant operations' or aspects of the work to other independent contractors. In that case, the developer/builder is the principal and they must operate RCT appropriately on payments to the sub-contractors. **Example 10.2** below illustrates how a person may be regarded as a principal contractor for RCT purposes.

EXAMPLE 10.2: PRINCIPAL CONTRACTORS

New Homes Ltd is a large building company operating primarily in Galway. It acquires undeveloped land and constructs houses as well as commercial properties for sale. It has a large number of employees and plant and machinery, and carries out a lot of the work itself. However, in order to complete construction, it generally needs to engage a range of contractors, including carpenters, electricians, painters, landscapers, etc. All of the contracts with these third-party contractors would generally be subject to RCT.

If one of the subcontractors in turn subcontracts out some of his work, then that subcontractor becomes a 'principal' in respect of the work he has subcontracted, and he too would be obliged to operate RCT on payments to his subcontractors.

So, it is possible, and indeed common, for an individual or company to be simultaneously a principal and a subcontractor.

EXAMPLE 10.3: SUBCONTRACTORS THAT ALSO ACT AS PRINCIPALS

To continue **Example 10.2** above, New Homes Ltd engages Carpenters Ltd to carry out a lot of the carpentry work on one particular development. Carpenters Ltd is very busy with several projects, so it in turn engages Woody Ltd to carry out some of the works on the New Homes site. As Carpenters Ltd is a contractor of New Homes Ltd, then Carpenters Ltd becomes a principal in respect of the contract it has with Woody Ltd and it must operate RCT accordingly.

It is very important to remember that RCT does not just apply to *full-time* builders/developers that are constructing properties for sale. You will note that from the wording of section 530A TCA 1997 above that a principal is a person whose business *includes* the erection of buildings or development of land and not just a person whose business *is* the erection of buildings or development of land.

Development to Land and Building/ Development for 'Own Use'

It is also worth noting that the term 'development of land' is defined quite broadly, as is the case in VAT legislation. However, there are sev-

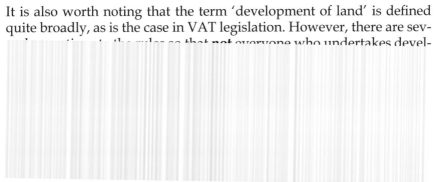

EXAMPLE **10.4**: DEVELOPMENT FOR OWN USE

Manufacturer Ltd makes goods in Cork, which are exported all over the world. Manufacturer Ltd needs a bigger factory for its business and it decides to engage a contractor to build it. At first glance, it appears that Manufacturer Ltd is a principal (for RCT purposes) as it is certainly in business and that business now includes the erection of buildings. However, section 530A(2) TCA 1997 states that Manufacturer Ltd will not be considered a principal as it is carrying out the works for use in its production process (i.e. it is for own use).

Tax Tip It is important to note that this 'own-use' exclusion only applies where the person would not otherwise be considered a principal under the legislation. If Manufacturer Ltd from **Example 10.4** was also involved in other development activities or was itself a construction company, then it would typically be obliged to operate RCT on payments to a contractor, even if that payment was in respect of works carried out on a building to be used in its exporting business.

'Connected-party Rule' As noted above, the principals listed in section 530A TCA 1997 include a person 'connected with' a company carrying on a business of land development or construction, etc. (or meat processing or forestry (section 530A(1)(c) TCA 1997). This is demonstrated in **Example 10.5** below.

EXAMPLE 10.5: CONNECTED-PARTY RULE

Michelle is both the director and the largest shareholder of a construction company (ABC Ltd). She personally buys a site and engages a different contractor (XYZ Ltd) to build an office block for letting purposes. RCT applies to this contract as Michelle is connected to another principal (i.e. ABC Ltd).

Section 530A(3) removes the obligation to operate RCT in certain cases where the only reason that RCT applies is by virtue of this connected-party rule, though the obligation is only removed in two scenarios:
(a) Where the person making the payment is considered a principal by virtue of being connected to a principal operating in the meat processing or forestry businesses, and the work is for 'own use'.
(b) Where the person making the payment is considered a principal by virtue of being connected to a principal operating in the development/construction business, the person is a company, the person is not otherwise a builder/developer and the work is being carried out for the person's own use or those of his employees.

EXAMPLE 10.6: CONNECTED-PARTY RULE

Taking Manufacturer Ltd from **Example 10.4**, the company is only engaged in manufacturing goods for export. Assume it is connected to a construction company as they are both subsidiaries of the same parent. Manufacturer Ltd pays a contractor to extend its factory in Cork. This contract would not be subject to RCT as Manufacturer Ltd is a company, it is not involved in construction/development (other than carrying out this extension) and the work is being carried out for its own use.

Building/Development for 'Letting' By concession, Revenue will accept that RCT does not apply where a person engages a contractor to perform relevant operations on a property with the sole intention of leasing the property (for a period not exceeding 35 years).

Example 10.7: Development For Letting

Landlord Ltd bought a site in Athlone. It entered into an agreement with a large company based in Cork which agreed to take a

wise a principal, i.e. construction for letting is not of itself principal construction it is involved in and it is not connected to other principals.

Small Value Payments and Connected Parties In 2009, Revenue issued *Tax Briefing* Issue 71 to remove the obligation for RCT to be applied in certain cases. These cases are described in the following extracts from that briefing.

Revenue Commissioners Tax Briefing Issue 71 – April 2009[1]

Relevant Contracts Tax (RCT)

Clarification on Connected Party Rules (Section 531(1)(c) TCA, 1997)
AND
Construction operations carried out in a private capacity by a sole trader or partnership

Introduction

This article sets out to clarify Revenue's position in relation to the operation of RCT by persons who are connected with construction, forestry and meat processing companies and to provide guidance to taxpayers and tax practitioners on this issue. It also provides clarification regarding the obligations of builders

---

[1] See www.revenue.ie/en/practitioner/tax-briefing/archive/71/relevant-contracts-tax.html (accessed August 2016).

operating as sole traders or in partnership in respect of construction operations carried out in a private capacity.

RCT and Connected Persons

Section 531 (1)(c) TCA 1997 provides that a person connected with a company involved in a construction, land development, meat processing or forestry business must operate RCT on payments made by that person to a subcontractor in the performance of a relevant contract. This connected person rule is an anti-avoidance provision introduced in 1981 to counteract the avoidance of the operation and application of RCT through corporate restructuring. A 'connected person' for this purpose covers both companies within a corporate group where one subsidiary is a principal under *Section 531 1(b)* and directors/shareholders with a controlling interest in such companies subcontracting as individuals or as part of a partnership.

It was recognised that this provision had inadvertently brought certain parties within the scope of RCT, in a way that was never the intention of the legislation. For example, a large Corporate Group with many subsidiaries could have one subsidiary involved in construction operations or the development of land. Under the connected persons rule, this would have been sufficient to require every other company in the Group to operate RCT in respect of any subcontractors engaged by them to carry out minor construction operations, electrical installations, plumbing work etc. Similarly, a person connected with a company involved in meat processing or forestry was, strictly speaking, required to operate RCT in respect of construction operations they carried out in a private capacity.

Finance Act 2008 Amendment

Section 35 of the Finance Act 2008 introduced a new subsection into *Section 531 TCA (subsection (2A))* that was designed to exclude some connected persons from the RCT provisions in respect of construction operations carried out in their own premises. Where the connection was with a meat processing or forestry company, the obligation to operate RCT in respect of construction work carried out in their own premises was removed from all persons connected with the company. Where the connection was with a company involved in construction or land development activities, the obligation was only removed from connected *companies*.

In this context, it is important to note that the obligation to operate RCT was only removed in respect of work carried out in the connected company's own premises. Where such connected companies were involved in letting out property, they were obliged to continue to operate RCT in respect of construction operations

New Treatment
(1) Companies, Shareholders & Directors

Revenue is prepared to regard the 2008 modification of the RCT legislation (introduced in *Section 35 of the Finance Act 2008*) as applying in certain *limited* circumstances to construction work carried out in premises that have been let out -
(a) by persons connected with companies in the meat processing or forestry businesses, and
(b) by companies connected with companies in construction and land development businesses.

The type of work which will qualify for this treatment (i.e. the obligation to operate RCT will not apply) is minor repair or improvement work to rented property where the total value of contracts awarded per property in any tax year in respect of such repairs or improvements does not exceed €20,000 (incl. VAT). Any contracts awarded in any tax year which would bring the total value of such contracts over the €20,000 threshold (per property) will continue to be subject to the operation of RCT in the normal way. A situation could arise where a contract is entered into during a tax year on the basis that it qualifies for this treatment i.e. the total value of the contract plus any earlier such contracts awarded does not exceed €20,000 (incl. VAT). However, if it subsequently becomes clear (at any stage after entering into the contract) that the value of the contract will/is likely to exceed the original contract price to the point that the contract will bring the total value of contracts entered into in the relevant tax year over the threshold of €20,000 per property, normal RCT requirements will apply to the contract from that point onwards.

The new approach outlined above will also apply in respect of minor repairs or improvements carried out in a *private* capacity on their own home (including outhouses and pleasure gardens), or private lettings, or other incidental private work (e.g. erection of a memorial monument) by a director/shareholder with a controlling interest in a construction company.

(2) Sole Traders & Partnerships

Building contractors operating as sole traders or in partnership are reminded of their obligations regarding the operation of RCT. A builder who is a sole trader or in partnership is a principal under *Section 531(1)(b)(i) TCA 1997* as s/he is 'a person carrying on a business which includes the erection of buildings'. S/he must operate RCT in respect of all payments made to subcontractors who carry out construction operations for him/her, including construction operations carried out in a private capacity (i.e. non-business related construction activities). However, the new approach outlined in *Paragraph 1* above (i.e. minor repairs or improvements where the total value of contracts in respect of such work does not exceed €20,000 (incl. VAT) per property in a tax year) will also apply in the case of a sole trader or partnership in respect of such work carried out in a private capacity on their own home (including outhouses and pleasure gardens) or private lettings, or in respect of other incidental private work (e.g. erection of a memorial monument).

General

Where the new approach above applies (i.e. where RCT is not operated in respect of certain minor work), records relating to payments in respect of such work should be maintained by the principal and retained for inspection by Revenue. Accordingly, all relevant invoices should be retained for a period of six years and must clearly show the address of the property or properties involved, the date of the relevant contract and the dates of all payments made.

This new approach represents a pragmatic approach in relation to the operation of RCT. However, Revenue reserve the right to impose the strict technical treatment set out in the legislation where, in the opinion of Revenue, there is a deliberate attempt to avoid the general operation of RCT, or there is an attempt or intention to avoid or evade tax by any of the parties to a contract.

Who or What is a 'Contractor' for the Purposes of RCT?

Although it will generally be obvious when a person has engaged a contractor, care must be taken to ensure that the person is genuinely a contractor and not an employee of the person.

fact an employee. For this reason, it is important that a person is satisfied that they are making a payment to a contractor rather than an employee, as failure to identify that a person is an employee can lead to PAYE and PRSI exposures for the person making the payment.

What are the 'Relevant Contracts' to which RCT Applies?

Section 530 TCA 1997 defines a relevant contract as follows:

> "*relevant contract*' means a contract (not being a contract of employment, or a contract between NAMA and a NAMA group entity, or a contract between a NAMA group entity and another NAMA group entity) whereby a person (in this Chapter referred to as 'the contractor') is liable to another person (in this Chapter referred to as 'the principal')—
>
> (a) to carry out relevant operations,
> (b) to be answerable for the carrying out of such operations by others, whether under a contract with the contractor or under other arrangements made or to be made by the contractor, or
> (c) to furnish the contractor's own labour or the labour of others in the carrying out of such operations."

We will now consider the 'operations' to which RCT applies, as referred to in subsection (a) above, namely construction, forestry and meat processing. (As already outlined, however, our focus is on construction operations, as the RCT treatment of these impacts on the VAT analysis.)

Construction Operations In a construction context, the following operations are included (section 530 TCA 1997):

> "'*Construction operations*' means operations of any of the following descriptions—
>
> (a) the construction, alteration, repair, extension, demolition or dismantling of buildings or structures,
>
> (b) the construction, alteration, repair, extension or demolition of any works forming, or to form, part of the land, including walls, roadworks, power lines, telecommunication apparatus, aircraft runways, docks and harbours, railways, inland waterways, pipelines, reservoirs, water mains, wells, sewers, industrial plant and installations for purposes of land drainage,
>
> (c) the installation, alteration or repair in any building or structure of systems of heating, lighting, air-conditioning, soundproofing, ventilation, power supply, drainage, sanitation, water supply, or burglar or fire protection,
>
> (ca) the installation, alteration or repair in or on any building or structure of systems of telecommunications,
>
> (d) the external cleaning of buildings (other than cleaning of any part of a building in the course of normal maintenance) or the internal cleaning of buildings and structures, in so far as carried out in the course of their construction, alteration, extension, repair or restoration,
>
> (e) operations which form an integral part of, or are preparatory to, or are for rendering complete such operations as are described in *paragraphs (a) to (d)*, including site clearance, earth-moving, excavation, tunnelling and boring, laying of foundations, erection of scaffolding, site restoration, landscaping and the provision of roadways and other access works,
>
> (f) operations which form an integral part of, or are preparatory to, or are for rendering complete, the drilling for or extraction of minerals, oil, natural gas or the exploration for, or exploitation of, natural resources,
>
> (g) the haulage for hire of materials, machinery or plant for use, whether used or not, in any of the construction operations referred to in *paragraphs (a) to (f)*."

As regards 'construction operations', the wide definition includes, or has been held to include:
- carpeting (as part of the completion of a building),
- erection of gravestones,

- removal of materials (e.g. site clearance), and
- external and internal cleaning of buildings in the context of construction works.

Also, haulage services (e.g. bringing materials or equipment) for construction, forestry or meat processing is one of the less obvious categories of relevant operations.

In August 2016, Revenue issued a revised guidance note to management of certain schools to understand their obligations under RCT legislation.[2] Certain schools are considered to be a 'principal' (for RCT purposes) as they were established under statute (see subsection (f) above in the list of principals (section 530A TCA 1997)). As it can be difficult to determine precisely what is and is not covered by RCT, some of the content of this leaflet has been reproduced in **Appendix 10.1** to this chapter as it provides some useful insight into Revenue's interpretation of some of the terms.

> **Tax Tip** You might also think that it is possible to argue that a contractor is not supplying any of the above services but rather is supplying labour/staff only. However, supplying labour/staff to carry out relevant operations is specifically catered for in section 530 TCA 1997 and falls within the remit of RCT.

As can be seen from the definition in section 530 TCA 1997, RCT needs to be considered in respect of all kinds of developments: residential or commercial buildings, infrastructure projects, golf course construction, car park construction, etc. It generally does not apply, however, to fees issued in respect of professional services.

Forestry Operations Section 530 TCA 1997 defines 'forestry operations' as involving any of the following:

"(a) the thinning, lopping or felling of trees in woods, forests or other plantations,

[2] Revenue Commissioners, *Guidance Note: Boards of Management: Relevant Contracts Tax/Value Added Tax* (Revised August 2016). See www.revenue.ie/en/tax/rct/guidance-boards-rct-vat.pdf (accessed December 2016).

(b)   with effect from the 6th day of October, 1997, the planting of trees in woods, forests or other plantations,

(c)   with effect from the 6th day of October, 1997, the maintenance of woods, forests and plantations and the preparation of land, including woods or forests which have been harvested, for planting,

(d)   the haulage or removal of thinned, lopped or felled trees,

(e)   the processing (including cutting or preserving) of wood from thinned, lopped or felled trees in sawmills or other like premises,

(f)   the haulage for hire of materials, machinery or plant for use, whether used or not, in any of the operations referred to in paragraphs (a) to (e)."

Meat-processing Operations Section 530 TCA 1997 defines 'meat-processing operations' as involving any of the following:

"(a)   the slaughter of cattle, sheep, pigs, domestic fowl, turkeys, guinea-fowl, ducks or geese,

(b)   the catching of domestic fowl, turkeys, guinea-fowl, ducks or geese,

(c)   the division (including cutting or boning), sorting, packaging (including vacuum packaging), rewrapping or branding of, or the application of any other similar process to, the carcasses or any part of the carcasses (including meat) of slaughtered cattle, sheep, pigs, domestic fowl, turkeys, guinea-fowl, ducks or geese,

(d)   the application of methods of preservation (including cold storage) to the carcasses or any part of the carcasses (including meat) of slaughtered cattle, sheep, pigs, domestic fowl, turkeys, guinea-fowl, ducks or geese,

(e)   the loading or unloading of the carcasses or part of the carcasses (including meat) of slaughtered cattle, sheep, pigs, domestic fowl, turkeys, guinea-fowl, ducks or geese at any establishment where any of the operations referred to in *paragraphs (a), (c)* and *(d)* are carried on,

(f)   the haulage of the carcasses or any part of the carcasses (including meat) of slaughtered cattle, sheep, pigs, domestic fowl, turkeys, guinea-fowl, ducks or geese from any establishment where any of the operations referred to in *paragraphs (a), (c)* and *(d)* are carried on, (fa) the rendering of the carcasses or any part of the carcasses of slaughtered cattle, sheep, pigs, domestic fowl, turkeys, guinea fowl, ducks or geese,

(g) the cleaning down of any establishment where any of the operations referred to in *paragraphs (a), (c)* and *(d)* are carried on,

Tax Tip Remember that the VAT reverse charge on RCTable services only applies to construction operations (except haulage for hire) and not to forestry or meat-processing operations.

What is a 'Relevant Payment'?

It is important to remember that RCT applies to payments made to contractors. Therefore, there is no issue from an RCT perspective (subject to the notification requirements outlined below) with a principal engaging a contractor, having the contractor carry out relevant operations and issuing an invoice for the works. RCT obligations only arise when a payment is made.

Generally, it will be clear when a payment is made. Most payments are made using cash, cheque, electronic transfer, etc. However, sometimes it is less clear when a payment has been made. For example, a contractor could agree to accept a property (or another asset) instead of cash. Alternatively, a principal may have given a loan of money to a contractor, but the parties agreed that the loan was not payment and it would only become payment when the works were complete. These types of arrangements can lead to difficulties in determining at what point a payment has been made.

Tax Tip It is important to be aware that payment can be made in many forms and not to assume that monetary payment is the only kind.

What Happens when Relevant Contracts Tax Applies?

A 'principal', for RCT purposes, should notify Revenue regarding the relevant contract (commonly called a 'contract notification')

electronically on ROS (Revenue On-line Services). The principal should also notify Revenue electronically on ROS (commonly called a 'payment notification') before paying a subcontractor. Revenue will then tell the principal to take one of three actions:

1. pay the subcontractor the full amount without deduction (i.e. 0% RCT);
2. withhold 20% of the payment; or
3. withhold 35% of the payment.

The 35% rate is likely to be applied where a subcontractor is not already registered with Revenue or where Revenue have identified there are serious compliance issues. Clearance should always be sought in advance of payment as Revenue can impose a significant penalty for each payment made to a subcontractor prior to clearance being received from Revenue (even where the subcontractor is fully tax compliant). The principal should not unilaterally decide to deduct 20% or 35% of the payment themselves; instead they should obtain confirmation from Revenue before making the payment and any deductions.

When a principal contractor submits a new contract notification via ROS, the principal contractor receives a system-generated 'site identifier number' (or 'SIN') for that site/project, which the principal contractor should use on all contracts that the principal contractor submits on ROS in respect of that site/project.

The Impact of RCT on the VAT Treatment of Certain Construction Operations

As already mentioned, where RCT applies to the supply of a construction operation, the VAT is generally dealt with by reverse charge, which means that the principal is obliged to self-account for the VAT arising, as demonstrated by **Example 10.8** below.

EXAMPLE 10.8: INTERACTION BETWEEN RCT AND VAT

A county council paid a company (Wee Building Services Ltd) to construct a portion of a new motorway outside Dundalk. The price agreed was €2 million and RCT applied to the contract. When the road was completed, Wee Building Services Ltd issued an invoice for €2 million with no VAT. Instead, a line was included on the invoice instructing the principal to self-account for the VAT. The county council was obliged to include €270,000 (€2m × 13.5%) of VAT in its VAT return for the relevant period and to pay the VAT amount to Revenue. As the county council was not entitled to reclaim any VAT on costs associated with road building, the total cost of this contract was €2,270,000.

not apply to all payments covered by RCT. This is because RCT applies to payments made under a contract that includes construction operations. Therefore, RCT can apply to payments for construction operations as well as other elements of a contract that are not construction operations (such as the supply of goods). VAT reverse charge would not apply to the supply of goods, even though they may be supplied as part of a contract that includes construction operations.

Tax Tip Even if services are not subject to RCT (commonly referred to as 'RCTable'), as we have seen in **Chapter 4** a reverse charge may apply for VAT purposes to certain construction services where they are supplied between connected parties (section 16(5) VATCA 2010).

The 'Two-thirds Rule' and Relevant Contracts Tax

Section 41 VATCA 2010 includes a particular rule known as the 'two-thirds rule'. This effectively dictates that where a person supplies goods as part of a supply of services, then the VAT rate applicable to the goods can apply to the entire consideration due under the contract. This generally only arises where the cost of the goods to the supplier exceeds two-thirds of the total price being charged to the customer for the goods/services combined.

The two-thirds rule does not apply to services that comprise RCTable construction operations where the recipient is obliged to self-account for VAT.

However, if a contractor supplies goods as well as services under a single contract, then it may be the case that RCT will apply to the entire payment but the VAT reverse-charge treatment will only apply to the services and not to the goods.

Relevant Contracts Tax in the Context of Insolvency

We looked at common VAT issues for insolvency practitioners (e.g. receivers) in **Chapter 8**. The issue of how RCT applies to receivers (or liquidators) is not specifically covered in the legislation. However, where an insolvency practitioner is appointed over the assets of a person who would be considered a principal and where an insolvency practitioner becomes involved in development works, then he would likely be considered a principal for RCT purposes. Therefore, where such an insolvency practitioner engages any subcontractors to carry out relevant operations, the insolvency practitioner should operate RCT. As outlined above, this is likely to apply to a range of subcontractors, including:

- building contractors;
- painters;
- electricians;
- carpenters;
- landscapers; and
- all the usual parties generally present when a development is being completed.

Tax Tip RCT may apply to payments made to contractors to erect fences or physically secure sites, even though the insolvency practitioner may not intend to carry out any development works.

Conclusion

In this our final chapter, we have considered some of the main aspects to consider in relation to relevant contracts tax (RCT), as this is a common area for practitioners and businesses alike. Care needs to be taken when analysing the RCT treatment of a contract, including being aware of the impact that the RCT position may have on the VAT analysis.

Throughout this book, which we hope you have found useful, we have considered a range of VAT issues and rules that commonly arise in practice. You will next find reference materials in the appendices which should also be helpful when considering the VAT treatment of transactions.

Appendix 10.1: Extract from Revenue Guidance Note for School Boards of Management on dealing with RCT/VAT

Boards of Management can be involved in a range including: Construction Projects, Summer Works, Emergency Works, Major Devolved Projects, Additional Accommodation Schemes as well as day to day repairs that bring them within the scope of Relevant Contracts Tax (RCT) and, as a consequence, Value Added Tax (VAT).

It is important that boards are aware of and understand their obligations in relation to these taxes. This note sets out to give general guidance to boards on RCT, how it can apply to contracts entered into by the board, how RCT operates and why VAT must be accounted for by the board.

Revised December 2016

What is Relevant Contracts Tax?

Relevant Contracts Tax (RCT) is a withholding tax system that operates in the construction, forestry and meat processing sectors. Where a principal contractor in those sectors makes a 'relevant payment' to a subcontractor, RCT must be operated. There must be a principal contractor making a relevant payment before RCT can apply.

Who is a principal contractor and what is a relevant payment?

Principal Contractor

Principal contractors are defined in the legislation (Section 530A, Taxes Consolidation Act 1997 as amended). The definition includes 'any board or body established by or under statute ... and funded

---

[3] www.revenue.ie/en/tax/rct/guidance-boards-rct-vat.pdf

wholly or mainly out of funds provided by the Oireachtas'. As such, school Boards of Management are principal contractors for the purposes of RCT.

Relevant Payment

A relevant payment is a payment made under a contract for relevant operations as defined in the legislation. Where a principal contractor makes a 'relevant' payment to a subcontractor, RCT must be operated, tax deducted if appropriate and remitted to Revenue. The whole contract is subject to RCT if any part of that contract is subject to RCT.

Construction Operations

The following are examples of the types of activities defined as 'Construction Operations' in Section 530 (a) to (g) Taxes Consolidation Act 1997, as they might apply to Boards of Management:

(a) *the construction, alteration, repair, extension, demolition or disman-tling of buildings or structures*

This paragraph includes building projects such as extensions, new buildings or additional accommodation. It also includes the erection of 'structures' such as gates, traffic lights, road signs, parking meters and sheds.

Alterations

'Alteration' is not defined in the legislation. Legal opinion is that there must be an element of materiality to the change in the building or structure. Examples of alteration include painting a building, replacing all the windows or doors in a building etc.

Minor changes such as painting one wall or replacing one door in a building would not be considered sufficient.

Repairs

As 'structure' is not defined in the legislation Revenue take the view that reasonably large items set in place on a permanent or semi-permanent basis are considered to be structures.

The repair of such structures and the repair of any part of a building, or of any system that has become a part of the fabric of the building, is also included and may encompass 'emergency works' carried out by a Board of Management.

Maintenance

Maintenance only contracts are outside the scope of RCT. Examples of maintenance include cleaning, removal of graffiti, unblocking of drains etc.

> *works forming, or to form, part of the land, including walls, road works, power lines, telecommunication apparatus, ... pipelines, reservoirs, water mains, wells, sewers, industrial plant and installations for purposes of land drainage*

This paragraph includes work relating to telecommunication apparatus but this only extends to masts, underground cabling, telephone poles etc. For other aspects of the telecommunications industry see paragraph (ca) below.

Also included is the building of new roads and footpaths and repairs to existing ones. However routine road maintenance, clearing blocked drains and cleaning of roads and paths (including the removal of chewing gum) would not be included.

(c) *the installation, alteration or repair in any building or structure of systems of heating, lighting, air-conditioning, soundproofing, ventilation, power supply, drainage, sanitation, water supply, burglar or fire protection*

This paragraph applies to the installation, alteration or repair of systems in a building or structure.

Alterations (the installation of 'add-on' or stand alone packages to systems already in place) must be 'material' to bring the work within the definition.

If a contract to service a system includes a liability to carry out repairs, then the contract is within the scope of RCT. Otherwise it is purely a maintenance contract and not subject to RCT.

233

(ca) *the installation, alteration or repair in or on any building or structure of systems of telecommunications*

This paragraph covers the installation of systems to facilitate two-way communication by phone, whether mobile, landline or via the internet. As with paragraph (c) it only applies to systems.

As 'systems of telecommunications' will continue to evolve over time, the provision is designed to accommodate this evolution.

(d) *the external cleaning of buildings (other than cleaning of any part of a building in the course of normal maintenance) or the internal cleaning of buildings and structures, in so far as carried out in the course of their construction, alteration, extension, repair or restoration*

Cleaning is only a construction operation when it takes place in the context of an overall construction operation i.e. the cleaning that is necessary after a building or structure is erected, altered, repaired etc.

Routine Cleaning

Normal day-to-day routine cleaning operations are not construction operations. Specialist cleaning jobs such as the removal of graffiti from buildings or structures are not construction operations. However if the removal of the graffiti involves a repair to the building or structure this repair would be a construction operation.

(e) *operations which form an integral part of, or are preparatory to, or are for rendering complete such operations as are described in paragraphs (a) to (d), including site clearance, earth-moving, excavation, tunnelling and boring, laying of foundations, erection of scaffolding, site restoration, landscaping and the provision of roadways and other access works*

This paragraph brings a whole range of activities that can be encountered on a building project within the definition of construction operations. Any activities that could be considered to be integral to an overall building project, not just the specific activities mentioned in the legislation, are covered. For example the hire of a crane with a driver, or where the subcontractor erects and dismantles the crane, would be covered by this definition, as would the erection of scaffolding and the hire of skips to remove waste material related to construction activity.

Site Investigations

Site investigation operations, except where these are imposed on the builder by regulation (such as archaeological investigations or environmental impact studies) would normally be considered to be construction operations where they involve a considerable

more of a professional services nature and the fieldwork is a very minor part of the investigations then RCT would not apply to any part of the contract. Where there is a significant amount of field-work (i.e. drilling, excavation etc) involved and the activity is integral, or preparatory, to the construction operation then a charge to RCT will apply to the full consideration where a single invoice is issued for the fieldwork and professional services.

Archaeological Digs

Archaeological digs are not considered an integral part of, or pre-paratory to the construction operation and are therefore not sub-ject to RCT.

Excavation, Drilling and Fieldwork

Geo-technical work involving excavation, drilling and other fieldwork to provide information necessary for the design and/or construction of a building or structure would generally be considered an integral part of, or preparatory to, construction. A contract for geo-technical services may involve significant fieldwork with some laboratory work and consultancy. Where the fieldwork is the significant part of the contract the full con-tract is subject to RCT.

Rendering Complete

A number of other activities also come within this paragraph. Where a new building is under construction or an existing building is being refurbished, all the activities necessary to render the building complete would be considered to be construction operations. These would include plastering, painting, fitting kitchens and bathrooms, tiling, laying carpets and the installation of certain types of fitted blinds. Some of these activities would not necessarily be considered to be construction operations if they took place outside the context of "rendering complete" for example certain painting jobs and the installation of blinds.

Landscaping

It should be noted that landscaping is only a construction operation when it is carried out as part of rendering complete a construction project. Contracts for landscaping work entered into by principal contractors such as boards of management where the landscaping is not part of an overall construction project are not within the RCT remit.

(f) *operations which form an integral part of, or are preparatory to, or are for rendering complete, the drilling for or extraction of minerals, oil, natural gas or the exploration for, or exploitation of, natural resources*

It is assumed that this paragraph will not apply in the context of school boards of management.

(g) *the haulage for hire of materials, machinery or plant for use, whether used or not, in any of the construction operations referred to in paragraphs (a) to (f)*

This paragraph includes all haulage operations related to the construction industry carried out by self-employed haulage operators. It includes the transportation of construction materials and machinery or plant used in construction operations. The delivery of ready to pour concrete to a building site by an employee of the manufacturer or distributor (irrespective of where or how it is placed at the site) is not considered to be a construction operation. It is considered to be the supply of building materials. However, where either the supplier or the builder hires a self-employed haulier to deliver the concrete, this operation is considered to be a construction operation.

Appendix A

European Union

As at 1 January 2016

Member State	Code	Standard Rate (in %)	Other Rates (excluding 0%)
Belgium	BE	21	6 / 12
Bulgaria	BG	20	9
Spain	ES	21	4 / 10
France	FR	20	2.1 / 5.5 / 10
Croatia	HR	25	5 / 13
Italy	IT	22	4 / 5 / 10
Cyprus	CY	19	5 / 9
Latvia	LV	21	12
Lithuania	LT	21	5 / 9
Luxembourg	LU	17	3 / 8 / 14
Hungary	HU	27	5 / 18
Malta	MT	18	5 / 7
Netherlands	NL	21	6
Austria	AT	20	10 / 13
Poland	PL	23	5 / 8
Portugal	PT	23	6 / 13
Romania	RO	20	5 / 9
Slovenia	SI	22	9.5
Slovakia	SK	20	10
Finland	FI	24	10 /14
Sweden	SE	25	6 / 12
United Kingdom	UK	20	5

Appendix B

Transfer of Business[1]

---

[1] November 2015. Available at http://www.revenue.ie/en/tax/vat/leaflets/transfer-business.html (accessed February 2017).

Introduction

1.1 Section 20(2)(c) of the Value-Added Tax Consolidation Act 2010 (the VAT Act) provides that a transfer of ownership of goods, being the transfer to an accountable person of a totality of the assets or part thereof, of a business, even if that business or part thereof had ceased trading, where those trans-

an accountable person and another person.

1.3 These two provisions, generally referred to as Transfer of Business relief (TOB), are important measures aimed at reducing compliance costs for traders. However, traders are advised that when they are involved in a transfer that could qualify for TOB they should, in cases of doubt, check with their local Revenue District before paying any VAT invoiced by the vendor in such circumstances. Where a transfer that qualifies for TOB takes place it is important to note that any VAT paid by a purchaser to a vendor in error will not be deductible since the transfer is deemed not to be a supply for VAT purposes.

1.4 Articles 19 and 29 of Council Directive 2006/112/EC (the VAT Directive) provide the vires for the provisions in section 20 and 26 the VAT Act. The definitions of accountable person and taxable person are set out in Section 2(1) of the VAT Act. For the purposes of TOB the term accountable person does not include a person registered for VAT only for the purposes of accounting for intra-Community acquisitions or received services.

1.5 This leaflet does not deal with the transfer of a business by means of the transfer of the shares in a company. The transfer of shares in a company is exempt from VAT in accordance with paragraph (6)(1) of Schedule 1 of the VAT Act.

What are transfers of business assets qualifying for the relief?

2.1 VAT law refers to the transfer of a totality of the assets, or part thereof, of a business. Where a business is transferred, the assets that may be transferred can normally be sub-divided as follows:
1. premises
2. employees

3. plant and machinery
4. stock
5. goodwill
6. intellectual property
7. debtors

The classic transfer of a business as a going concern will include the transfer of all seven. However, some businesses may not have all seven. For example, there may be no plant, machinery or stock where the business is a service business. The Courts have ruled that the relief does not cover the transfer of assets alone. The transferred assets must constitute an undertaking, or part thereof, capable of being operated on an independent basis.

Circumstances in which the relief applies to tangible assets

3.1 The relief applies where the transferred assets, or part thereof, are capable of being operated on an independent basis:
• to carry on the same or a similar taxable business,
• for the purposes of the acquirer's own taxable business, following the cessation of the transferor's business or
• to carry on a different taxable business in the premises using the assets acquired.

3.2 The relief applies even if the business or part of the business has ceased trading.

3.3 The relief does not apply to the sale of stock-in-trade on its own or the once-off sales of business assets. For example, the sale of an oil tanker by a garage owner who also delivers home heating oil would not qualify for TOB. In contrast, the sale of the entire home-heating oil distribution business which also includes that oil tanker would qualify for the relief.

3.4 The absence of any one of the component parts of the business from the transfer will not automatically preclude the application of the provision to the transaction.

3.5 Where a person acquiring a business, or part of a business, has applied for but has not yet received a VAT registration number, the vendor may apply TOB.

Circumstances in which the relief applies to intangible assets

4.1 Goodwill and intangible assets that are transferred as part of the transfer of a business may benefit from TOB and be deemed not to be a supply for VAT purposes.

4.2 The relief for intangible assets and goodwill applies both to the transfer from an accountable person to a taxable person who carries on a business in the State and to the transfer from a person who is not an accountable person to another person.

Transfers that may benefit from TOB

the accompanying assets being sold, comes within TOB.

5.3 In general, when a partner disposes of his/her interest in a partnership (as distinct from his/her interest in the assets of the partnership) there is no supply for VAT purposes. A disposal of an interest in assets of the partnership or of an interest in co-owned assets may constitute a supply for VAT purposes and, where applicable, may be subject to TOB provisions.

Transfer of a business to a non-established person

6.1 TOB does not extend to the transfer of a business to a person who is not registered or entitled to register for VAT in the State. The transfer of the goods out of the State may benefit from the zero-rating for EU intra-Community supply or export. The transfer of rights to intellectual property by a business in the State to a business established outside the State is generally not taxable in the State.

Sales by receivers and liquidators

7.1 A sale of goods forming part of the assets of a business of an accountable person under a power exercised by another person, including a liquidator or receiver, is generally deemed to be supplied by the accountable person under section 22(3) of the VAT Act. The disposal by way of TOB is deemed not to be a supply for VAT purposes. Therefore, where a liquidator or receiver or other person exercising a power disposes of the assets of an accountable person by way of transfer of business section 22(3) does not apply to the liquidator or receiver or other person.

Transactions after the transfer of assets

8.1 Where a transferor of a business issues an invoice to a customer and, subsequent to the transfer of the business, the goods are faulty and returned or where a discount or rebate is due to the customer against the price originally charged for the goods, then sections 39(4) and 67(1)(b) of the VAT Act (together with Regulation 20 VAT Regulations 2010) impose an obligation on the transferor to issue a credit note in respect of such transactions. Where a business has passed by way of TOB and the transferor had no tax liabilities outstanding in respect of that business Revenue concessionally allow the transferee, rather than the transferor, to issue a credit note in respect of such transactions.

8.2 Similarly, where a transferor of a business supplies goods issued under warranty and, subsequent to the transfer of a business, the customer returns the goods to the transferee for repair/replacement, the transferee is not entitled to recover input VAT incurred on expenditure relating to the fulfillment of the warranty since this expenditure does not relate to any taxable supplies made by the transferee. Where a business has passed by way of TOB and the transferor had no tax liabilities outstanding in respect of that business Revenue concessionally allow the transferee, rather than the transferor, input credit in respect of such transactions.

8.3 Where, as part of the transfer of a business to which TOB applies, the transferor of the business transfers debts that, subsequent to the transfer, are determined to be bad debts, the transferee has no entitlement to bad debt relief since transferee is not the accountable person who made the supply. However, bad debt relief subject to the normal conditions is available in respect of any debts retained by the transferor that are not included in the transfer.

Deductibility of input VAT

9.1 Section 59(2A) provides that a deduction of input VAT is allowable in respect of services directly related to the transfer of a business where that transaction would have been taxable but for TOB. Deductibility does not extend to a transfer of business where the parties agree that they would have acted differently, that is, they would have exercised a joint option to tax the transaction were it not covered by TOB.

9.2 No deductibility is available for services directly related to the disposal of a reversionary interest in accordance with Section 93(2).

9.3 There may be an entitlement to deductibility where the services bought in for the transfer of business represent inputs that are cost components of the general overheads of the business and, therefore, have a direct and immediate link to the taxable supplies of the transferred part of the business.

9.4 Some examples of deductibility of VAT charged on services related to the transfer of assets are set out in Annex 1.

Transfers of business that include property

10.1 Introduction

VAT rules for property transactions must be considered. These are set out in detail in the VAT on Property Guide (April, 2008) (as amended). The following paragraphs deal with the interaction between the TOB and the VAT on Property rules, in particular the Capital Goods Scheme (CGS).

10.2 The transfer of a property under TOB during the period when a property is considered new and taxable under the VAT on Property rules will give rise to the following:
• the transferor is treated as having made a taxable supply of the property; and
• the transferee is deemed to have been charged the VAT that would have been charged but for the fact that TOB applied. The amount of tax that would have been charged is treated as the total tax incurred. Where the transferee does not have full deductibility, the transferee must pay to Revenue the difference between the total tax incurred and the amount the transferee would be entitled to deduct if VAT had been charged on the supply of the property.

10.3 The transfer of a property under TOB outside the period where a property is considered new, that is, if the property were supplied at the time the transfer takes place its supply would be exempt from VAT, results in the transferee stepping into the shoes of the transferor for the purposes of the CGS. The transferee takes over from the transferor and inherits the adjustment period of the property. For example, if six of the 20 intervals have elapsed then there will be 14 intervals remaining in the adjustment period for the transferee.

10.4 The transferee steps into the shoes of the transferor where, under TOB, an assignment or surrender of a legacy lease takes place on which the transferor had an entitlement to deduct tax on the acquisition or development of the property and that transfer or assignment would be taxable in the absence of TOB. There is no new 20 year life and the transferee is liable for CGS obligations for the remainder of the VAT life of the capital good.

10.5 The sale of a property that is subject to TOB may trigger the cancellation of a waiver of exemption in accordance with Section 96(12). Where this occurs Revenue will give credit in calculating the cancellation sum as follows:
• Where the sale would have been taxable but for TOB, a credit is given for VAT at reduced rate, currently 13.5%, of the sales consideration.
• Where the sale would have been exempt but for TOB, a credit is given for the VAT taken on by the purchaser under the capital goods scheme, that is, the liability that would arise for the transferee if the transferee immediately diverted the property to an exempt use.

10.6 Exporters who qualify under section 56 of the VAT Act are entitled to have supplies to them zero-rated. A qualifying exporter, who avails of the zero rate on the costs of acquiring or developing property, including construction costs and refurbishment costs as a tenant, has the same responsibility within the CGS as if VAT has been charged at the rates appropriate to the goods or services concerned and fully deducted by the exporter.

10.7 The concepts of 'undertaking' and 'business' include the exploitation of tangible and intangible property for the purposes of obtaining income therefrom on a continuing basis. It follows that the transfer of a let property is a transfer capable of qualifying for TOB since the transferred asset is capable of being operated on an independent basis. TOB will only apply when the person acquiring the let property is an accountable person but not necessarily accountable in respect of the asset being acquired. TOB does not apply to vacant property that has never been let or partially let.

10.8 TOB relief may apply in the following circumstances:
• the transfer of properties that are let, or that have been let, for a period of time on a continuing basis. This can include a transfer of a property, such as a shopping centre or office block, where some units are let or have been let on a continuing basis and some are vacant; and
• the transfer of a portfolio of distinct properties, including some that are or have been let on a continuing basis, where the portfolio of properties is being sold in one lot to one purchaser. Where a portfolio of properties is being divided and sold to more than one purchaser, each individual sale will be treated separately and TOB may apply to none, some or all of the sales.

TOB cannot apply to land or properties held as trading stock. However, where that stock is tangible property that has been exploited for the purposes of obtaining income therefrom on a continuing basis, such as the let properties in the preceding paragraph, TOB may apply.

10.9 There is a taxable supply of services where a property on which an input credit would have been allowable but for the operation of TOB is appropriated to private or non-business use before 1 January 2011 but during a period of 20 years following the acquisition or development of the property. Section 27(2) and section 44 of the VAT Consolidation 2010 Act and regulation 7 of the VAT Regulations 2010 set out details of the charge and the method to be used to identify the extent to which the goods are to be used for private or non-business purposes.

10.10 Where a property acquired or developed on or after 1st January 2011 forms part of the business assets that pass under TOB and the property, of part of the property, is subsequently used for private or non-business use, a CGS adjustment arises.

the person that retention is not required.

11.2 The change in the property rules in 2008 introduced the Capital Goods record. The vendor must pass a Capital Goods record to a purchaser including when the supply of immovable goods is deemed not to be a supply by virtue of TOB provisions. In such circumstances, the transferee steps into the shoes of the transferor in relation to Capital Goods obligations.

11.3 The Capital Goods record should reflect new buildings in the last 20 years and refurbishments in the last 10 years, since each has a distinct capital goods life. The task of creating a Capital Goods Record for periods prior to 1 July 2008 usually involves looking back in time by reference to available documents and corporate memory. Documents, such as planning applications and fixed asset additions in accounts filed with the Companies Office, that are on the public record may be available going back over the potential 20 year life of the capital good. These should be obtained, where available, as they will give a good indication of when the building was constructed, its intended use and changes in use, some of which may have been refurbishments. Accounts prepared using recognised accounting standards should be available for the last 6 years since this is the required retention period for tax purposes. These should be consulted to identify additions to fixed assets that will generally relate to a new capital good or a refurbishment.

11.4 Where it proves impossible to identify all items of capital expenditure a practical approach must be adopted where individual items cannot be specifically identified. For example, the fixed assets schedule of a business shows there were additions totalling €150,000 in 2007. From the accounts it is clear that €120,000 was the cost of a building extension and €20,000 the cost of carpark layout, the balance of €10,000 refers to the cost of other unidentified capital expenditure on buildings. This balance of €10,000 may be treated as a separate single 2007 capital good.

11.5 Where capital expenditure is not shown on the Balance Sheet practitioners may assume that capital goods are not reflected in Profit and Loss items unless the practitioner has concerns about the accounting standards used in the preparation of the accounts, or other matters. In such cases, the practitioner should contact the vendor's Revenue District.

Further information

Enquiries regarding any issue contained in this Information Leaflet should be addressed to the Revenue District responsible for your tax affairs. Contact details for all Revenue Districts can be found on the Contact Details Page [See www.revenue.ie/en/contact/index.html].

VAT Interpretation Branch,
Indirect Taxes Division,
Dublin Castle.

Annex 1

Examples of deductibility of VAT charged on services directly related to the transfer of assets subject to TOB

1. A developer developed a block of apartments with the intention of selling them on completion. The developer was unable to sell the apartments on completion and rented them for a period. The block of apartments is subsequently sold to an accountable person and is subject to TOB. VAT charged on services directly related to the sale is deductible because the sale would, but for TOB, be subject to tax.
2. A manufacturer sells its taxable business which consists of a factory, which is not new, together with plant. The VAT charged on services directly related to the sale is deductible because the services are cost components of the general overheads of a fully taxable business.
3. A VAT-exempt person sells its business which consists of a building that is not new together with equipment. The VAT charged on services directly related to the sale is not deductible because the services are cost components of the general overheads of an exempt business. Neither are they covered by Section 59(2A) as the sale would not be taxable even in the absence of TOB.
4. The owner of commercial property that is not new and has been let or partially let sells the property and the sale is subject to TOB. A number of scenarios arise.
   a. VAT on services directly related to the sale is deductible if all the property or all its units were subject to taxable lettings;
   b. VAT on services directly related to the sale is partially deductible if only some of the units were subject to taxable lettings;
   c. VAT on services directly related to the sale is not deductible if none of the units were subject to taxable lettings;

d. In the case of a transfer of a development where some units are let on a taxable basis, some units are subject to exempt lettings while other units are vacant;
   - VAT is deductible in respect of the taxable lettings
   - VAT is not deductible in respect of exempt lettings
   - VAT may be partially deductible in relation to the vacant units depending on factors including the intended use of the units and

- TOB applies to properties that are let at the time of transfer. For example, a developer developed a block of apartments with the intention of selling them on completion. The developer was unable to sell the apartments on completion and rented them for a period. The developer subsequently sold the block of apartments to an accountable person. TOB rules apply to this sale. However, if the developer had sold the same apartments to private individuals TOB would not apply.
- TOB applies where a property has been let on a continuing basis and is being sold to a tenant who is an accountable person.
- TOB applies where a portfolio of properties, some or all of which are let or have been let on a continuing basis, is being sold as one lot by one vendor to one purchaser, who is an accountable person. Where a similar portfolio of properties is being divided and sold to more than one purchaser or where a number of vendors are selling a portfolio of properties to a single purchaser, each sale should be treated separately in respect of TOB provisions.
- The sale of a mixed development, which includes some let units, some vacant units, some incomplete units and some development land, by a single vendor in one lot to a single purchaser is capable of TOB treatment. The appropriate CGS treatment should be applied to each portion of the development.

Vacant Properties

- TOB applies in the case of a vacant property that was let or partially let on a continuing basis in the past.
- TOB applies where a vacant property was used for the purposes of a business in the past and has the necessary quality and attributes to be used for a similar business again immediately after transfer. For example, TOB applies to a factory that is vacant at the time of transfer but has all the necessary fixtures and fittings to be operated as a factory again following transfer.

Appendix C

Bad Debts
(excluding hire-purchase)[1]

---

[1] October 2013. Available at http://www.revenue.ie/en/tax/vat/leaflets/
bad-debts-relief.html

General

Bad debt relief arises when a customer defaults in full or part on payment to a supplier where that supplier has accounted for VAT in respect of the supply. The conditions under which bad debt relief is allowed are set out in Section 39(2) of the VAT Consolidation Act 2010 and regulations 10(2) and

What debts are covered by the relief?

For business purposes, a debt is regarded as bad when the decision has been made that it is irrecoverable. This decision is usually arrived at when all reasonable efforts have been made, without success, to collect the debt in question and the supplier is in a position to reduce the amount of debts in his/her accounting records by the amount of the debts regarded as bad.

The expiry of the supplier's trade credit period is not, on its own, sufficient to trigger an entitlement to bad debt relief. In general, an accountable person who has accounted for VAT on a supply (other than to a connected person) may claim relief for the VAT attributable to the supply where he/she is in a position to demonstrate that:
- He/she has taken all reasonable steps to recover the bad debt.
- The bad debt is allowable as a deduction in arriving at the tax-adjusted profits for income tax or corporation tax.
- The bad debt has been written off in the financial accounts of the accountable person and the obligation to keep relevant records in relation to the debt have been fulfilled (see: Records to be kept).
- The person from whom the debt is due is not connected to the accountable person.

The VAT bad debt relief should be calculated in accordance with the VAT analysis of the transactions outlined in the paragraph "How to calculate bad debt relief" below.

Bad debt relief is available only to traders who account for VAT on the invoice basis.

Bad debt relief is available only for bad debts actually written off and is not available in respect of specific or general provisions for bad or doubtful debts.

255

What are 'reasonable steps'?

Reasonable steps will depend on the facts and circumstances of each case and can comprise a number of actions undertaken to recover the debt, including correspondence with the debtor, referral of the issue to a solicitor or a debt collection agency or other action undertaken, resulting in objective evidence that the trader is in a position to reasonably consider that the debt is bad and to reduce the amount of debts in his/her accounting records by the amount of the debts regarded as bad. Correspondence from a liquidator stating that there are no funds to pay non-preferential creditors would constitute such evidence and would justify the writing off of a debt.

A trader is required to retain evidence of action taken, including all correspondence, in attempting to recover the debt.

What does written off as a bad debt in the financial accounts mean?

The bad debt must be written off in the day-to-day records of the business and transferred from the debtor's account to a separate bad debts account. A trader is not required to wait until his financial year-end to write off a debt but may do so in the VAT return for the taxable period in which the debt is transferred to the bad debt account.

Obligations in relation to record keeping

A trader's records of all transactions in relation to bad debts written off must include:
* particulars of the name and address of the debtor,
* the nature of the goods or services to which the debt relates,
* the date or dates on which the debt was incurred, and
* the date or dates on which the debt was written off.

A trader seeking bad debt relief is required to keep copies of the relevant VAT invoices and evidence that the VAT had been accounted for. All records relating to bad debts written off must be kept for 6 years from the date of the write off.

Unpaid debts from connected persons

Bad debt relief is not available where a debt is due from a person connected to the supplier. Section 97(3)(b) of the VAT Consolidation Act 2010 determines the criteria for establishing whether or not a person is connected with another person.

Credit notes

VAT law provides that a trader, including one operating on the cash basis, is obliged to issue a VAT credit note for a reduction in consideration or the allowance of a discount after the issue of a VAT invoice. However, the question of issuing a credit note does not arise in the case of a bad debt

VAT invoice or, in the case of a supply to an unregistered person, at the rate in force at the time of supply.

How to calculate bad debt relief

Where no payment has been received in respect of a supply, the relief will be in respect of the total amount of VAT accounted for on that supply.

Where a partial payment has been received in respect of a supply the relief will be based on the amount of VAT that is still outstanding in accordance with the following formula:

A × B / 100 + B

where:

A is the amount which is outstanding from the debtor in relation to the taxable supply; and

B is the percentage rate of VAT applicable to the supply.

Example:
Bad debt relief for a supply, other than a supply under hire purchase:

Sale Price of the Goods: €24,600 (€20,000@23% = €4,600)
(B) VAT rate: 23%
VAT amount accounted for on the supply: €4,600
Amount received from debtor: €14,520
(A) Amount outstanding from debtor: €10,080

The VAT adjustment for bad debt relief is €1,884, calculated as follows:

(€10,080 × 23) / (100 + 23) = €1,884

What if a customer pays everything but the VAT?

If a customer pays the VAT-exclusive amount charged for goods or services but refuses to pay the VAT charged, the relief should be calculated by entering the total unpaid amount at A in the formula in the preceding paragraph.

Accounting for VAT on the recovery of a bad debt that has been written off

If after claiming bad debt relief, an accountable person receives payment of any part of the debt he/she must make an adjustment to the bad debt relief already claimed. The adjustment should be made by reducing the VAT on purchases figure in Box T2 on the VAT return form for the period in which the payment is received. The amount of the adjustment should be calculated by using the formula in paragraph 10 where A is the total amount received from the debtor.

Property transactions

Bad debt relief is not allowable in the case of leases, of ten years or more, which were created prior to 1 July 2008.

Bad debts determined after a transfer of business

Where, as part of the transfer of a business in accordance with Sections 20(2)(c) or 26 of the VAT Consolidation Act 2010, the transferor of the business transfers debts that, subsequent to the transfer, are determined to be bad debts, there is no entitlement to bad debt relief. However, bad debt relief subject to the normal conditions is available in respect of any debts retained by the transferor that are not included in the transfer.

Insured debts

An entitlement to receive compensation payment under a policy of insurance against bad debts does not affect entitlement to bad debt relief. This is not affected by any condition of an insurance policy that may assign the right to recover the debt to the insurer.

Third-party payments, payments in kind and mutual debts

No bad debt relief can be claimed to the extent that any payment is received by any third party in respect of a debt owed by a customer, e.g. payment by a guarantor or payment by a director of a debt owed by a company.

Payments in kind, e.g. goods or services bartered in exchange are also con-

Where a debt is assigned by one person to
as part of a factoring or invoice-discounting arrangement or otherwise, the originator ceases to have an entitlement to any bad debt relief in relation to that debt. In a factoring or invoice-discounting arrangement, with recourse, the originator may be entitled to bad debt relief where all the other conditions in this leaflet are satisfied. Please refer to VAT Information Leaflet: **Factoring and Invoice Discounting**.

Reservation of title

The sale of goods under an agreement for the reservation of title until the goods are paid for does not affect entitlement to bad debt relief.

Hire-purchase

Special rules apply to determine the amount of the relief in the case of hire purchase or credit sale. Please refer to VAT Information Leaflet: **Hire-Purchase Transactions**.

Further information

Enquiries regarding any issue contained in this Information Leaflet should be addressed to the Revenue District responsible for the taxpayer's affairs. Contact details for all Revenue Districts.

VAT Interpretation Branch,
Indirect Taxes Division,
Stamping Building,
Dublin Castle.

Appendix 1

a. any question of whether a person is connected with another person shall be determined in accordance with the following:
   i. a person is connected with an individual if that person is the individual's spouse, or is a relative, or the spouse of a relative, of the individual or of the individual's spouse,
   ii. a person is connected with any person with whom he or she is in partnership, and with the spouse or a relative of any individual with whom he or she is in partnership,
   iii. subject to clauses (IV) and (V) of subparagraph (v), a person is connected with another person if he or she has control over that other person, or if the other person has control over the first-mentioned person, or if both persons are controlled by another person or persons,
   iv. a body of persons is connected with another person if that person, or persons connected with him or her, have control of that body of persons, or the person and persons connected with him or her together have control of it,
   v. a body of persons is connected with another body of persons –
      I. if the same person has control of both or a person has control of one and persons connected with that person or that person and persons connected with that person have control of the other,
      II. if a group of 2 or more persons has control of each body of persons and the groups either consist of the same persons or could be regarded as consisting of the same persons by treating (in one or more cases) a member of either group as replaced by a person with whom he or she is connected,
      III. if both bodies of persons act in pursuit of a common purpose,
      IV. if any person or any group of persons or groups of persons having a reasonable commonality of identity have or had the means or power, either directly or indirectly, to determine the activities carried on or to be carried on by both bodies of persons, or
      V. if both bodies of persons are under the control of any person or group of persons or groups of persons having a reasonable commonality of identity,
   vi. a person in the capacity as trustee of a settlement is connected with –
      I. any person who in relation to the settlement is a settlor, or
      II. any person who is a beneficiary under the settlement.
b. "control", in the case of a body corporate or in the case of a partnership, has the meaning assigned to it by section 4(2) of the VAT Consolidation Act 2010;
   "relative" means a brother, sister, ancestor or lineal descendant.

Index

abuse of rights principle 202–4, 205
accommodation expenditure,

supply of services through
10–11, 61
undisclosed 11, 38–9, 61
annual returns of trading
details 24
anti-avoidance provisions
base erosion and profits shifting
(BEPS) project 208–9
mandatory disclosures regime
206–8
overview 205–6
protective notifications 205
surcharges 205
apportionment methods 126–9
aspect queries 155–6
asset finance 150
audit notification letters 156–7,
158, 175
audit review periods 159
audit selection 158
audit settlements 164–70

bad debt relief
and insolvency situations 187–8
and taxable value 144–5
Revenue guidance 253–60
barter transactions 147

base erosion and profits shifting
(BEPS) project 208–9
broadcasting services

cancelled deposits 145
Capital Goods Scheme (CGS)
CGS adjustments 102–3
inheriting liabilities from tenant
107–8
and insolvency situations 179,
182, 183
intervals of VAT life 99–100
operation of scheme 100–102
overview 99
VAT life of property 99–100
capitalised value (long leases) 80
careless behaviour with significant
consequences 166
careless behaviour without
significant consequences 166
case law
on abuse of rights 203–4
on anti-avoidance provisions 205
*Argos Distributors Ltd v.
Commissioners of C&E* 146
*Boots Company Plc v. Commissioners
of C&E* 146
Bupa Hospitals case 203–4
*Card Protection Plan (CPP) v.
Commissioners of C&E* 140
Cibo case 15

case law—*Cont.*
  on composite and multiple
    supplies 140
  on concept of establishment 64
  Cussens & Ors v. Brosnan 205
  Elida Gibbs Ltd v. Commissioners of
    C&E 146
  EMS-Bulgaria Transport OOD
    case 201
  on fiscal neutrality 200
  Halifax plc case 203
  HMRC v. Bridport and West Dorset
    Golf Club 200
  HMRC v. The Rank Group Plc 200
  Inspector of Taxes v. Cablelink Ltd. 140
  Kretztechnik AG v. Finanzamt Linz
    15, 121
  on legitimate expectation 201–2
  Marks & Spencer plc v.
    Commissioners of C&E 201–2
  Part Service case 204
  on proportionality 201
  on taxable value for retailers 146
  on VAT groups 26
  on VAT recovery 15–16, 121
  see also Court of Justice of the
    European Union (CJEU)
cash-flow issues 151–2
cash receipts basis of accounting 148
chain supplies 39
charities 14
Code of Practice for Revenue Audit
  and Other Compliance
  Interventions 157
completion of development,
  definition 89–90
composite supplies 13, 139
compulsory purchase orders
  (CPOs) 39
connected building agreements 92
connected parties
  construction services received
    from 8, 108

definition 114–16
and determination of 'new'
  property 90
impacts on property transactions
  108–9
imposition of market value of
  property by Revenue
  109, 148
option to tax restrictions
  94–5, 108
potential clawback of VAT under
  CGS 109
and relevant contracts tax 217–18,
  219–22
waivers of exemption 98, 111
consignment stock relief 10
construction operations, definition
  for RCT 224–5
construction services received from
  connected parties 8, 108
contract notifications (RCT) 227–8
contract work involving handing
  over of goods, non-deductible
  23, 125
contractors, definition for RCT 223
co-ownerships 13
Council Implementing Regulation
  61, 64, 68, 197
coupons 146–7
Court of Justice of the European
  Union (CJEU) 15–16, 26,
  64, 121, 140, 146, 198–204;
  see also case law
credit notes *see* VAT credit notes
cultural events, place of supply 69
cultural services, place of supply 69

data protection 159
deemed non-supplies 42–3
deemed supplies 37–41
deliberate behaviour 166
deposits 145
deregistration 29, 187

development of land
    connected party rule 217–18,
        219–22
    definition for RCT 217–22
    development for letting 218–19
    development for own use 217

disclosed agents 10–11, 61
discounts 144
distance sales
    place of supply 46–7
    registration requirements 9, 46
    turnover thresholds 46
dual-use inputs 125–9

economic value test (EVT) 79
electricity, time of supply 25
electronic audits (e-audits) 159–61
electronic invoicing 149
electronic services
    MOSS system 10, 71–2
    place of supply 70
    registration requirements 9–10
electronic VAT reclaims (EVRs)
        73, 123
entertainment expenditure,
        non-deductible 23, 125
establishment, definition 63–4
EU Directives 196
EU emissions trading system
        (EU ETS) 9
EU law
    abuse of rights principle 202–4, 205
    case law see case law; Court of
        Justice of the European
        Union (CJEU)

Council Implementing Regulation
        61, 64, 68, 197
    Directives 196
    fiscal neutrality principle
        199–200
    impact on Irish VAT system
        3, 195
    Regulations 197
    role of the CJEU 198–9
EU Regulations 197
EU VAT rates 237–9
examinership 188
exempt transactions 4–5
exports to non-EU countries 45–6
expressions of doubt 149–50

farm buildings 12, 123
farmers
    flat-rate addition 11–12
    registration requirement for
        certain activities 11
    VAT recovery on construction/
        alteration of farm buildings
        12, 123
financial services
    common VAT issues 150
    place of supply 71
    use and enjoyment rules 71
fiscal neutrality principle 199–200
fishermen, VAT recovery on
        specified equipment 123
flat-rate addition 11–12
food and drink expenditure,
        non-deductible 23, 124
foreign currency transactions 143

forestry operations, definition for
RCT 225–6
freehold equivalent sales 41, 86

gas, time of supply 25
gifts 39–41
goods *see* supply of goods
goods and services sold together
case law 140
composite supplies 139
and joint ventures 13
multiple supplies 139–40
overview 139
and relevant contracts tax 229–30
two-thirds rule 140–41, 229–30
greenhouse gas emission
allowances 9
*Guidelines on Tax Consequences of
Receivership and Mortgagees
in Possession* 179

hire of transport, place of supply
69, 71
hire-purchase transactions 38, 42
holding companies 15–16
holiday homes 112

imports of goods from non-EU
countries 52–3
innocent errors 169
insolvency practitioners
see liquidators; receivers
insolvency situations
bad debt relief 187–8
deregistration from VAT 187
entitlement of practitioner/MIP to
input credit 184–5
examinership 188
liquidators' VAT obligations
181–2
MIPs' VAT obligations 183
overview 179
receivers' VAT obligations 182–3

relevant contracts tax implications
188–92, 230
transfer of business relief 185–6
VAT groups 186–7
VAT issues particular to property
transactions 183–4
VAT review on appointment of
practitioner/MIP 179–81
insurance companies, disposal of
assets 43
intangible assets, transfer of business
relief 60
intending traders 16–18
intermediaries *see* agents
intra-Community acquisitions (ICAs)
new means of transport 7, 48, 49
place of supply 48–51
recording on VAT 3 return 22–4, 52
registration requirements 7, 48
reverse charge of VAT 48–51
triangulation relief 50–51
intra-Community supplies of goods
conditions for zero-rating 44–5
INTRASTAT returns 52
invoicing 44, 45
place of supply 44–5
recording on VAT 3 return
22–4, 52
VIES returns 52
intra-Community transport of goods,
place of supply 69
INTRASTAT returns 52
invoices *see* VAT invoices

joint ventures (JVs) 13–14

land-related services, place of
supply 68
landlords' expenses 82–3
leases *see* long leases; short leases
legitimate expectation principle
201–2
licences 112

liquidators
  deregistration 187
  entitlement to input credit 184–5
  registration 184
  and relevant contracts tax 188–92
  and VAT groups 186–7

transfers in ...

old VAT rules
  accounting for VAT 81–2
  capitalised value 80
  economic value test 79
  extension or break options 80
  landlords' expenses 82–3
  service charges 83
  transactions involving 79–80
transitional VAT rules
  assignment or surrender of
    leases 97

mail order sales see distance sales
mandatory disclosures regime 206–8
margin schemes 146
market value imposition 109, 148
meat processing operations,
    definition for RCT 226–7
Mini One Stop Shop (MOSS) 10, 71–2
minor development, definition 89
mortgagees in possession (MIPs)
  entitlement to input credit 184–5
  registration 184
  and relevant contracts tax 188–92
  VAT issues particular to property
    transactions 183–4
  VAT obligations 183
  VAT recovery 184–5

VAT review on appointment
    179–81
motor vehicles expenditure,
    non-deductible 23, 125
moveable goods, working on,
    place of supply 69
    ... supplies 13, 139–40

to VAT 87
exceptions to two- and five-year
    rules 92
tenant works make building
    'new' 108
two- and five- years rules 87–91
no loss of revenue situations 167–8
non-deductible VAT 23, 124–5
non-Irish established traders 10
non-monetary consideration 147

occupied property, definition 90
opening meetings (Revenue
    audits) 164
options to tax
  connected party restrictions
    94–5, 108
  letting of property 94–5
  sale of property 92–3, 110
  situations where not possible 93,
    94–5, 110

partial VAT recovery 125–9
partnerships 12–13
passenger transport, place of
    supply 68
passive holding companies 15
payment notifications (RCT) 228

penalties
    for failure to file returns 20
    for failure to make mandatory
        disclosures 206
    for incorrect returns 20
    for incorrect VAT reclaims 119
    prosecution 172
    publication 171
    statutory fixed penalties 170
    tax-geared penalties 165–9
petrol expenditure, non-deductible
    23, 125
place of supply
    EU law 197
    goods
        distance sales 46–7
        goods exported to non-EU
            countries 45
        goods sold on journeys 48
        intra-Community acquisitions
            48–51
        intra-Community supplies 44–5
        overview 43–4
        supply and installation 47
    services
        business-to-business
            supplies 62–6
        business-to-consumer
            supplies 66–7
        exceptions to general rules 68–70
        overview 61–2
        summary of rules 67–8
        use and enjoyment rules 71
Pre-Contract VAT Enquiries (PCVEs)
    104, 112
premises providers 8
premiums paid in relation to
    leases 113–14
prepayments 145
pre-trading expenses
    see intending traders
price adjustments 143–4
principals, definition for RCT 214–16

profile interviews 156
prompted qualifying disclosures 162
property transactions
    cancellation of waivers of
        exemption 111
    Capital Goods Scheme 99–103,
        107–8, 183
    changes in timing 104–5
    connected parties issues 108–9
    co-owned 13
    determining property history
        103–4
    disregarded transfers 105
    holiday homes 112
    inheriting CGS liabilities from
        tenant 107–8
    and insolvency situations 179–81,
        183–4
    leases versus licences 112
    new VAT rules (post-1 July 2008)
        connected building
            agreements 92
        determining if a property is
            'new' 87–92
        determining if a sale has taken
            place 85–6
        determining if a sale is subject
            to VAT 86–93
        exceptions to two- and five-year
            rules 92
        letting of property 93–5
        option to tax letting of
            property 94–5
        option to tax sale of property
            92–3, 110
        residential property
            developers 92
        transfers in substance 41, 86
        two- and five-year rules 87–91
    non-business use of property 113
    old VAT rules (pre-1 July 2008)
        accounting for VAT on long
            leases 81–2

landlords' expenses with long
leases 82–3
overview 77–8
requirements for VAT to
arise 78–9
supplies of immovable goods

sales within a VAT group 26–7, 28
situations where option to tax is
not possible 110
tenant dilapidations 112–13
tenant works make building
'new' 108
transfer of business relief 105–7
transitional VAT rules
assignments or surrenders of
long leases 97
overview 95
sales of reversionary
interests 96–7
supplies of freeholds 96
waivers of exemption 98
VAT clauses in sales contracts
111–12
waivers of exemption 84–5, 98, 111
proportionality principle 201
prosecutions 172
protective notifications 205
public bodies 9
public-private partnerships (PPPs) 13
publication of defaulters 171

qualifying activities 120–21
qualifying avoidance disclosures 205
qualifying disclosures 161–3

Recast Sixth Directive 196, 197,
199–201
receivers
deregistration 187
entitlement to input credit 184–5
registration 184
and relevant contracts tax 188–92

registration
deregistration 29, 187
determining if required 3–5
difficulty of backdating 16, 17
persons required to register 5–18
registration process 18
using ROS 18
TR1 form 18
TR2 form 18, 31–4
turnover thresholds 6, 41–2
of VAT groups 25–8
relevant contracts tax (RCT)
application to joint ventures 14
definition of construction
operations 224–5
definition of contractor 223
definition of development of
land 217–22
definition of forestry operations
225–6
definition of meat processing
operations 226–7
definition of principal 214–16
importance of correct operation
213–14
and insolvency situations
188–92, 230
interaction with VAT 228–9

relevant contracts tax (RCT)—*Cont.*
  nature of the tax 213
  operation of the tax 227–8
  overview 213
  rates of tax 228
  relevant contracts 223–7
  relevant payments 227
  Revenue guidance on 189–92,
    231–6
  and reverse charge of VAT 8,
    189, 213, 228–9
  and the two-thirds rule 229–30
residential property developers 92
restaurant and catering services,
    place of supply 69
retailers' special VAT scheme 146–7
returns
  annual returns of trading details 24
  filing dates 20–21
  INTRASTAT returns 52
  non-deductible VAT 23
  penalties for failure to file 20
  penalties for incorrect returns 20
  VAT groups 26
  VAT 3 returns 20–24, 52, 65–6,
    122–3
  VIES returns 26, 52, 65
Revenue assessments 171
Revenue audits and interventions
  actions on receipt of audit
    notification 157
  audit notification letters 156–7,
    158, 175
  audit process 157–9
  audit review periods 159
  audit selection 158
  audit settlements 164–70
  data protection 159
  e-audits 159–61
  inability to pay 170
  innocent error 169
  location of audit 158–9
  no loss of revenue situations 167–8

  opening meetings 164
  overview 155
  preparation for an audit 163–4
  prosecutions 172
  publication of defaulters 171
  qualifying disclosures 161–3
  Revenue powers 170–71
  self-corrections 168–9
  statutory fixed penalties 170
  tax-geared penalties 165–9
  technical adjustments 169
  tips for handling the audit
    process 172–3
  types of interventions 155–7
  unannounced visits 158
Revenue On-line Service (ROS)
  deregistration 29
  electronic VAT refund claims 123
  Mini One Stop Shop (MOSS) 71–2
  RCT contract notifications 227–8
  RCT payment notifications 228
  registration 18
  VAT 3 returns 20–21
  VIES returns 52
Revenue powers 170–71
reverse charge of VAT
  business-to-business services
    62–3, 65–6
  construction services received from
    connected parties 8, 108
  construction services subject to
    RCT 8, 189, 213, 228–9
  greenhouse gas emission
    allowances 9
  intra-Community acquisitions
    48–51
  long leases 81, 82
  option to tax sale of property 92
  scrap metal sales 8
reversionary interests 80, 96–7
Risk Evaluation, Analysis
    and Profiling (REAP)
    software 158

scrap metal sales, reverse charge of
VAT 5, 8
section 56 authorisation 27, 53–4
self-accounting *see* reverse charge
of VAT
self-billed invoicing 149

old VAT rules 78, 83–5
site identification numbers (SINs) 228
special VAT schemes 146–7
statutory fixed penalties 170
supply and installation
place of supply 47
registration requirements 8
supply of goods
chain supplies 39
compulsory purchase orders 39
deemed non-supplies 42–3
deemed supplies 37–41
definition of goods 37
disposals of assets by insurance
companies 43
distance sales 46–7
exports to non-EU countries 45–6
gifts 39–41
goods and services sold
together 139–41
goods sold on journeys 48
hire-purchase transactions 38, 42
imports from non-EU
countries 52–3
intra-Community acquisitions
7, 48–52
intra-Community supplies 44–5, 52
INTRASTAT returns 52

overview 37
place of supply 43–51
recording on VAT 3 return
22–4, 52
section 56 authorisation 53–4
self-supply of goods 39–41

turnover threshold 6, 41–2
VAT invoices 44, 45
VIES returns 52
supply of services
business-to-business
supplies 62–6
business-to-consumer
supplies 66–7
determining if services are being
supplied 59–60
goods and services sold together
139–41
MOSS system 71–2
overview 59
place of supply 61–70
receipt of services from abroad 7,
62–3, 65–6
recording on VAT 3 return 22–4,
65–6
recovery of foreign VAT 72–3
reverse charge of VAT 62–3, 65–6
self-supply of services 60
through agents 10–11, 61
time of supply 24
transfer of business relief 60
turnover threshold 6
VAT invoices 65
VIES returns 65

tax avoidance *see* anti-avoidance
    provisions
tax-geared penalties 165–9
taxable amount
    bad debts 144–5
    buy one, get one free
        promotions 143
    cancelled deposits 145
    discounts 144
    foreign currency transactions 143
    margin schemes 146
    non-monetary consideration 147
    overview 141–2
    prepayments 145
    price adjustments 143–4
    self-supplies 143
    special schemes 146–7
    tipping 142
    unjust enrichment 145
    vouchers and coupons 146–7
technical adjustments 169
telecommunications services
    MOSS system 10, 71–2
    place of supply 70, 71
    registration requirements 9–10
    time of supply 25
    use and enjoyment rules 71
time of supply
    continuous supplies 25
    goods 24
    services 25
tipping 142
TR1 form 18
TR2 form 18, 31–4
transfer of business relief
    and insolvency situations 185–6
    and intangible assets 60
    Revenue guidance 241–51
    and supply of goods 42
    and transfer of property 105–7
    and VAT recovery 121
transfers as security for loans 42
transfers in substance 41, 86

transfers of own goods abroad 41
triangulation relief 50–51
turnover method (VAT
        apportionment) 126–8
turnover thresholds
    distance sales 46
    not applicable to non-Irish
        established traders 10
    reduction for VAT on purchases
        of stock for re-sale 6
    supply of goods 6, 41–2
    supply of services 6
two-thirds rule 140–41, 229–30

unannounced Revenue visits 158
undisclosed agents 11, 38–9, 61
unjust enrichment 145
unprompted qualifying disclosures
    162–3
use and enjoyment rules 71

VAT 3 returns 20–24, 52, 65–6, 122–3
VAT 4A procedure 81
VAT 60E claim forms 123
VAT 60OEC claim forms 73, 124
VAT apportionment methods 126–9
VAT clauses, property transactions
    111–12
VAT credit notes 144
VAT-exempt activities 4–5, 129–31
VAT-exempt traders 4–5, 131–2
VAT groups
    case law 26
    conditions to be satisfied 25
    head offices and branches 26
    impacts of registration 26–8
    imposed by Revenue 26
    insolvency situations 186–7
    intra-group sales of property
        26–7, 28
    not recognised in all EU Member
        States 26
    payment 26

registration of 25–6
returns 26
section 56 authorisation 27
VAT invoices 26–7
VIES statements 26
VAT invoices

VAT rates
applying the correct rate 138–9
in EU Member States 237–9
for goods and services sold
together 139–41
livestock rate (4.8%) 137
reduced rate (9%) 137, 138
reduced rate (13.5%) 137, 138
standard rate (23%) 137
zero rate (0%) 137–8
VAT recovery
case law 15–16, 121
on construction/alteration of
farm buildings 12, 123
of foreign VAT paid 72–3, 123
general rules 119–22
holding companies' share
transaction costs 15–16
by insolvency practitioners and
MIPs 184–5
landlords' expenses 82–3

non-deductible VAT 124–5
by non-EU traders 124
partial recovery 125–9
penalties for incorrect
reclaims 119
qualifying activities 120–21
reclaim process 122–4

timing of VAT-recovery rate
calculation 129
and transfer of business relief 121
by unregistered claimants 123
VAT apportionment methods
126–9
VAT-exempt activities 129–31
VAT-exempt traders 131–2
VAT-recovery rates
apportionment methods 126–9
timing of calculation 129
VAT Refund Orders 123
VAT review periods 126
VIES returns
VAT groups 26
supply of goods 52
supply of services 65
vouchers 146

waivers of exemption 84–5, 93,
98, 111